HOMELESSNESS AMONG YOUNG PEOPLE IN PRAGUE

A NARRATIVE ANALYSIS OF DEVELOPMENTAL TRAJECTORIES

MARIE VÁGNEROVÁ
LADISLAV CSÉMY
JAKUB MAREK

CHARLES UNIVERSITY IN PRAGUE
KAROLINUM PRESS 2014

Reviewed by: Prof. PhDr. Zdeněk Helus, DrSc.
Doc. Paedr. Eva Šotolová, Ph.D.

CATALOGUING-IN-PUBLICATION – NATIONAL LIBRARY
OF THE CZECH REPUBLIC
Vágnerová, Marie
  Homelessness among young people in Prague : a narrative analysis of developmental
trajectories / Marie Vágnerová, Ladislav Csémy, Jakub Marek ; [English translation
by Phil Jones]. – 1st English ed. – Prague : Karolinum Press, 2014
Translated from the Czech. – Published by: Charles University in Prague
ISBN 978-80-246-2517-1

364.682.42 * 364.682.42-051 * 316.346.3-053.81 * 316.64 * 364-786 * (437.3)
– homelessness – Czechia
– homeless persons – Czechia
– young adults – Czechia
– life attitudes – Czechia
– social integration – Czechia)
– Prague (Czechia)
– collective monographs

361 – Social problems and social welfare in general [18]

ISBN 978-80-246-2517-1
e-ISBN 978-80-246-2587-4 (pdf)

CONTENTS

FOREWORD TO THE ENGLISH EDITION

The generosity of Karolinum Press has made it possible for an English translation of this book on the lives of young homeless people to be made accessible
to a wider readership. The Czech edition of the book came out in 2013 and was
the first comprehensive analysis of the psychosocial and developmental psychological context of homelessness in the Czech Republic. As the authors, we feel
it incumbent upon ourselves to offer a short foreword to the book for readers
living in other countries.

Readers in more advanced economies may well be surprised to discover that
the first publication on homelessness was only published in the Czech Republic
in 2013. A short historical detour might be useful in this respect. After the Second
World War what was then the Czechoslovak Republic, along with other Central
and Eastern European countries, found itself within the sphere of influence of the
Soviet Union. In 1948 the Communist Party came to power and a period of sin-
gle-party government began that lasted four decades. One of the basic attributes
of the totalitarian regime was the attempt to control the way that people thought
by means of communist ideology and the imposition of draconian restrictions
on access to information. The way that people behaved was subject to the same
control. The right to work was transformed into a statutory duty to work. The
farcical nature of this situation was epitomised by practically full employment
and the criminal prosecution of those who for whatever reasons avoided this
duty. Another instrument for enforcing control over people was the duty to report one's permanent or temporary residence. Needless to say, homeless was not
and could not be a social problem under the conditions of the totalitarian social
system. The rapid collapse of the totalitarian regimes of Central and Eastern Eu-
rope in autumn 1989 revealed not only the internal weaknesses of the system, but
above all people's craving for freedom. The turning point in the Czech Republic
was the Velvet Revolution, personified by the charismatic figure of Václav Havel.
The country immediately set about reintroducing democratic social principles
and economic transformation. The quarter of a century that has elapsed since
that time has shown how difficult this is. The restoration of freedom was accompanied by both pleasure in the large gains made and anxiety resulting from
the necessity to deal with the social problems that accompany freedom and a
modern social organization. These problems include unemployment, new forms
of criminality, corruption, drug abuse and homelessness. Society was forced to
reflect upon these problems and to begin taking various measures to resolve
them. Homelessness was never regarded as a priority. From the very start it was

left to charities and NGOs to sort out. It gradually became clear that dealing with homelessness would require greater integration into the system of state-supported social services. The systematic resolution of homelessness is part of the Social Inclusion Strategy 2014–2020 unveiled by the government at the beginning of 2013. Another input was the results of the Census of People, Houses and Apartments 2011, which included a census of homeless people. In terms of homelessness, 11,496 met the criteria of the Czech Statistical Office. However, these results must be regarded as approximate, since they included only persons in contact with an institution at the time the census was taken, and the Czech Statistical Office itself says that the genuine number of homeless people in the Czech Republic may be far higher. Our research, which was conducted from 2010 to 2012, must therefore be regarded in the light of what has been written above.

Why have we focused on young homeless people? The findings of employees working at centres for the homeless indicate that young people comprise a relatively high proportion of the homeless. When defining the objectives of our research project we were aware that our findings regarding the lives of young homeless people could be valuable in respect of the process of their reintegration into society. Our research took in older adolescents and young adults aged 18 to 26. We did not include younger teenagers and minors, i.e. persons below the age of 18. This is because these young people are covered by the Act on the Social and Legal Protection of Children. Under this law and the provisions relating to it, minors cannot practically speaking remain on the street for any longer period of time. Of course, there are cases in which a dysfunctional family is incapable of looking after an underage child or a young person runs away from home and finds themselves on the street. However, in such cases after a certain period of time has elapsed they are returned to their family or placed in institutional care, usually in a children's home or juvenile detention centre.

As far as research methodology is concerned, we combined a qualitative and quantitative approach. We based our work largely on analyses of structured interviews and responses to visual stimuli (selected thematic apperception tests (TAT) and original pictures created especially for this project). During the qualitative part of the research we administered the Eysenck personality questionnaire and the Brief Symptom Inventory (BSI), with the aim of supplementing the quantitative analysis with the personality characteristics of those questioned and their psychopathological profile.

We will leave it to our readers to judge to what extent we managed to contribute to the recognition and understanding of the causes and course of homelessness among young people. We believe that this book will be of interest to students and teachers involved in the humanities, professionals working in the caring professions, and those members of the general public interested in the social problems of our time.

The authors   Prague, 17 September 2013

1. THE LIFE STORIES OF YOUNG HOMELESS PEOPLE

1.1 INTRODUCTION

Chronic homelessness can be perceived as a **syndrome** characterised by **comprehensive social failure**, which is manifest in an inability to accept and deal with everyday social requirements. It is usually accompanied by many other problems caused by the interaction of undesirable personality traits and adverse life experiences, i.e. an accumulation of stressful situations that a person finds difficult to deal with subjectively. Homelessness is a complex phenomenon that is not simply about the lack of shelter. This is now accepted by most specialists in the field. Průdková and Novotný (2008) point out that, along with the loss of accommodation, homelessness is linked with the **loss of a home**, **social exclusion**, and relegation to the margins of mainstream society. This in turn can lead to a homeless person becoming detached from the system of societal values and norms and to a fundamental change in their lifestyle. Social exclusion is manifest in all spheres of life:

- through job loss and hence legal access to financial resources,
- through the fracturing of close relationships and the collapse of social networks,
- through a drop in the standard of living and increased dependence on the support of charities, begging, scavenging, or criminal activities.

From a psychological standpoint the most significant loss is that of the sanctuary of a home and the people to whom an individual is close and who share his or her life. Mallett et al. (2010) maintain that the lack of a place that an individual feels part of and where he or she is wanted and supported by others is also important (though it is true that very often this does not apply to the home that these young people left or were expelled from). Home is associated with a certain privacy. It is a place that strangers cannot enter and it therefore represents both symbolic and real security. The loss of a home tends to lead to **deracination**, rootlessness, and the lack of a sense of belonging and allegiance to someone or something. This is often accompanied by an inability or unwillingness to act in accordance with generally accepted rules and with consideration for other people (Robinson, 2002).

Homelessness is associated with higher levels of stress brought on by the constant necessity to deal with the hazards that life on the street involves. It is not simply that a homeless person does not have a permanent residence, but that they lack people to whom they belong (or such people are changing too frequently) and a place where they feel safe and which they are willing to work on. On the one hand homelessness removes the pressure from a person to meet various requirements. On the other it deprives them of the protection that standard social integration provides. Opting for a life on the streets is very often the start of a declining life trajectory that can be irreversible. Homelessness is often linked with a **process of gradual desocialization**.

Homelessness also results in **social stigmatisation**. Mainstream society regards life on the street as an unequivocally negative deviation from the norm. For most people it is undeniable proof of social pathology. Their attitude to homeless individuals is one of disapproval and condemnation (Marek, Strnad and Hotovcová, 2012). Farrington and Robinson (1999) found that, to begin with, homeless people attempt to maintain an acceptable degree of self-respect by denying they belong to the homeless community and emphasising their own dissimilarity from it. The subsequent adoption of a homeless identity, which the authors claim takes place after approximately two years of sleeping rough, signals increased indifference and a continued personal and social decline.

A significant part of the homeless community comprises young people below the age of 26[1]. As Darbyshire et al. (2006) point out, approximately half of all homeless people belong to this age category. There may be **many reasons why these young people took to the streets**. One of them is the need for freedom and independence and the desire to experiment. Sometimes sleeping rough is merely a temporary glitch in the course of life. Other times it may signal the start of a gradual decline that the individual is unable to control whatever the reasons for their failure. On the threshold of adulthood, opting to sleep rough can represent a way of searching out new experiences and limits, a kind of variation on the adolescent moratorium, which does not have to last long. However, it may also be the result of serious and often long-term problems, over which a young person has no control and to which they are incapable of reacting otherwise than through escape and resigned acceptance of the lack of a more effective solution. In any event it is a risky decision that leads to further difficulties. These can impact negatively on the personal development of the individual in question, change their approach to life and their conduct, and militate against reintegration into society.

Young people most often belong to the category of the **concealed homeless**. Though living on the street, they cannot at first sight be differentiated from members of mainstream society (Průdková and Novotný, 2008). Most of them adhere to conventional social standards, i.e. they take care of their appearance, they are clean, and their conduct does not mark them out in any particular

---

1 M. van den Bree et al. (2009) state that homeless people comprise 7.4% of the adult American population. It is not known how many homeless people there are in the Czech Republic since precise data does not exist.

way. Even though they live a homeless lifestyle, for the time being they distance themselves from that community. Their social decline has not yet inured them to the opinions of people around them. They are usually convinced that street life is simply a temporary stage and that they will return to mainstream society at some point in the future. For the moment they do not accept that this is something they may not manage. Young people are in a better position to change their lives, and for this reason it is worthwhile ascertaining how best to work with them so as to ensure that they do not become chronically homeless. This was one of the main objectives of our study, the results of which we will present in the text below.

1.2 RESEARCH OBJECTIVES AND METHODS AND A DESCRIPTION OF THE GROUP UNDER EXAMINATION

As D. McAdams (1996, 2001, 2006) shows, one way of understanding a person is via their **life story**, i.e. the method by which they perceive themselves and interpret their life. This is not about the depiction of real events, but how these events are subjectively understood. A personal story provides interesting information, not only about the individual in question, but also about the incidents they recount. In their life story an individual may express their opinion of themselves, other people that were significant to them in some way, and their relationship to the world. What other people an individual chooses to include in their story, how they assess them, and what role they attribute to them in relation to themselves are all important. The events that are included in such a story have some personal significance and can be regarded as landmarks influencing the course of subsequent actions. The subjective principle is also manifest in the way that an individual explains the causes and consequences of various events and what conclusions he or she draws from them in respect of the future. Also of interest is the dynamic of a story linked with a transformation in the understanding of certain events and the evaluation thereof (e.g. an adult might evaluate the conduct of their mother differently than they did as an adolescent, etc.). The information cited does not have to be true. Some information is distorted (either consciously or not), other information might be omitted, etc. A life story is subjective truth and must be viewed in this light. Nevertheless, it represents very important information (Vágnerová, 2010).

Experiences from childhood and adolescence lead to the creation of patterns that actuate certain **ways of perceiving and evaluating other people and ourselves**. (This is how it was explained by G. Kelly, one of the representatives of social cognitive theory.) What is important is how a person understands their surroundings and how they interpret the various actions of other people, which, in light of their personality traits and the experiences they have had, may be very dissimilar. Not even social patterns must fully correspond to reality. Certain aspects may be accentuated and others repressed or simply overlooked. Someone may, for instance, idealise their mother and see only her positive traits, while evaluating their father in a generally negative way simply because he left his wife and children and started a new family. According to J. Bowlby (and his attachment theory), early experience is important in terms of the development of our opinions and relationships to other people (and ultimately to ourselves). The child acquires this experience on the basis of its emotional bond with its mother or other primary caregivers. Each individual projects their experience with their parents into their self-identity and relationships with other people. **Primary experience with a secure, reliable person** and with clearly differentiated social signals is a good basis for the continued development of social adaptability and the personality as a whole. If such experience is lacking, this development is disturbed and distorted. In the case of certain young homeless people the basis of future social decline may reside in such a lack.

The aim of the research was to **identify the method by which young homeless people understand the course of their own lives** and to determine the landmarks and people that most influence them. If work with the young homeless is to have the desired effect, we need to know what they are like as people, what problems they have, and what led them to a life on the street. Such findings can be acquired by means of **narrative-based, semi-structured interviews** that respect the chronological sequence of their lives. The life story is also a suitable method for grasping even such a complex phenomenon as the process of adaptation to a fundamental change in a person's existence. It can provide information on how the subject perceives and experiences such a change and which events or decisions they regard as crucial. The interviews included the following spheres:

- **The course of childhood and adolescence.** Important here is the subject's opinion of the family they grew up in, their relationships with their biological or foster parents and siblings, their school and scholastic success, and finally their relationships with their peers.
- **The moment they left home for the street** and an explanation of the circumstances that led to this. What is crucial here is the opinion the subject has of their current lifestyle, how they cope with it, and their relationships within the homeless community.
- **The subject's opinion of themselves**, including the changes that have taken place as a consequence of sleeping rough and the degree to which their own identity and self-satisfaction has changed. It is important to ascertain any shift in their moral thinking and current hierarchy of values.
- **Their ideas about the future** and the possibility of reintegration into society. Better understanding in this sphere would be achieved by knowing the opinion of these young people regarding possible assistance and its anticipated effectiveness.

The stories told by young people contain many inaccuracies, especially chronological. Sometimes the information provided is self-contradictory. Only in exceptional cases were we able to access other sources and cross-check the accuracy of the information we received. Certain inaccuracies and memory lapses can be put down to the consequence of long-term use of psychoactive substances, as well as the lifestyle in question, which makes no demands on accuracy.

During the course of an interview clients were given sufficient space to say everything they wanted. The outputs were extensive and yielded a wealth of information. Individual interviews lasted 2 to 2.5 hours on average. The interview was recorded and then transcribed. We analysed the information acquired structurally and thematically according to how the respondents described individual events and the conduct of various persons, as well as how they interpreted the assumed causes of a given event and its future consequences. We specified the frequency of individual variants and added this to the qualitative evaluation in order to improve the final overview. We also drew on the experience and knowhow of employees of the organisation Naděje [Hope], who have long been working with young unemployed people and have gathered a lot of information on them.

We used the **short-form revised Eysenck EPQ/S questionnaire**, the validity of which has been confirmed on the Czech population (Kožený, 1999), to acquire a basic typology of the personalities of young homeless people. The questionnaire contains 48 items, with 12 items devoted to the evaluation of each of 4 subscales (extraversion-introversion, neuroticism-emotional stability, psychoticism and social desirability). The psychometric parameters of the short-form test remain relatively stable and can be used without problem for research purposes (Kožený, 1999).

We also used **H. Murray's projective thematic apperception test (TAT)**, specifically three pictures from this test (see the appendix) and two new pictures created especially for this research. This method is intended to obtain information on interpersonal and family relationships, and to address the theme of the future and life orientation. The underlying premise of the method is that the individual processing of a theme will assist in understanding a given personality. The individual under examination has to create a story for each picture that in their opinion best corresponds to their circumstances. They say what they think is happening in the picture and what the person or persons shown are doing. They also have to say what is going to happen, what the people are thinking about, what they would like and what they will do, i.e. what the outcome of the story is. Even though we used this method only on a semi-projective basis, i.e. we prompted responses from clients by posing general questions, we can assume that the clients will identify with a certain figure and project their opinions, needs and feelings into their stories. The aim is to identify how they perceive the surrounding world, other people, and their own position in the world. However, this is not only about what intentions and motives are ascribed to different figures.

What is also interesting is which of these is the most frequent and can therefore be deemed important for the client in question. Impediments and problems that might befall the central character are also examined, as well as the client's suggestions regarding how these might be dealt with and how the story will end, i.e. whether the outcome be positive or negative (Svoboda 1999; Vágnerová, 2010).

The group under examination comprised 90 young homeless people, 60 men and 30 women, aged between 19 and 26 (the mean age of the men was x=22.90, SD=2.25, the mean age of the women was x=22.63, SD=2.40). These people had been homeless for 2.43 years on average (SD=2.33). Most were aged between 19 and 22 (73.3 % of the group) when they lost their home, left home, or were expelled. They were individuals who visited the drop-in centre run by the charity Naděje in Prague, where they were offered food, clothing and warmth. All the persons contacted agreed to be interviewed, a fact that was probably influenced by their positive experience with the interviewer (an employee of Naděje) and the small fee (CZK 150/USD 7.50) they received for their participation.

1.3 THE LIFE STORIES OF YOUNG HOMELESS PEOPLE

Getting to know the life story of young homeless people can increase our understanding of their current situation. This situation is characterised by the lack of any direction in life, failure to deal with the demands of adulthood, superficial and unstable relations with people, and an insecurely defined life territory with the minimum of privacy. The end of adolescence and emerging adulthood represents a crucial period of time in terms of a young person's future, even when it does not develop as it should, i.e. if freedom of thought and deed are not harmonised and responsibility not accepted for decisions and actions. As Whitbeck (2009) says, opting for a life on the street shuts down access to many possibilities (in terms of both professional life and relationships) that could contribute to the more effective development of a young person's life, and can fundamentally distort the way their personality matures.

Many foreign studies are devoted to the issue of youth homelessness, e.g. research by Lynn Rew (2003), J. Hyde (2005), L. Whitbeck (2009), S. Mallett et al. (2010), and many others. Czech specialist literature does not yet offer much information. Where such information exists it tends to be in the form of a synopsis of empirical experiences of working with young homeless people. This is so in the case of Hradecký (2007), Průdková and Novotný (2008), and Marek, Strnad and Hotovcová (2012). We can assume that in many respects the results of research conducted under different socio-cultural conditions will correspond to our own, though this may not always be the case or apply to all spheres.

Our research outputs show that **youth homelessness is caused by many different circumstances**. It is not usually the result of a sudden change provoked by an isolated event, but is the consequence of the long-term accumulation of adverse influences. Sometimes there may be a genetic component that prevents these young people from dealing with many burdens in an acceptable way or without assistance. Such assistance is not always available. There are many paths to homelessness and the life stories of our clients differ. The common denominator may well be simply the fact that they have dropped out of mainstream society and been consigned to its margins. They may have come from very different social backgrounds and the extent of their personal failure may differ. They may or may not acknowledge their own culpability in the matter. The descent into homelessness is often associated with an accumulation of problems that the individuals concerned are unable or unwilling to resolve. The **family** plays a pivotal role in their stories, either as a source of support and assistance or, on the contrary, as a source of suffering and stress.

The period of emerging adulthood, during which a young person gradually gains their independence, is critical from the point of view of a possible descent into homelessness. The sources of the problems that Hyde (2005) maintains act as a **trigger for young people to opt for life on the street** tend to involve conflicts between parents and children, failure to respect parents' requests, poor communication, insufficient supervision of a young adult who is allowed to do whatever they want, a lack of interest on the part of their parents, disproportionate corporal punishment, and the use of drugs or alcohol. Whitbeck (2009) points out that people who grew up in a problematic environment, without a feeling of security and safety and without the opportunity to acquire the necessary social skills, are not sufficiently prepared for friendship and partnerships. They behave to other people in the same way as they do to their relatives or friends at home or within their group, and end up being rejected or deemed unacceptable by the rest of the population. This in turn leads to their being further relegated to the margins of society. As Johnson et al. (2005) says, the social network of such people is smaller and is restricted to similarly problematic individuals, and this in turn creates the risk of a downward spiral of social failure.

Even though each young homeless person tells a different story, certain themes reoccur: a less than happy childhood, an unsatisfactory family environment, unhealthy relationships with parents, behavioural problems already apparent at school age, and an incomplete education leading to problems finding work. These young people are not willing or able to meet so much as the basic requirements of life such is their lack of social skills, and often act in an unusual, sometimes antisocial way. They are less resistant to pressure (perhaps only of a certain type) and display various psychological problems, which they attempt to deal with by means of passive escape strategies. Their problems are intensified by the use of psychoactive substances and their relationships with individuals who also use drugs or alcohol. These conclusions have been reached in research carried out by Votta and Manion (2003), Johnson, Whitbeck and Hoyt (2005), Bearsley-Smith et al. (2008), Shelton et al. (2009), Marianne van den Bree et al. (2009), and many others.

2. THE CHILDHOOD AND EMERGING ADULTHOOD OF YOUNG HOMELESS PEOPLE

2.1 FAMILY – THE OPINIONS OF YOUNG HOMELESS PEOPLE REGARDING THEIR HOME LIFE AND THEIR CHILDHOOD

The families of young homeless people are many and varied. They may be intact and functional, or broken and problematic in some way. They may be extended by other members or so changeable that it is not even clear who is and is not part of the family, in which case they cannot operate as an acceptable emotional base. Some young homeless people grew up in foster families or institutional facilities because their parents were not able or willing to look after them. However, in some cases not even the foster family delivered the desired outcomes, sometimes because it was not given the opportunity to intervene in good time.

Work carried out by many researchers (Cauce et al., 2000; Votta and Maniona, 2003; Tyler, 2006; Bearsley-Smith et al., 2008; Coward-Bucher, 2008, and Ferguson, 2009) shows that young homeless people most often come from **families that do not provide a secure, safe background**. Their parents were incapable of dealing in an acceptable way with their partnerships, parenthood, and sometimes their professional responsibilities. They were often involved in substance abuse, and this increased the risk of their failure as parents. Sometimes they suffered mental health issues or personality disorders and were unsuccessful even within the framework of their own socialisation.

Life in a dysfunctional family often entails young people feeling overlooked and underappreciated. They are convinced that they do not matter to anyone. The family does not represent sanctuary: sometimes, indeed, the opposite. A lack of support and a sense of belonging, compounded by the accumulation of traumatic experiences, **means these young people look to leave home as soon as possible and head anywhere**, even the street. The breakup of the family incites them to seek independence earlier and to leave the environment which, from their subjective perspective, is not providing them anything positive (Mallett et al., 2010). Issues linked with the mother acquiring a new partner who is unwilling to tolerate the problematic conduct of his partner's adolescent children are a frequent cause of stress. If these replacement fathers are themselves not completely well balanced – if, for instance, they regularly consume alcohol and are of a violent nature – then they merely exacerbate conflicts.

A dysfunctional family background represents a serious burden. However, other children have to deal with similar problems and do not become homeless. The reason may be greater resistance, a more favourable genetic disposition, or the support of a particular person (e.g. their grandmother), etc. Those who fail may have **less propitious hereditary characteristics** acquired from their problematic parents. This may involve, for instance, a tendency to be impulsive, to lack empathy, to display overly emotional or aggressive reactions, etc. Such adverse traits are clearly the reason why these young people cannot profit from the positive incentives they have at their disposal.

Negative experience and a feeling of insufficient support increases overall insecurity and reinforces any tendency to risky behaviour. In these cases the course of the life story is quite similar: an emotionally unsatisfying and stressful life in a non-functioning family leads to a flattening out of emotional development and the reinforcement of undesirable habits and forms of conduct. In later childhood and emerging adulthood this may be manifest in various ways, e.g. through an individual's tendency to compensate for their problems by using psychoactive substances, joining a group or gang with an antisocial profile, making a living in non-standard ways, lazing around and sponging off others, through aggression and insensitivity to other people, and sometimes through criminal activities. Desirable forms of conduct are not created, or at least not to the necessary extent. These young people lack positive experiences, and under these circumstances they have no chance to assert themselves in society in an acceptable way. Their problematic behaviour may represent an **imitation of their parents' behaviour** and be the consequence of neglect, emotional poverty and traumas experienced. The negative experiences they have suffered with their own parents are reflected in their relationships with other people. The conditions are created for inappropriate forms of reaction (individuals who are tyrannised and abused as children often regard inconsiderate behaviour as something completely normal) and the creation of defensive barriers in the presence of other people. Leaving home for the street represents simply another stage on the path to deeper and often irreversible social decline.

The same conclusion was reached by L. Rew (2002), who drew attention to the significance of feelings of loneliness, alienation and rejection within the family. According to Marie Robert et al. (2005), almost 70% of homeless adolescents come from dysfunctional families and in 60% of cases the relationship between parents and child was seriously disturbed. Similar conclusions were reached by K. Tyler (2006) and M. Taylor-Seehafer et al. (2007). Kristin Ferguson (2009) regards an unstable family environment, the departure of one or both parents from the home, and the lack of support from any member of the family as negative factors preventing the creation of a feeling of security and safety in a young person. This is compounded by the parents' inability to look after their children because they have to deal with their own problems. Addictions of various kinds, whether to alcohol or drugs, represent a serious burden that undermines more than just parental capabilities. The results of research conducted by A. Nesmith (2006) show that frequent and fundamental changes of people and environment, including a later placement in foster care, can also be risk factors.

According to Patterson et al. (in Whitbeck, 2009), children acquire the basis of asocial conduct in dysfunctional families in which they are physically abused and neglected. Their reactions are derived from their experiences with their parents. They become convinced that inconsiderate, aggressive reactions are desirable because the person who acts in this way is usually successful. During childhood and above all adolescence they mix with similarly inclined people and act in accordance with the same rules. The tendency to be inconsiderate creates problems with adaptation at school and results in a split with their more conventional peers and failure in their professional training and actual employment. Ryan et al. (2000) draw attention to the possible negative consequences of an undesirable model of conduct in the sphere of social cognition. Such individuals lack empathy, are unable to orientate themselves in the behaviour of other people, possess a hostile attributional style (i.e. they see malicious intent in every action), and tend to resolve anything and everything aggressively. There is no doubt that the conduct of the parents, not only to their children but to each other and other members of the family, influences the development of the child's personality, sometimes more than an occasional beating.

An important part of any life story is the method by which the subject **perceives and evaluates their own home**. Young homeless people often describe the families they grew up in as being very problematic and subjectively unsatisfactory from the start and as not improving over time. Sometimes this involves broken homes, new partnerships formed (often undesirable for the subject), or families that were in the process of breaking up at various times in the subject's life. The reaction to family breakdown was often explosive. There are many reasons why as children they reacted in this way. It might have been the result of an accumulation of stressful experiences or the manifestation of a more complex disadvantage entailing an inability to deal with the loss of a certain security (albeit only symbolic at this time). These explosive reactions may have been a signal of the fact that there was nobody around who could offer any security. The stories told also feature families that, though regarded by the client as the source of their problems, were not so dysfunctional as to be the sole cause of the client's social failure. A young homeless person's subjective perception of their home life does not have to correspond to reality or even match the opinions of other family members. However, for the person concerned it has this significance and their subsequent actions derive from it.

In order to understand young homeless people better, we have to ascertain where they believe the negative influence of the family or parents resides.
- One possibility is that the parents **did not look after the children, neglected them**, and displayed no interest in them.

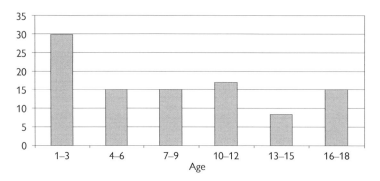

Graph 1. Family break-ups classified by the age of the child (the graph shows relative frequency).

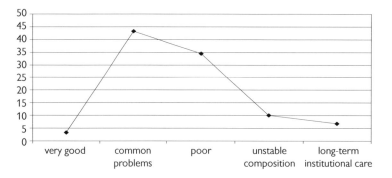

Graph 2. The clients' evaluation of their family (the graph shows relative frequency).
NB. Certain clients were in institutional care from birth and never lived in a family.

- Another category involves parents who are **less well off, with a poor education and often addicted to alcohol**, who represented an **undesirable role model** that the child imitated. The child logically began to experience similar problems. Forms of undesirable conduct imitated by the child include unreliability, irresponsibility (debts, unemployment, sponging off people), unscrupulous and violent behaviour, and a tendency to substance abuse.
- The third variant involves parents who were **unable to deal with their child during adolescence**, even though they tried to and did not condone its behaviour. What is important here is the reason why the family ceased (or never started) functioning and whose fault this was, or rather whom the subject (narrator) regards as the main culprit. If the cause of family dysfunction is the problematic personality of one of the parents and their tendency to inappropriate conduct, then this cannot be resolved through changing partners. This parent's idiosyncrasies will continue to influence the child who lives with them.

As is clear from graph 2, a **third of clients (34.4%) describe their family environment as being very unsatisfactory**. Their stories feature families that were unable to provide the children almost anything – an emotional background, basic upbringing, or even the bare material necessities. Under these circumstances it is practically impossible to learn everything necessary to master the basic demands of socialisation, and so these children stood no chance of success at school, among their peers, or in later life.

2.1.1 THE PROBLEMS OF ALCOHOLIC, VIOLENT, OR MENTALLY ILL PARENTS

Stories involving genuinely problematic families very often featured the **consequences of excessive alcohol consumption**.[2] *"All I know about the time I was born was that my parents were always quarrelling. My father stole from my mother and vice versa, so there were always court cases going on. My three siblings lived with mum and only I lived with dad. And then everything took a turn for the worse and my father turned into an alcoholic. The truth is that **for 13 years I never saw him sober.** I was put into various children's homes, a psychiatric hospital and a youth detention centre. To tell you the truth, I had a better life in a children's home. My father used to beat me and I couldn't deal with it. He blew everything out of proportion and was always after me for something. Everything was caused by alcohol. I never saw him sober enough to talk things through with me. Mum found herself a boyfriend and became different. She was subservient to him and **I realised that they'd given up on me** and that mum didn't want to see me anymore."* (PV, male) An alcoholic father and a mother with no interest in her son cannot be good parents and cannot offer their child a secure background. In addition, they offer them an undesirable model of conduct that reinforces the idea that drinking alcohol and acting aggressively is normal in life. At present their adult son is a homeless drug addict who is serving a prison sentence.

It is not always an alcoholic father who is the cause of family breakdown. **A mother who drinks excessively may be unable as a result to look after her children.** *"To begin with we were a decent, respectable family that functioned normally. When I was five dad started to drink a lot. Mum didn't, she carried on as usual, but **because he was drinking he started to beat us**, and then things went from bad to worse. Mum stuck it out for about a year and a half and then they both started to booze. We lived in that apartment about six years. For 18 months it was fully furnished, but then my parents started to sell things in order to buy drink and the whole place began to look like a squat. Me and my brother started to play truant and nobody knew where we were. And then **dad was put in prison** for five years and the apartment owner evicted us. For a week or two we slept with mum in the laundry room in the cellar, but then the social services arrived and took me and my brother out of school and put us in a youth*

---

2 Young homeless people in other countries also have alcoholic parents. Thompson et al. (2007) state that more than half the homeless have one parent who was an alcoholic, with both parents alcoholic in the case of 20%.

detention centre in Krč." *(MT, male)* The basic problem in the case of this family was alcohol and the domestic violence ensuing therefrom. This eventually led to the breakdown of the family. The client is also an alcoholic and has been living on the street for eight years.

Domestic violence represents a specific form of negative experience. Whether the victim is the mother, grandmother, sibling or the child itself, it always **diminishes feelings of security and safety**. As various studies have shown, young homeless people often come from families where violence is commonplace, and they are both victims of and witnesses to this violence. Many of them have seen their parents abusing each other and rowing and often resorting to physical attacks. The mother is most often the victim, though the children can be too. At least half of them were repeatedly and disproportionately beaten, mainly by their biological or substitute father. Though fathers tend to be more violent than mothers, a third of young homeless people stated that their mothers also hit them. The experience of domestic violence can be so traumatic that it results in the child running away from home as soon as possible. It can lead to a change in the way a child experiences and thinks about the world (and in certain cases to post-traumatic stress disorder). There is no doubt that such experiences will impact negatively on an individual and distort their conduct. They may become anxious and withdrawn or belligerent and aggressive.

Tyler and Cauce (2002) state that 47% of homeless youth were subject to excessive physical punishment as children for more than five years. The Spanish paediatrician Olivan (2002) discovered that 48% of homeless youth were severely beaten. Stewart et al. state that 44% of homeless youth had to ensure disproportionate capital punishment. According to J. Hyde (2005), 59% of homeless youth were subject to physical abuse as children and 50% were repeatedly witness to various conflicts and domestic violence. Ferguson (2008) discovered that 39% of homeless youth had witnessed domestic violence and 50% had been physically abused by the parents. Taylor-Seehafer et al. (2008) quote even higher figures, according to which 74% of youth homeless had been emo-

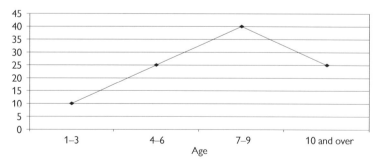

Graph 3. The age at which clients first encountered domestic violence, i.e. when they first became aware of it (the graph shows relative frequencies).

tionally tyrannised in their original family and 70% were frequently and severely beaten. According to Crawford (2009), 57% of girls and 80% of boys were subject to severe corporal punishment. Rachlis et al. (2009) state that 48% of young homeless people were physically tyrannised. Shelton et al. (2009) arrived at similar results, with 50% of youth homeless being repeatedly beaten. K. Tyler (2006) cites the same figures. Mallett and Rosenthal (2009) discovered that 34% of young homeless people were subject to severe physical punishment by the father, either their biological or stepfather, and 13% had been hit by their mother too. Maternal aggression is mentioned in the study by Pears and Noller (1995), who found that this applied to 30% of the mothers of young homeless people. Similar results were reached by Tyler and Cauce (2002). Ferguson (2009) summarises the situation by stating that 50–83 percent of youth homeless have encountered some form of violence in their family. As is clear, the authors of various studies arrive at different conclusions, probably depending on the cohorts selected for examination. Nevertheless, there is no doubt that people who go on to become homeless often experience a less than standard childhood and it is difficult to imagine that this negative experience would not manifest itself in their outlook, conduct and in relation to other people.

Almost a third of clients (28.8%) have encountered some form of violent conduct exhibited by the father or stepfather. Often the attacker was an **alcoholic father**. *"To begin with, when we were little, things were ok. But when we began to grow up we realised it wasn't going to be so cool. Mum was also sometimes horrible, but kind of appropriately. For instance, she'd punish us by making us kneel in the corner. But dad broke four cooking spoons on us and beat us with a belt on the backside, which isn't something a normal parent does. Sometimes, when he came home pissed, he didn't need a reason. Perhaps he didn't have much money left or he didn't have a cigarette. My father was a bastard. **He broke my arm when I was eight**, and that really hurt, because I had stuck up for mum. When I was about 10 or 11 **he threw mum through glass doors into the pantry**, and every month we had to buy new dishes, because there was nothing to eat from."* (KM, female) The client herself did not become aggressive, but has problems with self-respect, anxiety and insecurity. Her story does not continue well, and she has been living on the street for five years.

An **older stepbrother**, who adopts the role of dominant bully from his father, can also be involved in domestic violence. This was so in the case of TŽ (female), who was especially frustrated by the fact that her mother did not stand up for her. *"From when I was about four or five my brother began to tyrannise me psychologically and physically. I suffered a broken rib and serious concussion. Basically everything that dad did to my brother, my brother did to me. The worst was in a pub, when I had left the playground to buy some cola and my brother beat me up so badly that **he nearly strangled me. A couple of seconds longer and I would have died**. And then I bullied people at school. Whatever my brother did to me I took out on those around. I beat them up."* This girl continued the circle of violence and beat up her peers. Even as an adult she was repeatedly the object of someone's aggression and is in the dual position of a victim who herself has a tendency to react with violence.

The story of domestic violence in the family of KV (female), which finally fell apart, continues with **a description of her own aggression**: *"They beat us both (siblings). When I was six or seven I was put in a children's home. That was mainly because of my father, who was **always hitting me**, sent me to school in a t-shirt during the winter, **kicked me, took a lash to me**... When he had drunk a lot he became aggressive and frenzied. If he didn't like something at work, he didn't shout there but waited until he got home. I was pleased, I said that I wanted to go to a children's home, that I'd be better off there. At junior school I punched one girl twice because she called me a bastard from an orphanage. I had problems. I think I slapped or punched the teacher, but I'm not sure why. In seventh grade I got a B or a C for conduct. That was for the girl I punished, and in the second term I also got a B for attacking the school principal."* It is not clear whether the aggression against the adults actually took place or whether it is simply a wish fulfilment. However, there is no doubt that this client thinks about violence and has a tendency to act accordingly.

People who have been repeatedly exposed to violence can come to regard such conduct as the norm. As a result they themselves act aggressively and accept the rudeness of others as **something ordinary that has to be expected**. Living a homeless life they encounter violence frequently and this strengthens their conviction that it is not worth expecting anything different.

Stress related to domestic violence can ensue from the **feeling of helplessness and awareness of their inability to defend themselves against the threat** that a child experiences when it is unable to help its mother or grandmother. *"The worst experience was seeing violence against my mum, my father hitting her and kicking her head. You can't see anything worse in a family. As a young boy I ran away, because I was little and couldn't do anything about it."* (PV, male) However, despite the client's revulsion he learned by example, and later very often reacted in a similar way to his father. Currently he is in prison for this very reason.

Sexual abuse. In the case of girls not only physical but sexual abuse within the framework of the extended family was involved. Experience of abuse leads to a disruption of family relationships and to the loss of feelings of security and safety.

Foreign studies offer varying results. L. Rew (2002) discovered that 43% of girls and 32% of boys were sexually abused as children, though the Spanish paediatrician Olivan (2002) claims the figure is only 11%. Tyler and Cauce (2002) state that 29% of young homeless people were sexually abused as children, with the figures higher in the case of girls (44%) than boys (18%). Most of these were abused before they were 12 and the abuse continued over an average of two years. Stewart et al. (2004) found that 31% of young homeless people were subject to both severe physical punishment and sexual abuse, and that 6% were sexually abused only. M. Taylor-Seehafer et al. (2008) state that 55% of the young homeless were sexually abused. According to Crawford (2009)

20% of boys and 57% of girls suffered sexual abuse. Shelton et al. (2009) found that a third of young homeless people had been sexually abused. Rachlis et al. (2009) put this figure at 24%.

In the stories recounted by Prague-based homeless people this topic was referred to by slightly less than 7%, perhaps because it was something some clients did not want to talk about. **The sexual abuse was most often carried out by the stepfather or uncle**, and in one case by a foster parent, and **the victims were mainly girls**. Thirteen percent of girls said that they had been sexually abused.

An experience of sexual abuse that led from the client's perspective to an interesting outcome is described by IH (female). She tries to repress and forget what happened, though without much success. *"I had a kind of crazy uncle, though I don't really want to discuss him. I had a wonderful childhood and I'm going to kid myself of that all my life. Well, it was about abuse, though we don't want to enquire into that in more detail.* **I was really small, I wasn't even school age,** *and he's now in a wheelchair, which is what he deserves. That just happened. I'd always wanted it from when I was little. And then suddenly I hear that our uncle was in a wheelchair. He was my grandfather's brother and none of the family knew. Ever since then I decided that justice exists."* The punishment that represented a higher justice for the client helped her deal with the trauma she had experienced. The person who had abused her had been duly punished, and so everything was as it should be.

The traumatic experience of being sexually abused by her uncle forms part of the life story recounted by MH (female), who was taken into care when she was 15. *"Things worked out badly with my uncle. For two years he abused me. I ended up in Bohnice. I ended up there because he was the only relative to whom I could be sent. I wanted to go, I didn't know him, I'd never seen him before.* **He was really kind to me and I thought that he meant it normally. The problem was he didn't.** *After six months of living with him he started to take liberties and so on. I collapsed at school, I was completely psychologically damaged. And then I went to the police because some of the psychologists found out about it. The main thing was I wanted to commit suicide."* This case involved the clear abuse of the client's dependence. Sexual abuse was only one of the many traumas from childhood that the client had to come to terms with, and it is no surprise that she continues to suffer psychological problems as an adult.

The mental illness of a parent can mean they are incapable of coping with their parental role. This was so in the case of EK (female), whose mother suffered a mental illness that got worse when EK was 11[3]. *"My mother suffered badly from depression. Three times she was in Bohnice. In all she was there four times over three years. Her craziest period was three months before she died. She discharged herself*

---

3 It is not completely clear what mental illness this woman suffered from. The client speaks of depression and schizophrenia. From the description of her conduct one might infer that an element of psychosis was involved.

*against medical advice and she died shortly after. She overdosed on antidepressants. It was horrible **when mum started to experience these depressions. She locked me in our apartment saying I wanted to steal money from her**, that kind of thing. When she wasn't depressed she was really nice. It all depended on when it afflicted her."* This client's situation was made worse by the fact that her father was no longer part of the family. Her parents divorced when she was four. At present the client's main problem is drug addiction. It is difficult to say what influenced her the most: her mother's mental illness, the absence of her father, or the negative example set by her older sister who was herself a drug addict.

LB (male) had a mother who was a schizophrenic and unable to deal with her children. *"When I was eight the social services placed me with my father because my mother was ill. She had schizophrenia and I know that when I was little we visited her in Bohnice. She would be ok for a while, then she would suffer another attack and go back to Bohnice. She died two years ago. I didn't have problems with my mum. She was simply ill. I don't know how to describe it. **You can do whatever you want and someone who is ill doesn't notice.** Because she was ill, I could tell her that I smoked or took drugs and she accepted it."* The client's alcoholic father was incapable of raising his son and the client became a homeless drug addict.

2.1.2 THE RELATIONSHIP OF YOUNG HOMELESS PEOPLE TO THEIR PARENTS

From the interviews with certain clients it is clear that an **emotional relationship with the parents**, or at least one of them, can be formed even when from a general perspective the parent is problematic and neglects the child. Such people are incapable of functioning more effectively, often because of alcohol or psychoactive substance abuse. The parents offer a **negative model of how not to adjust to adulthood** and the client has nothing to learn from them. Nevertheless, even these parents can be emotionally accepted.

This was so in the case of the family of JB (male), who comes from a Slovak Roma community. *"My mum, both parents in fact, are happy with the fact that mentally they are kind of classic Gypsies, if I can put it that way. **Both my parents booze,** mum a lot, and that influenced me as a child. The household operated in such a way that the television got switched on and that was the only entertainment there was. They cooked something when there was something to cook. **Dad is an amazing person.** You throw a glass at his head and he wipes away the blood and asks if you're hungry. He's really amazing, simply because of how he is, his character. Maybe it's that reticence. He says almost nothing, only when he drinks. **Mum is more the shouting type.** She shouts at dad too. I have actually only just begun to see my parents through normal eyes. Previously I used to blame them for everything, when I was small, because we really had nothing. It was never ending. Even though they worked, when they had money they drank it all. They didn't know how to save, it was totally crazy. There was no learning from them.*

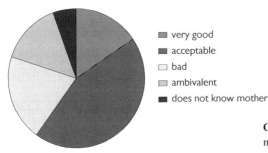

■ very good
■ acceptable
□ bad
▨ ambivalent
■ does not know mother

Graph 4. Clients' relationship to their mother (the graph shows relative frequency).

*When your parents don't teach you how you should deal with things… Overall their method of bringing me up damaged me, though the feelings they had toward me helped me. **They both have a huge heart**. These days paradoxically I see them as my children."* The client has no education or any of the necessary habits. He takes drugs and drinks alcohol. His relationship with his parents is exemplified by the fact that he paid for a hostel for them from the last money he had. At present his parents are unemployed alcoholics.

Other young homeless people come from **families that function without any great problem** and in which the parent-child relationship is not distorted in any way. In these cases the cause of social decline most often involved adverse personality traits and the devastating influence of alcohol or drugs. *"As far as I know the situation at home was fine, there were no problems. I fucked things up myself. I fell in with a certain crowd. Then **I began to booze** and that was the beginning of the slippery slope. No, nobody else drinks at home, I'm the only alcoholic. Mum would like to help me with everything. She always wants to look after me. But I don't want that, so **I moved out so as not to cause them worry**."* (IK, male) Until the client decides for himself to give up drink and to undergo treatment, his situation will not improve. Even though his family, especially his mother, tries to help him, they are powerless.

Young homeless people's opinion of their mother and their relationship with her

While the mother can be very problematic in reality, she can nevertheless be of great emotional significance for the child. Sometimes an ambivalent relationship to her is formed along the lines of: *"I love my mum, but I wish she were different. Sometimes I feel ashamed of her, though I also feel sorry for her."* This, for instance, is how MH (female), who was born out of wedlock, perceives her mother. She does not know who her father was. To begin with she was looked after by her grandmother and subsequently in a children's home, because her mother was an **alcoholic and drug addict**. *"From the age of six I was in a children's home. For me this was a relief. It's my mother, she gave birth to me, but it was simply better to live in a children's home. It ended up with **her beating and hitting me frequently**, so they took me away from her. She used to visit me, maybe once every six months, and she had me over the holidays. But it was horrible, because she hit me and she was always drinking and* *taking drugs. **The whole of my life I wanted to do everything for her** in order to make her show me some love. I used to steal things for her, I did the rounds of pubs with her, I put up with everything, but **she still gave priority to booze and drugs.**"* The client's mother died during the client's emerging adulthood, clearly as a consequence of the serious abuse of drugs and alcohol.

Many young homeless people **describe the relationship they had with their mother as being more problematic** than in the case of other people of the same age. They are convinced that the mother **was uninterested in them, rejected them, and was not willing to look after them** and offer them their love, for whatever reason. This is the subjective opinion of clients and there may be many reasons for this opinion. We do not know whether these were genuinely such bad mothers (though several certainly were) or whether the child's inability to differentiate plays a role in their evaluation. For instance, was the child able to understand that a mother who enforces certain rules and makes them attend school or work is not necessarily a bad mother? The development of the relationship with the mother may have been influenced by the inability of these individuals to cope with more difficult situations and the resulting feelings of frustration and insecurity, and their inability to come to terms with the fact that they had stopped being the centre of the mother's attention. Several young homeless people were unable to leave go of the mother and were not willing to share her with anyone. They often justify a **negative or ambivalent relationship with the mother** as being a reaction to the disappointment ensuing from their conviction that she was uninterested in them and preferred someone else, either a partner or a younger sibling (usually a stepsibling). Such clients believe that their mother betrayed them and did not stand by them as she should have or as they feel she should have. They experienced her new partnership as the loss of her love, a love they felt they had an inalienable right to. The mother continues to be regarded as an important person, but now as the **agent responsible for their failure**, because she did not respond to the signs of dissatisfaction and disappointment that they provided her. In these and similar cases there is often a misunderstanding in operation: the child acts provocatively in order to receive the mother's attention, but does so in an unacceptable way that aggravates the situation.

The clients' evaluation of the relationship with their mother and her conduct **is often extremely critical**. Several clients describe how they took revenge on their mother for some presumed grievance (though they are often unable to say exactly what). *"I don't know what it was with my mum. We were always arguing, we couldn't stand each other, we did it deliberately. She couldn't stand me from the start. She'd help me because she's my mother, but she screams at me as though I'm an idiot and then waves goodbye and leaves. I so wanted to take revenge on her that they locked her up in Bohnice, because she couldn't keep me under control. **I did everything I could to harm her**. It wasn't as though I wanted to hurt her. I wanted to bring her down a peg or two. Because I can't stand her. Yeah, of course she occasionally said something reasonable,* *she warned me that something would happen and it did."* *(JP, male)* This man's story is dominated by a powerfully ambivalent relationship with the mother. He blames her for the loss of his stepfather, with whom he had a very good relationship. This case clearly does not involve a bad mother but rather a disproportionately defensive reaction on the part of the client. The question remains as to what he was aiming for through his provocative conduct and what his mother could have done to satisfy him. The client is someone who even in adulthood has not formed any kind of deeper relationship and feels himself to be misunderstood by everyone around him.

Some young homeless people are unable to admit that rejection by the mother might have been caused by **their own intolerable conduct.** *"I don't even feel the need to communicate with her. Yes, I have communicated with her. But then when I was there on a visit I learned that I allegedly burgled her apartment and stole certain items, including money. So she reported me, I was prosecuted and escaped with a suspended sentence. That annoyed me the most. I didn't burgle her, and since then **I haven't been in touch with my mother.**"* *(PV, male)* The client has a problematic relationship with both parents. In his case the emotionally important person was his grandmother.

Some clients **are aware that the deterioration of the relationship with their mother is also down to them** and the way they behaved towards her. They know that they disappointed her, but despite all the problems have a positive emotional connection with her and believe that this is reciprocated. *"The relationship with my mother unfolded in stages, first good, then bad. **I disappointed her** and that was that. Mum loves me and I love her, but I disappointed her and it will be a long time before she trusts me, because I disappointed her several times."* *(JJ, male)* The good relationship maintained with the mother contributed to a positive resolution of the client's situation. Eventually he returned home and no longer sleeps rough.

Sometimes the relationship with the mother reflects a client's disappointment that she did not help and support them as she should have done, even though it is clear that this was not due to a lack of interest but fear of an aggressor. This is so in the case of TZ (female), who was tyrannised by an older stepbrother (in other cases it is the father or stepfather). *"I loved mum a lot, but the fact that **she didn't help me with that brother of mine** hurt me. She just looked on and didn't raise a finger. There was a kind of uncertainty between us. I stopped believing*

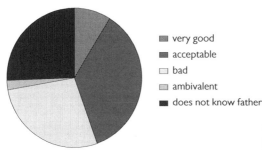

very good
acceptable
bad
ambivalent
does not know father

Graph 5. Clients' relationship to their father (the graph shows relative frequency).

in her, she became like a stranger to me. I really loved her but she hurt me too. She didn't help me. I think she was afraid of my brother. Twice he hit her." At present the client lives on the street and is not in contact with anyone from her family.

A third of clients gave their mother (including adoptive) an unambiguously **positive rating** as someone who had done a lot for them. She was the one person they could rely on, who supported them and tried to give them a good upbringing. *"Mum (adoptive) **did everything she could for me**. When I was little I had problems, and she really helped me. The worst thing that ever happened to me was when she died, because I was dependent on her." (LP, male)* The client's adoptive father rejected him after the mother's death and the client ended up on the streets. If his mother had not died this would probably not have been the case.

In many cases the relationship with the mother is **realistic and stable.** Such clients take into consideration her positive and negative aspects as is usual in adulthood. *"I loved mum a lot and my childhood was basically happy. I can't really complain since many people have it a lot worse than me. Of course, there are lots of things I don't like to remember." (TN, male)* Even though the mother could not cope with her role, as an adult the client is able to forgive and understand her. *"Mum always tried to give us a proper upbringing, but the alcohol meant she couldn't really cope. Slowly she began to forget she even had children." (MP, male)* In these cases we can assume that the primary relationship with the mother was sound, that the mother was basically a kind person but later failed. In the case of client MP this was because the mother drank to excess.

Clients' opinion of their father and their relationship with him

Several of the clients questioned had a very **positive relationship** with their father. Some even adored and idealised him. They are convinced that their father loved them, but are unable to see that his influence was not always positive. This

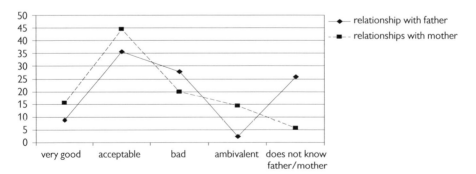

Graph 6. A comparison of clients' relationship to their mother and father (the graph shows relative frequency).

can be the case even within families in which childcare is substandard. *"**Dad liked me best of all**. Dad's ok. He's good fun, he likes me and helped me in everything. From the age of thirteen onward dad taught me how to drink. He would pour drinks for me and my brother." (DV, female)* JB (male), who came from a similarly problematic family, also loved his father. *"I would run away from mum to dad, because he protected me. **He was your typical charming dad**, if I can put it like that that. Kind… that's too weak… maybe stupidly kind."* Not even this father was a guarantee of a good upbringing. He was probably incapable of this, though he clearly genuinely loved his son.

Other clients were more critical. They believe that, though their father's conduct **was not exclusively positive**, it was not catastrophically bad. Many people hold this opinion, including those who are successful in life and do not end up on the street. *"**Dad didn't have time for me**. He was always at work. I reckon it would have been good if he had been stricter and had somehow set me an example and paid more attention to me. Instead, when I wanted something he would promise me it or simply give it to me. But I can't complain. I travelled to the seaside and skied every year with his firm. But because he was so rarely at home I guess I have nothing to say to him." (JJ, male)* The client expressed disappointment at the fact that his father did not display sufficient interest in him and believes he did not care for him. He is convinced that he was not as important to his father as he should have been, and this sense of grievance and injury remains with him to the present day. *"He disappointed me most when he split up with mum. Ok, these things happen, but even so I was disappointed. **He didn't want to see us every weekend**, he found his own family and focused his attention on them."*

An unequivocally **negative evaluation** usually means that the father was an alcoholic and violent (see the stories recounted by clients PV and MT on page 21). Ambivalent feelings toward such a father are not unheard of. *"**When he was sober my dad was one in a million**. You could do anything with him. We used to go on holiday. But he was only like that when sober. You could talk about anything, play games, muck around, do anything you liked. Everything was cool. But the moment he started boozing he turned into a monster." (MŽ, male)*

Now adults, some clients are able to view their father objectively. They forgive him and display an **understanding of his conduct**, even though it bothered them and still does. But they now realise that they were not simply passive victims of family relations. They are capable of understanding the causes of these problems, problems that they were unable to perceive in a more comprehensive way as children. *"You know what? Dad had me when he was eighteen or nineteen. If I had had a child when I was eighteen, I wouldn't have had much of a clue as to how to bring it up. Plus at that time he played sport, he had a life of his own. I can't hold it against him. Of course they let me grow into the maverick I am, maybe that's what they wanted. But maybe I didn't offer them much room. I regret the lack of interest from dad. But I don't know. If dad hadn't been at work every day – but then at least we had money." (JJ, male)*

2.1.3 PROBLEMS ARISING AS A CONSEQUENCE
OF THE BREAKUP OF THE ORIGINAL FAMILY

Some young homeless people regard the **breakup of the family** as a milestone event in their lives that triggered other problems. It is clear that such an event can take place at any point during the course of childhood and adolescence. It does not ensue from the clients' stories that the earlier the breakup the more serious the consequences. The impact can be subjectively significant even if the family splits up when the client is somewhat older. Anything can provide a concrete reason for a feeling of insecurity: the concentration of the married couple on their own problems, the disruption caused to family background, the feeling that the parents are uninterested in or even reject the child, or the arrival of a new member of the family, often a stepfather, who is unwelcome to the child. It is not only the fact that a family breaks up that is important, but the reason why it broke up and what the consequences were.

Some clients do not speak of the collapse of their own parents' marriage but of the problems that arose after another man joined the family who was introduced to them as their **mother's new partner**. (46.7% of clients report having had this experience, with 13.3% having experienced the repeated arrival and departure of their mother's new partners.) Many problems arose from the fact of having to live with this person, and some because of their departure (the child became fixated on them and could not understand why they had to lose them) or the fact that their mother changed partners frequently, thus increasing feelings of insecurity. A more detailed analysis of the stories of young homeless people shows that the primary cause of dissatisfaction in the child is not always the unacceptability of the stepfather or his hostile conduct to his stepchild. The source of the problems was sometimes the unacceptable behaviour of the client themselves, who ran away from home, played truant, stole, took drugs, etc. The mother then finds herself forced by circumstances to adopt an unambiguous stance that for her represents a painful choice. She is either on the side of her own, albeit problematic child, or on the side of her partner (who may on occasion be in the right, though this is difficult for the mother to accept).

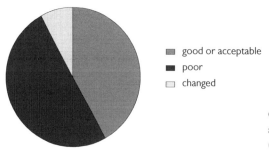

- good or acceptable
- poor
- changed

Graph 7. Clients' relationships to their stepfather or their mother's new partner (the graph shows relative frequency).

An unwillingness to accept their mother's new partner, who represents an **unpleasant intervention in family relations**, is an important feature of the life story told by ŠP (male), whose father left home when he was 10. ŠP and his mother lived on their own until he was 17, when his mother brought home a boyfriend he was unwilling to accept. *"Practically nothing changed. Mind you, the fact that dad had left was apparent from the atmosphere, which was completely different when we weren't all together, when I was there only with mum. She was all alone when me and my sister went to bed, it was completely different. Everything was basically normal until she found a new boyfriend when I was 17. We ignored each other. I had a great relationship with my mum, no problems with my sister. We haven't had any serious conflicts in life. But **he is simply horrible to me**, I find him unpleasant. I used to smoke a joint occasionally and that really bothered him. I asked him what business it was of his, and he accused me of not communicating with him. I couldn't get on with him because he would come home drunk and knock my mum about. So **I punched him** and broke his jaw in three places. I was in prison for three months for that, and while he remains at home I'm not setting foot in the place. I don't think there's any way I could get on pleasantly with him. I guess I know why I don't like him. Because he hit my mum. **I guess we just didn't hit it off and a concrete reason for disliking him arrived by chance.**"* At the time he was interviewed the client had been living on the street for three years. He did not want to return home and was probably unable to.

LB (female), whose family was far more problematic than that of the previous client, is another who did not accept her mother's new partner. Her parents separated when she was two and shortly afterwards all three siblings were placed in a children's home. However, her mother regained custody of her children. LB also felt that a strange man had taken her mother away and **represented a new threat to her** already undermined sense of **security**. *"Then mum took us to live in Ústí until I was 10. And then she found herself a bloke. I was in Borstal because of him. We couldn't stand each other, we went at each other with knives. I don't talk to my mum. I don't want to. She wanted a bloke, and now she's got one. **He took our mother away, she didn't notice us anymore**, and when she did, she simply beat us and that was all. Before that things had been fine. She brought us up on her own. We were dependent on her, simply on her and nobody else. I really took it to heart. Mum's marriage pushed us away completely. Before that, even though we didn't have what we wanted, or we didn't have everything that other children have, we simply envied them, but that was ok. The problems started when he appeared on the scene and they stopped noticing us."* This mother was clearly flawed in many ways. She did not always look after her children as she should have. However, the client's interpretation of her conduct is probably an oversimplification. Nevertheless, this is how she explains her problems and that is the crucial fact.

Our group of young homeless people includes people who were **unable to forgive their mother for finding a new partner** and thus disturbing what had formerly been a harmonious family. Though for them the stepfather is an undesirable person, the main problem lies on the side of the mother, who allegedly gave priority to him over them. The relationship with such a mother is characterised by ambivalence: she was (and probably is) loved, but is also disliked for what she did to her children. It would appear that there is an inability to deal with such a fundamental transformation of family life. This is not an unusual situation and most children manage to deal with it without too many problems. But not PČ (female). *"I had a normal family. My parents divorced when I was about eight. Until then my childhood was relatively good. Then they divorced and mum was on her own for a while. We wanted to see dad, but he just seemed to disappear. Then mum found herself a **real fucking dickhead**. He's seven years younger than her and wanted to create a revolution in our home. I began to run away. I was searching for love, the love you don't have in a family when it's breaking up. Mum was the kind – sorry for saying this – who lost the remains of her brain when she had her first orgasm. So she falls in love with a bloke who's seven years younger than her. **I'll never forgive her for giving him priority over us kids**."*

The client admits that the tension and problems in the family were often the result of her behaviour and feels guilty. *"My parents were always arguing. Mum would nag dad, saying he wasn't providing for her. I started to understand that they were arguing because of me, and I always felt that if I wasn't there things would be better. When I was 12 I started to run away from home. Once, when they caught me, I told them I didn't want to return home, that I'd prefer to be in a children's home."* There is a question mark over how the family functioned in reality, since the client's younger brother grew up without problems. This could be due to his age and greater adaptability. He was not so used to his real father and was able to accept someone else more easily.

A mother's new partner was an important figure in the families of homeless youth. However, their relationship with this person was not simple. It definitely did not involve the classic structure of the evil interloper and the suffering child, even if the new partner was often perceived as an intruder. However, a similar attitude is far from exceptional and regularly appears in the case of people who do not become homeless. Some clients were clear from the outset: they did not accept their mother's new partner. However, in many cases **the stepfather was accepted** and rated very highly. He was the person who looked after them (which their own father had not done), was kind to them and supported his partner's children. (This was most often the case when the real father had never lived with the family or had behaved so badly toward the child that it was a relief when he left home or when the mother left him). The stepfather in the story told by JP (male) played this role. JP does not know who his real father is. He formed a close relationship with his stepfather and took it badly when his mother and stepfather split up. He is convinced that his mother did him great harm by taking away his father surrogate. *"After I was born we were alone for three years. And then mum found someone and lived with them for four years. This man was **possibly the best father**. He was kind, really kind. And then they split up. I don't know exactly why, mum never told me. It would have been better if she had never introduced me to such a* *great person. After that there was a new father every six months. I still keep in touch with him and visit him every week."*

Both the arrival of an unwelcome stepfather and the loss of a person who functioned as a substitute father in the family and was very important for the child can be stress factors. The **departure of such a person** entails the **loss of someone important**, a blow to feelings of security, and sometimes a stimulus to undesirable behaviour. A change of substitute fathers is always difficult, and if a child accepts one, it will not find it easy to accept another. The mother's new partner is then perceived as having caused the loss of the previous one, who was viewed positively and perhaps even idealised.

Over the course of time the relationship between a child and its substitute father changes, and even though he may have been accepted to begin with, he does not always retain this positive role. This is usually because he is **incapable of coping with the fact that his partner's child, who may sometimes be problematic, is growing up**, and so difficulties arise that may be more serious than in the case of a conflict between the real father and his offspring. This is so in the case of TN (male), who is aware that he is also responsible for the negative transformation of the relationship with his substitute father. *"My parents split up when I was seven years old. A few months after the divorce mum brought home a new partner. He remained with us for ten years.* **To begin with the relationship was reasonably good,** *but when I got a bit bigger things started going wrong. He started humiliating me in front of my friends. We ended up by simply saying hullo and then ignoring each other.* **I was insolent to him.** *He never hit me, but took the piss out of me and I saw a big difference between the way he acted to me and my sister and to his own children. In time* **I developed an aversion towards him** *and gave up even noticing him. When conflicts arose, mainly because of me, mum would defend me when she saw that he was acting unfairly towards me. But it was at that time that things started to go wrong. In the end he split up with mum and she put the blame on me. She got really depressed and when I came home she would start to moan at me, saying it was all my fault. That lasted a long time, six to nine months. Then we started arguing a lot and the relationship* (between mother and son) *completely collapsed."* The client's opinion was influenced by a sense of injustice at the way that his stepfather behaved differently to him than to the other children (either less problematic children or his own offspring from an earlier marriage). It is difficult to say whether this was really the case. However, what is fundamental is that the client felt himself being rejected and behaved accordingly. (The belief that a negative stance is fair may be a rationalisation of a child's own not always reasonable conduct.) At present the client has resolved his relationship with his stepfather and rates him more objectively in retrospect. He now believes his stepfather to be a pretty good person. *"We didn't like each other.* **In hindsight I reckon he wasn't that bad.***"*

Some clients have an **objective view of the reasons the relationship with their stepfather deteriorated** and are aware that they themselves were partly to blame. They realise that their own behaviour was not always perfect and that it was not only about their stepfather behaving badly towards them. *"My stepfather behaved to me as though I were his own child. There was a peaceful transition to this second father and I have a lot more respect for him than I do for my biological father. He brought me up and provided for me. Nowadays I have a poor relationship with my stepfather. I started to have conflicts with him because I was stubborn and because I stopped respecting him."* (MM, male)

When the composition of a family is constantly changing and it is not clear who belongs and does not belong to it, **this can be a source of insecurity** for a child. New people are constantly turning up, usually the mother's partners, and previous partners are leaving, and so the child has no chance to create a more stable relationship with someone. **The stability and reliability** that a child needs, because it defines itself by the people to whom it belongs and upon whom it can rely, are missing. JP (male) had an unstable family in which his mother got through various partners. His position was made worse by the feeling that it was always he that was overlooked in favour of the other children. *"I never knew my real father. My mother had already taken up with my sister's father by the time I was born. As far as I remember everything was fine until I started to be a son of a bitch and a bastard in the words of my dad* (his first stepfather)*, who started to hit me. I don't know when it all started, maybe when I was in 2nd grade. Suddenly I was the bastard and my sister started to be the favoured one because I wasn't his biological child. They split up when I was in 4th grade and mum found herself another boyfriend. This one was nice.* **He was really nice until he and my mum had a daughter together**, *another sister for me. And then the arguments began between us. For instance, he didn't tell me what I had to do and then after a week would complain that he had to do everything himself and that I was useless and wouldn't help him and so on. The situation got worse and worse until it collapsed completely."* There is a question as to why this highly unstable family kept breaking up and whether the problem was not more to do with tension in the relationships between the adults and the oldest child rather than rejection by the stepsibling. What is important is that the client felt himself overlooked within the family.

An unstable family background, in which **substitute fathers came and went and the mother was unable to cope with life,** features in the story told by TD (female). *"I lived with mum and dad until I was six, and then they split up. But we lived in one apartment together until I was 11, when* **mum found another boyfriend** *and we moved out. Her new bloke was almost completely uninterested in me, he couldn't care less. We lived like that for five years. Then they split up and for a while it was just me and mum, before she found herself another bloke. We lived with him for three years, but then* **they split up and mum found yet another**. *I lived with them for a short while and then moved in with my father. I got on well with my mum's second boyfriend. He was really nice, more of a friend than a father. As far as that husband was concerned, I didn't get on well with him to begin with, though things are better now. When mum split up with her first boyfriend,* **she started to drink**. *She also drank with the second boyfriend and we didn't get on at all. I think that's when it all began. Alcohol has had a terrible effect on* *mum. Otherwise she's a really nice woman. By now I didn't want to go home, so I would spend weekends sleeping at friends'. I don't like seeing my mum when she's drunk."* This case is not so much about the mother's partners but more how she responded to repeated split-ups by resorting to alcohol. A later relationship that was finally functional remedied the situation, though for the client this was by now too late.

2.1.4 A HOME WHERE THE CLIENTS FELT UNWANTED

The stories of young homeless people often feature a **feeling of being unwanted and unaccepted by their parents**, be these their biological or stepparents, and the ensuing insecurity that encourages them to look for stability and gratification elsewhere, often in problematic conduct or relationships. Many homeless youth feel they were rejected, overlooked, unwanted and unloved. We do not know whether this was true or not. However, the important thing is that this is how they felt. These clients say things like: *"I was the one nobody took any notice of, nobody was interested in me and I wasn't important for anyone".* This rejection does not have to take an extreme form, e.g. *"they didn't want me and hit me".* It can involve much more subtle manifestations that did not even have to exceed the boundaries of the normal. What is important here is the client's interpretation. The fact that they are convinced that their parents have no interest in them and do not love them enough serves as a justification for their undesirable conduct. Feelings of being overlooked, emotionally rejected and negatively evaluated were reported by 50% of homeless youth in the group examined by K. Ferguson (2010). The figure was not as high in our group (see graph 2), though there is a clear tendency to feel unaccepted. For the homeless in our study home does not provide the background it should and it is therefore easy to leave it.

Some young homeless people said the family in which they grew up was insufficiently receptive and that their parents did not provide them the necessary support. It mattered to them that their parents had no time for them and, as they see it, no interest. They did not pay any attention to them, were unable to appreciate the fact the child had been successful in some way, and simply criticised them. *"Nobody ever praised me for anything I did at home. No matter how hard I tried they always simply criticised me. **They never praised me for anything**, or if they did I certainly can't remember it. And I needed to hear that." (TN, male)* In later life this client felt that he was not sufficiently accepted even by his peers. He has psychological problems and has received psychiatric treatment. His relationship with his mother has gradually improved.

A feeling of being unwanted, rejected and inferior is a basic motif running through the story told by MS (female), who is the last of three children (the older two being brothers). *"They* (her grandparents) *didn't want me, they wanted just two grandchildren. But mum ignored them because she wanted a little girl. I was completely in my brothers' shadow, **I couldn't listen to anything** (music). I wasn't* allowed to listen to anything or watch television. Whenever mum and I argued she always told my father. What I've learned, what I know how to do, is accept blows." This girl's family is far from ideal. The parents drink to excess. The father resorts to corporal punishment more often than is appropriate. However, the family is not so pathological as to be able to regard it as the cause of their daughter's social ostracism. The family included two older brothers who applied themselves at school and have jobs. In addition, the client's parents are managing to look after her daughter, now five years old.

JP (male) also felt overlooked and undervalued. "You're good at sports, say, and your parents don't even come to watch you play. You do something you're good at and they couldn't care less. It's horrible." His feeling of being overlooked and rejected increased when his sister was born. "It was clear from the start that everything had changed, that nobody was going to behave as they had up until them. The upshot was that **nobody took a blind bit of notice of me**. My sister is the darling of the family, not me. All of the care simply evaporated. I just sat and stared as mum played with V., how she played with the dog, and **nobody so much as noticed me**." It is impossible to say whether this simply involved a regular focus on caring for a small child that an older sibling tends to be jealous of, or genuinely preferential treatment being given the child of both parents over the problematic little boy from the mother's previous relationship. What is important is how the client experienced it.

A feeling of being overlooked and having no interest taken in them, combined with a conviction that a sibling is receiving preferential treatment, was a strong feature of the life story recounted by ZK (female). "Up until I was eight I was basically an only child. Then a younger brother came along. I found it difficult, because **he received all the attention**. I looked forward to him, I was glad to have him. But then I discovered that my parents were only looking after him. I'm eight years older than him and he was a right little arse-licker, he knew exactly what to do to make them worship him." The client still has an unresolved relationship with her parents to the present day. "I can't remember anything nice. They blamed everything on me." Her relationships with other people are also problematic, and she still lives on the street.

A feeling of being unwanted and the insecurity this provokes can lead a person to seek support elsewhere (e.g. in a gang) or to behave in a provocative way in order to attract attention. However, the results of such efforts tend not to be satisfactory. The parents do not respond in the desired way or the client is unable to interpret their reactions correctly. Provocative and often intolerable conduct can in many cases be a sign of dissatisfaction or even desperation and the inability of a child to cope. The unresolved problems persist and relationships gradually deteriorate.

In many families described by clients as problematic (almost 80%), their **siblings**, either biological or stepsiblings, grew up **without any problems** and do not suffer any now. (Indeed, there are few people who had similarly problematic siblings, just under 15%, and all of these cases involved a severely dysfunctional family.) The question arises as to why the family environment impacted so negatively on one child, causing them to fail in so many ways, while others dealt with this burden without significant detriment (unless a negative subjective interpretation was involved of what was basically a standard family environment). It is of course possible that the parents did not behave to all of their offspring in the same way, perhaps simply because they were different personalities and responded in different ways. Stepsiblings might represent competition. A stepfather who was the biological father of their siblings may have displayed greater interest in them than in his partner's children. Another important fact may be that the **dysfunctional individual is often the oldest child in a family** (regardless of whether they are a boy or a girl), on whom the parents might have greater demands, yet to whom they pay less attention.

Another cause of problems could involve a less advantageous combination of genetic dispositions that contributes to a failure to cope with a given situation and sets off a process of gradual social decline. This possibility is backed up by the fact that, for instance, young homeless people often (in a third of cases) have **in their family someone who was also a problematic personality** (be this father, mother, uncle or grandfather). Such figures may have been alcoholics, gamblers or criminals who had problems with the law (we can assume that this might be the manifestation of a personality disorder) or were mentally ill. It should again be emphasised that this involves the subjective opinion of the client recounting

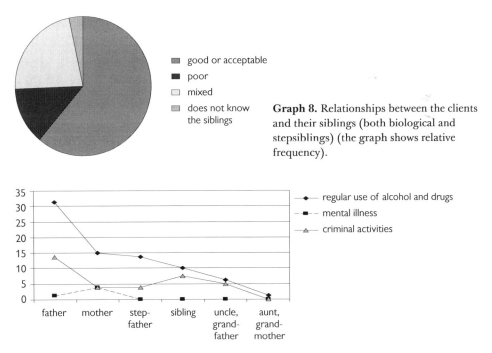

Graph 8. Relationships between the clients and their siblings (both biological and stepsiblings) (the graph shows relative frequency).

Graph 9. The frequency of problematic individuals in the clients' families (the graph shows relative frequency).

their life story and describing these people in a certain way. It is very possible that there were more such cases or, on the contrary, that many of these were not so problematic.

Information is lacking on 10 people, because from early childhood they lived in an institution and do not know their relatives.

Cauce et al. (2000) discovered that 55% of the mothers of young homeless people drank alcohol or used drugs and 84% of them had problems with the law. The fathers were similarly problematic: 52% drank alcohol or used drugs and 70% had been prosecuted. Ryan et al. (2000) reached similar conclusions: 39% of young homeless people had a father who had committed a criminal act and 21% had such a mother. Mallett et al. (2005) discovered that one of the parents of 26% of young homeless people drank alcohol or used drugs, and when the family split up the mother's new partner was similarly disposed. Thompson et al. (2007) say that in half of the families of homeless youth at least one of the parents drank to excess, and in 20% of cases both parents drank and more than one third of them used hard drugs. Ferguson (2009) discovered that 42% of the parents of young homeless people consumed drugs or alcohol to excess. According to Tyler (2006) the consumption of alcohol and drugs in such families is commonplace and was part of life for 92.5% of the parents of young homeless people.

2.1.5 GRANDPARENTS AS A SUBSTITUTE SOURCE OF SECURITY AND SAFETY

For many clients the **grandmother** (and sometimes the grandfather) was an important person and reliable source of emotional security and safety. Approximately one third of the group (28.8%) said that their grandmother played a positive and important role in their life, while only 2.8% thought otherwise. For the most part it was she who focused her attention on the children, protected them, helped them, and brought them up. Grandmothers coped with even the more problematic grandchildren by using the carrot rather than the stick. *"The best of the bunch was grandma. Grandma influenced me by making me realise that I had to get an education. She made me complete my schooling so that I got out of the rut in which I'd been. Grandma really helped me in this respect because she saw that I wasn't coping psychologically. So she was the one person I told everything. **I always trusted grandma** and I always will."* (PV, male) Unfortunately the client failed in his attempt not to disappoint her. The reason was his drug addiction, which finally destroyed this relationship too.

It was the grandmother who brought up TN (male). *"**Grandma was a wonderful woman**. She gave me good advice about life, except she was somewhat two-faced, she didn't say things openly, there was no pressure on me as there was from granddad. I liked it that way."* The same goes for MŽ (male). *"My grandma **stuck by me** and suffered everything. If it hadn't been for her I would have ended up in a children's home,* *because nobody took any notice of me, none of my relatives, and it was only she who said that as long as she lived I wouldn't go to a children's home. She looked after me, re-educated me. When I was with dad I was a right little bastard. I'd steal money from his wallet. I didn't do anything like that to grandma."* The client's grandmother died when he was 16 years old.

The client's grandmother represented a security that was constant and unchanging, that would only be lost when she died. The death of a grandmother is often cited as a negative experience. *"The most important person was grandma. She was a fantastic woman. You could say that she brought me up, since I didn't listen to mum. **The best time was while grandma was still alive,** and when she died I felt completely empty without her." (JP, male)* The client has a very problematic relationship with his mother, whom he blames for divorcing his favourite stepfather and the birth of his younger sister. He feels betrayed by her. His grandmother never let him down and so remains a positive figure for him. It is also possible that he has idealised her over the course of time.

2.1.6 FOSTER PARENTS OR INSTITUTIONS

A relatively high number of young homeless people have lived for at least a certain period of time in **foster care**. Sometimes the child does not even know its real parents, but knows that they had no interest in him or her. At other times the child undergoes a phase of neglect or even tyranny before being placed in a more peaceful environment. None of this can be regarded as positive, which is why it is no wonder that such individuals are prone to failure later in life. The new environment is not always ideal and sometimes foster parents cannot cope with bringing up a child. At other times there are problems ensuing from an insufficient link being formed with the new family.

> The results of foreign studies are diverse. Lara Embry et al. (2000) state that more than half of the young homeless people in their group had been in foster care. (However, these were individuals who had also suffered psychological problems and had been placed under psychiatric supervision). Cauce et al. (2000) discovered that 33% of young homeless people had spent a certain time in a foster family, and that some were only found such a family when already in the prepubescent phase. M. Kushel et al. (2007) say that in their group of homeless youth 40% had grown up in a foster family. The same results were reported by A. Nesmith (2006). In the case of K. Shelton et al. (2009) this figure was only 12%.

Whatever the reason, some adolescents run away from or leave their foster families relatively early and often end up on the street. Sometimes they become homeless because after leaving a children's home or youth detention centre they do not know how they should live and have no financial or social support that would get them through the period during which they belong nowhere. Their social decline can also be hastened by the baggage they carry from the past, from the family in which they lived in early childhood. In most cases there is an **accumulation of risk factors**, including both the personality of the individual in question and the negative influence of the environment to which they were exposed from birth (Nesmith, 2006).

The lack of interest shown by the biological parents is manifest by the abandonment of the child immediately after its birth or insufficient care that results in the child being removed from the family. If the foster family also fails, the child returns to a children's home. If the foster family later breaks up (the mother dies or the parents divorce), an adolescent may not have to return to institutional care but will not always deal with the situation acceptably. It is obvious that not even adoption or foster care can be 100% successful, whatever the reasons (the personality of the foster parents, their death, the breakup of the family or the problematic personality of a troublesome child). In our group of young homeless people, **20% grew up in an institution or a foster family**. This is a relatively high figure that is well in excess of statistics for the population as a whole (which is 1% at most).

A foster family can compensate for rejection or negligence on the part of the biological parents. However, if the child is only placed in a new family at preschool age or as they are starting school, it may already be too late to effect a remedy. The child's **problems associated with emotional insecurity** and the lack of any bond with another person can persist and undermine relationships with the other members of the new family. At this age children cannot so easily accept the family and create links with it, even though they do not feel unwanted and are aware that the new family is looking after them well. It is easy to leave such a family, because it does not represent the kind of background that a person never fully leaves even as an adult.

A foster child cannot always overcome its **disappointment at being abandoned by its own mother**. Even when foster care works well and the child is aware of this fact, it remains split between the two mothers, its biological and foster. Such individuals find it easy to leave their foster family, even though they have no objective reason for so doing. Their problem simply resides in the fact that they do not belong anywhere. *"When I was born I was basically with just mum and my uncle. I never met my father. Then me and my brother were in a children's home from the age of three to five and then **we were adopted. This helped me a lot, in the most positive sense of the word.** But I started asking myself why things had panned out in this way. Who did I love more? Well, my adopted parents, of course. But when I was little I spent night after night in tears. This went on a long time. I asked my adopted parents why she* (the client's biological mother) *had put us in a children's home. They told me that it was because she was always involved with some bloke or other. I'd like it if things were different with my own mum. I'd definitely like to meet her. Adoption was the most important thing and the suspension of contact with my own mother."* (JH, female)

The client did not experience significant problems with her foster parents, and yet at the age of 18 decided to leave home with a group of her peers, without knowing where she was heading, and ended up on the street.

A **lack of the necessary life experience** can result in an unwillingness and inability to accept authority or any restrictions. This in turn can be manifest in poor grades at school, truancy and running away, as well as other problematic conduct. Individuals who did not experience any kind of satisfactory relationship in their childhood do not trust anyone and in many situations are **unable to react in an appropriate way**. They never learned to take responsibility for themselves and resolve their own problems, i.e. to reach decisions with an awareness of and consideration for the possible consequences, to be thoughtful toward other people and empathise with them, etc. None of this creates a sound basis for dealing with an independent life as an adult.

This is to be seen in the story recounted by LD (female), which represents a **sequence of disappointment, distress and rejection**. It becomes apparent how various burdens accumulate that in the end a person cannot deal with. The family rejected her, she was abused by her foster parents, and her own father did not want to meet her. She ended up spending her childhood in a children's home. *"When I was still a baby I was put in a children's home. When I was three I was placed with foster parents, but they abused me when I was still only three. It's really horrible. You're little and an older person shows you these disgusting things. I tried to forget it, not think about it, but it's always with me. **For me the children's home was family**, and the carers there, because they were the ones that brought me up, taught me cleanliness and so on. When I was 13 I began running away because I wanted to be at home, **I wanted to get to know my parents**. But dad wasn't interested. **That astonished me**, the fact that he had no interest in what had happened to his daughter, how she was and what she was doing. I was in a youth detention centre, a juvenile home, a children's home, I was aggressive, rude, I did whatever I wanted, I didn't listen."* The lesson she learned from her experiences was not to take anyone else into account. The realisation that her parents had no interest in her and had rejected her provoked various defensive reactions, many of which led to yet further problems.

IB (male) tells a very similar story. He looks like the typical product of institutional care and exhibits the symptoms of **early emotional deprivation and adaptation problems**. He had no interest in meeting his biological parents. From his point of view this made no sense. *"From the age of three **I was stuck in a children's home**. All I remember are the policemen who took me to some building or other where I remained. I never learned why I was put there, because when I was little it never occurred to me. I never actually learned the truth, just that my mother and father had been in prison many times, both when they were young. My father was in for 15 years, though I don't know what for. **I didn't lack anything in the children's home**, I had everything I needed, though the regime was strict. **I didn't even notice I didn't have parents**. What was nice about the home was that I travelled abroad several times, something I would never have done with my parents. It never occurred to me that I should run* away. I didn't have anywhere to run. I think the children's home could have taught me more about life, how things should be done, so that I didn't end up as I did." The client's social decline began after he left the children's home, when under the influence of a gang he gave up his job and began to use drugs.

KV (female) only entered a children's home after her family split up when she was seven. Her mother ended up homeless and her father beat the children and so they were removed from his care. She describes her time in the home as a relatively positive period in her life (several clients were of the same opinion). For people in her situation, a **children's home** can offer a **reliable, albeit impersonal base**. *"In the children's home they wanted to help us with everything*, even upbringing. They taught us how to behave politely. Everyone wanted to help us and teach us that life is complex and that we had to find work, a base, everything. But some kids ignored them. I was one of the kids that ignored them. I would always be thinking of something else, I was never interested, so I was like byeee! and off doing my own thing. However, when I ended up on the street I regretted the fact that I hadn't listened to them."* This client is aware that she made mistakes and does not look for the cause in her complex family relations, even though they unquestionably impacted negatively on her.

The life story recounted by LP (male) differs from those we have examined so far. His adoptive family was functional and only fell apart **after the death of his adoptive mother**. If this had not happened, his life would have probably headed in a different direction and he would not have ended up on the street. *"The main problem is that I never knew my own family. After I was born I was put in an infant care centre, then a children's home. I stayed there until I was three, and then I was adopted. **When I was 12 my adoptive mum died**. A year later my father found himself a boyfriend, and that was the end of the family. So mum died when I was 12 and I ran away for the first time when I was 13. The worst thing was when mum died. It had a huge and lasting impact on my psyche, because I had been dependent on her. **Conflicts began between me and my father**."* The client's adoptive father did not care for him and his entire support base collapsed. This is a person who needed guid-

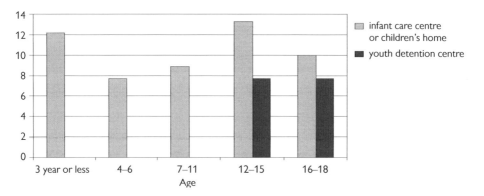

Graph 10. The time spent by the clients in different institutions (the graph shows relative frequency).

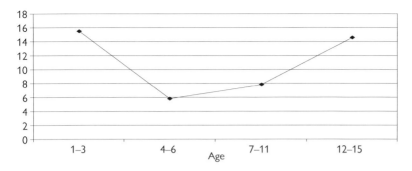

Graph 11. The age at which fundamental changes most often took place (the graph shows relative frequency).

ance, and when he had it was capable of meeting his duties. Alone, he was unable to deal with life and ended up on the street, though this had never been his intention.

Another variant is to be found in the life story of LR (male), who was adopted. There was never any problem with his adoptive family. His parents did not divorce and they took care of their children. However, **the client's personality** made it impossible for him to develop in at least an acceptable way. He does not enjoy a warm relationship with either his adoptive parents or his siblings, even though he was placed with the family as a baby and had the opportunity to form a strong emotional bond. *"Mum is permanently pissed off with me, she's disappointed. With dad things are on what you could call a professional level.* ***If I need something I go to him, but if I don't need anything I ignore him.*** *I have a better relationship with my mother. They were really kind to me, they gave me a lot of leeway. And the* ***relationship with my siblings?***[4] ***Nothing to speak of with any of them.*** *I see them once every six months or so when I meet them by chance somewhere. When I lived at home it was ok, normal. Until I was fourteen I was obedient, and then defiant, disobedient."* The client ended up as a homeless drug addict.

Being moved from place to place frequently can place a significant burden on a child, prompting them entirely logically to believe they do not belong anywhere. A change of environment is usually brought about by the parents splitting up or having another type of problem (alcoholism, time spent in a psychiatric hospital or prison, etc.). The child is not always capable of dealing satisfactorily with these events, especially if they are repeated. **Moving from one dysfunctional family or institution to another** has very negative consequences. Well intentioned attempts to return a child to their original family, i.e. their biological parents or other relatives, can be stressful and unsuccessful (see the story of MH (female), who was abused). Under such circumstances a child can

---

4 These siblings are the biological children of his adoptive parents, who were born only after he arrived in the family.

lack even the little a good carer can offer. PČ (female) believes her carer offered her more than her own mother. *"I think of my carer as my mother, and I remain in touch with her. In one year in a young offenders' institution she did more for me than my mother did in her whole life."* Our group included several such people, who are convinced that they were better off in an institution. At least they had a sense of security, life had set rules, and nobody hit them. *"In all honesty, I was better off in a children's home than at home with an alcoholic father." (PV, male)* **At a certain age**, at the dawn of adolescence, **an impersonal institution may be more appropriate** and easier to adapt to than a new foster family that finds an older child difficult to accept.

2.2 SCHOOL – THE OPINIONS OF YOUNG HOMELESS PEOPLE REGARDING THEIR SCHOLASTIC SUCCESS

Homeless people tend to be unwilling or unable to respect society's norms and meet the duties placed on them. This tendency is already apparent in childhood and is clear above all in relation to school. A poor education and the lack of any qualifications, the inevitable result of their approach to school, becomes a permanent obstacle to achieving better social status. A fact that complicates efforts to abandon street life is that there is no interest in an unqualified person. According to C. Bearsley-Smith et al. (2008) and Marianne van den Bree et al. (2009) failure at school, problematic conduct and a low level of education are significant risk factors that contribute to social decline, including homelessness.

The stories recounted by our young homeless people did not feature school as an important topic, even though for understandable reasons their relationship to school was poor, as indeed were their grades. The most frequently offered explanation for this state of affairs is a lack of motivation (the children did not enjoy school and did not want to learn). They admit that failure at school was their own fault because they were lazy, **did not meet their duties**, and made no effort to succeed. Few of them concede that the reason for their lack of success was a lack of ability and that it was not actually within their power to learn more. As part of a defensive rationalisation they say things like: *"I didn't do anything because I had no reason to do anything"*. It is clear that an unwillingness to work, later manifest in their descent into homelessness, was already influencing their conduct in childhood and adolescence.

The stories recounted by young homeless people contain many **similar descriptions of their lack of educational success**. A milestone was often attained upon reaching puberty, at the end of basic school or immediately afterwards. It is not entirely clear whether this is the consequence of a general rejection of duties and an unwillingness to accept the associated restrictions, or an inability to cope with more and more difficult curricula and a resignation to receiving poor grades. Both possibilities probably play their part.

Adolescence is accompanied by increased criticism of norms that have been hitherto respected. This is reflected in a negativity that expresses the adolescent's need to have their opinion heard. The adolescent breaks away from the family and the world of superior adults. Purely formal authority no longer controls them, since they cease to recognise it, and often nobody socially acceptable embodies any kind of genuine authority for them. This is the period during which individuals who lack a strong base and whose parents do not care for them or display an interest in them break away from the family definitively. They no longer have any reason to respect their parents and are physically strong enough not to tolerate corporal punishment. Such adolescents can begin to act in a completely uninhibited way. Their parents do not represent authority and school has no power to influence their conduct in any fundamental way (Vágnerová, 2006). We can expect several young homeless people to conform to this description.

When young homeless people speak about school, they all say roughly the same thing: *"**We didn't enjoy ourselves, we didn't want to study, we were lazy**"*, and this is how they remain. Nothing much changes in this respect. They did not acquire the ability to work systematically as children, and this is difficult to acquire as an adult:

*"I had pretty poor grades at school. Mostly Cs, a few Ds. I basically couldn't give a fuck, **I didn't want to learn**." (TD, female)*

*"I had poor grades. I only just about scraped through. **I was a slacker. I'm lazy**. I didn't enjoy sitting on a bench in school." (MP, male)*

*"I didn't have very good grades. I didn't study much. I could have coped if I'd wanted to. But I didn't want to. **I've been like this the whole of my life. It's sheer indolence**." (KS, female)*

Such sentiments were repeated again and again.

Not all clients adopted such a negative attitude to studies, at least at basic school. In the stories of several young homeless people there is a clear decline from an initially problem-free school career, and this decline is **associated with problematic conduct**. If someone plays truant on a regular basis, it is unlikely their grades will be good. One of the clients who studied assiduously to begin with but then dropped off was PČ (female), who had problems more with con-

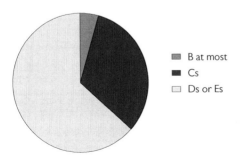

■ B at most
■ Cs
☐ Ds or Es

Graph 12. The grades attained by young homeless people as far as they remember at the end of basic school (the graph shows relative frequency).

duct than with grades. *"I didn't have any great difficulty in studying and if I had gone to school I'd have had ok grades. But most of the time I was average. I never had a worse grade than C. But as far as conduct was concerned, from sixth grade onwards I was always on a C, though I can't remember what I did to deserve it.* **What happened was I ran away from home and so didn't go to school.** *"*

It is by no means exceptional for **drugs and alcohol to be the cause of scholastic failure**, even though this would usually involve the accumulation of more than one problem. *"At basic school things were really bad. I had to repeat eighth grade twice. When I was in seventh or eighth grade* **I began to sniff toluene and smoke grass**. *That was possibly the worst thing I could have done, because* **I was completely out of it**, *I didn't know what I was doing. This was because firstly I couldn't cope with it and secondly because I didn't even want to cope, I was off my head, I saw drugs everywhere and only thought about where to find the money to buy them."* (PV, male) This young man was taking drugs even during the interview, and apart from his behavioural problems, his addiction was the main reason he ended up on the street.

MK (male) was expelled from school for drinking alcohol. *"To begin with I studied electronics and mechanics. I hated that and dropped out of it, and then I transferred over to cookery, where I got straight As and Bs. School was ok, but incredibly boring, which was why* **I used to drink from time to time, even at school**. *I always got on fine with the teachers and they always praised me. Later on they started to nag me because of the booze. And finally they* **chucked me out, again because of the booze.** *"* Alcohol remains this client's main problem and the reason he ended up homeless.

Sometimes the reason for poor grades is to be found in a **dysfunctional and uneducated family**, which is unable to support its children and does not represent any kind of positive model for them. JB (male) was not successful at school because he lacked basic knowledge and skills, as well as the necessary habits and guidance. His parents were on such a low intellectual and educational level that he could not expect any assistance from them whatsoever. For their part they demanded nothing from their son and it is therefore no wonder that his grades were so poor. *"***I flunked school**. *I left in the eighth grade and then went to a school for kids from special school and basically I flipped. They threw me out because I stole a thousand crowns from one office in change. I didn't even complete one year."* The client found himself on the level that is customary in his family. None of his family blamed him for this, but equally nobody was able to assist him.

Similar reasons lay behind an inability to complete middle school. The trigger as far as an inability to complete professional training was concerned was a **general apathy**, an inability to be engaged by anything, to set a target and/or to **fulfil the basic requirements** (to turn up at school and do at least the minimum work). The clients recounted how they were often allocated a certain study sphere by other people and were unable to study the subjects they wanted to. This is one of the reasons they cite for their lack of motivation to graduate. Their subsequent failure was usually the consequence of a lack of interest in the activities in question combined with an inability or unwillingness to respect the rules of the school. From the stories recounted by the clients it is clear that they were indifferent to the consequences of such conduct. *"**I began bunking off school**. I didn't know what I wanted, but I didn't want to attend school, so I skipped it. Work experience didn't interest me so I just thought sod it."* (TN, male)

*"I stopped going to school and then never went back. I don't know why, **I simply had no desire to**. I didn't go to work, I simply sat at home."* (SP, female)

Several clients failed repeatedly, most often because they did nothing and made no effort to learn anything. *"I went to two different middle schools, one to be a vehicle body repairer, that was at Škoda, and one to be a confectioner in Karmel. I was at Škoda for a year and got absolutely nothing from it. The school didn't suit me at all. **I did no studying whatsoever**, just farted around for a year. Then I went to Karmel. I thought it would be easier. **I had to repeat** first and second grade. The problem was the work experience."* (JŠ, male) The client did not complete his apprenticeship and ended up homeless. If he works at all, it is only as an unskilled labourer.

Some clients cite **conflicts with authority and failure to abide by rules** when explaining the premature termination of their education. *"**At the end of the year I ran away** from middle school to be with my boyfriend. That was completely crazy because it wasn't necessary. And the school was pretty strict on attendance. Fourteen days later I ran away again. This time I fucked it up completely and they chucked me out."* (PČ, female)

*"When I left basic school I went to study to be a chef cum waiter, a profession I'd chosen myself. I studied for six months or so, and then I gave it up because during work experience on fast food **I argued with the supervisor** and they told me that either I left of my own accord or they would boot me out. So I left. Then I trained as a bricklayer in this youth detention centre, but I didn't complete the course because I ran away."* (MP, male) In all of these cases expulsion from school was simply the start of a series of other problems.

MM (male) **did not have problems with school**. He studied and acquired qualifications. *"At basic school I had good grades. At middle school things went pretty well apart from German, because I have no talent for foreign languages. I enjoyed school. I wanted to be a chef, I enjoy cooking. Apart from German, which I had real problems with, and with the teacher too, everything went well. I was something of a favourite among the teachers. Nobody ever complained about me."* His problems only began after he found himself on the street because of extensive criminal activities.

It is rare for failure at school to be caused by a more serious intellectual impediment. On the basis of the stories recounted by young homeless people we estimate that a slight mental handicap is present in approximately 5%. This figure does not differ much from the population at large. There was a higher number of neglected individuals coming from families with a very poor educational and socio-cultural level, and in these cases it would be difficult to anticipate great success at school. However, most clients had parents who had at least received some form of education or training and could have been a guarantee that their

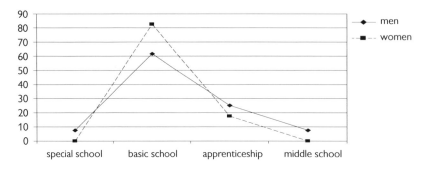

Graph 13. The education achieved by young homeless people (the graph shows the relative frequency).

children would attain at least the same level. The group studied also contained individuals who had better than average prerequisites but whose continued development was blocked by some form of **mental illness** (schizophrenia).

The most frequent cause of failure at school on the part of young homeless people was a **combination of unfavourable personality traits and insufficiently developed regulatory functions** associated with their inability to work systematically. These are individuals who were unwilling or unable to apply themselves because nobody had ever shown them how. Many had no reason to study since school grades were not important to them (as they were often not to the parents). Most were not even interested in the reasons for their failure. They give the topic no thought and accept their lack of an education as a given.

2.2.1 THE BEHAVIOURAL PROBLEMS OF YOUNG HOMELESS PEOPLE AT SCHOOL AGE AND DURING ADOLESCENCE

Homelessness is regarded as a negative social deviation associated with an inability or unwillingness to adapt to the requirements of mainstream society and respect its rules. Young homeless people have a range of problems in this sphere and admit that they already had them during childhood and adolescence, when it was a case of not respecting the requirements of their family and school. This was so in the case of the majority of clients (81%). Only just under a fifth of the clients think that they did not suffer serious **behavioural problems**. From the stories told by young homeless people it is clear that they felt no need to control their behaviour, often did not reflect upon it, and were indifferent to its consequences.

An example of a story that includes the **accumulation of various behavioural problems** that appeared as far back as childhood and continued during adolescence is that recounted by AK (male). *"I used to get a B in classroom conduct, even a C. In fourth grade I received a C for conduct because I had told the teacher to fuck* *off, and in third grade it was because I had burgled the changing room. Then there would be Bs for stupid things like causing a disturbance during class. At vocational school I was in the shit when they found grass on me that I wanted to sell."* This is a person who did not enjoy a good family environment. He felt unwanted and was convinced that nobody had any interest in him. He continues to have problems respecting rules and laws as an adult. His main problem is drug addiction, and he has been prosecuted for this.

Behavioural problems were sometimes linked to a client's relationship with authority, which at school age was represented by their parents and teachers. Given that a teacher requires that duties be met and that conduct correspond to stipulated norms, one might expect that young homeless people would at the very least feel distant from their teachers. However, this is not always the case. Some think that basically they had a positive or at least problem-free relationship with their teachers. Others did not accept the teacher as an authority figure or accepted only a specific person. Their stories reveal a **tendency to see the relationship with the teacher in extremely personal terms**. Such a perception may be the result of feeling unwanted within the family and needing to obtain the interest of someone else. Sometimes we can infer from the description of the relationship with teachers future difficulties in social adaptation and an unwillingness to respect anything that might restrict a person. *"I had a good relationship with school, but not with the teachers, because they bossed me around." (ZK, female)*

Young homeless people make clear their **need for a teacher to have reasonable requirements** and to be fair and wise. The legitimacy of a teacher's authority is not given simply by their formal position. They must be deserving of respect. This opinion is common, especially among adolescents. *"I simply don't like authority and I'm the kind of guy who's going to do what he wants. **I respected my teachers to the degree to which I thought they had a right to be respected**. If I thought they were blowing things out of proportion, I didn't respect them." (MM, male)* This client refused to take other rules into account and has been repeatedly prosecuted for criminal activities.

Perhaps the only difference is that some young homeless people **arrogate to themselves the right to decide when to listen and who to listen to**. It will

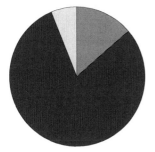

■ Level 1 basic school
■ Level 2 basic school
□ Secondary school and later

Graph 14. The period of their lives when clients say they began to exhibit behavioural problems (the graph shows relative frequency).

be their choice and will not depend on the opinion of some superior figure or accepted rules. Sometimes they exhibit a personal aversion and sensitivity to a certain teacher's way of behaving, though this of course is not only a problem experienced by children who go on to become homeless. There may be a reduced tolerance to negative reactions on the part of adults to their problematic behaviour. *"I was something of a rebel in this regard, because **whenever a teacher shouted at me I hated it**. They shouted at me at home, and that was enough for me. I sometimes answered back. I wasn't vulgar or anything, but **I simply defended myself**." (TN, male)*

*"Yeah, it depended who it was. But I had no problem in telling a teacher to fuck off if he annoyed me. I accepted him **until the moment he insulted me in some way**." (LR, male)* Both clients had behavioural problems later in life and ended up on the street as a result.

Nevertheless, young people distinguish between and **take into account how an individual acts toward them**. PV (male) did not view all of his teachers in the same light. *"I had a good relationship with my class teacher. She was always able to advise me on what, where and how I could organise things. She helped me a lot. I didn't like the other teachers, we used to argue all the time. When I didn't want to do something I told her so."* The client had to repeat eighth grade twice and left school prematurely. He took drugs as far back as basic school and had quite serious behavioural problems.

Some clients rate their relationship with their teacher as positive and are **grateful to the teacher for what they did for them**. One reason could be the fact that the teacher behaved in a much more friendly way to them than their parents and exhibited an interest in them. *"My parents were not very loving and didn't help me with my homework. If I needed an explanation, I went to my friends and neighbours or to a teacher who lived across the street, who explained what I had to do." (JV, male)* The client did not even complete basic school and his mental abilities are limited.

2.3 CONTEMPORARIES – RELATIONSHIPS WITH PEERS DURING CHILDHOOD AND ADOLESCENCE

Though young homeless people rate the relationships they had with their contemporaries at school differently, it is clear that these relationships were **often of a more extreme character**. Some clients claim that they were the class authority and were not satisfied by anything. Others felt they were overlooked, rejected or even bullied. MP (male) believes he enjoyed a high status in his group, which he puts down to his ability to impress and amuse those around him. *"I suppose you could say I was the **class leader**. I was always getting in scrapes and having a laugh, so all in all I was popular with the other kids."* He is of the opinion that he still enjoys good relationships with those around him even now as a homeless person. LC (male) also believes he was popular. *"You could say that **I was the comedian of** *the class, the clown, the entertainer. The others liked me."* At present the situation is somewhat different and LC says that he has stopped being so trusting.

The way young homeless people assess their status among their contemporaries during childhood and adolescence shows that many of them already had certain problems with social adaptation. Some of them concede that, **while their behaviour gave them a certain power and influence within the group, it did not bring them the sympathy of others**. The possibility cannot be excluded that, in certain cases at least, their status was worse than they are prepared to admit. A high status in the classroom, or rather a client's conviction that they enjoyed such a status in their group, often ensues from the fact that they were older and more experienced and were able to impress the rest in some way (or were able to manipulate them more easily). A combination of various disadvantages was manifest in relation to their contemporaries, whether related to personality traits or the negative effects of the environment in which they grew up. Their parents did not teach their children to recognise the feelings of those around them and to react to them in an acceptable way. Many of the parents themselves probably lacked this skill. Leaving aside any doubts we might entertain, the fact that a third of the young homeless people questioned say that they enjoy a good relationship with their peers can only be a good thing. Such people do not always have to have difficulties forming relationships, especially of the shallower kind from which no commitments ensue.

Individuals who were not accepted and felt that they did not fit into a group or could not get on with other people **comprised on third of the group**. They dealt with this problem – if, indeed, they regarded it as such – in various different ways: through aggression, provocation and pretence. However, the tendency to establish a status for themselves through problematic behaviour or playing the fool does not always have the desired effect and many young homeless people are aware of this fact as adults. *"I was always the clown of the class, and so I was accepted and always had lots of people around me. **But I began to realise that they weren't friends.**" (TN, male)* JP (male) also felt he was not accepted, though his problems forming relationships were more general in nature and persist to this day. *"Even in second grade **I knew that I didn't belong**, not with anyone, and so I*

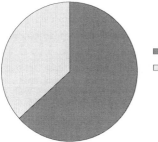

■ good or acceptable
□ poor

Graph 15. Peer relationships during childhood and adolescence (the graph shows relative frequency).

was happiest on my own. I only spoke to those I wanted to, mainly with girls because I get on best with them. I wasn't bullied but I was a kind of loner and closed off within myself."

LD (female), who lived in a children's home, did not enjoy stable peer relationships. *"Sometimes I had friends, sometimes not. It depended on how I was with them. They didn't speak to me much, they thought I was horrible to them. **They didn't like how I behaved to them so they didn't talk to me**."*

JB (male) had similar problems. *"I was on the margins of the class. **I was aggressive, I didn't like anything or anyone**. I even had to see a psychiatrist because my teacher couldn't figure out why I was so nasty."* JB now realises that his only friends were those who, like him, were on the margins of the group. *"I was someone who back then was incapable of finding normal people, the kind who go to school and have hobbies."*

The approach followed by MS (female), who is convinced that nobody cared for her and attempted to make friends through bribes, submission and tolerance of their unpleasant conduct or even aggression, also failed to have the desired effect. *"I didn't have any friends at basic school. **I bought myself friends. They hit me** because I was fat. One time they pushed me under a car and I was in hospital two weeks. I didn't tell on them because that would have made the situation worse and they would have wanted revenge. I didn't do anything about it. It seemed normal to me after the children's home, where everyone behaved horribly to everyone else. My problems began, I don't know when. **Nobody wanted to talk to me**, I was fat, ugly, I was rubbish at sports, all because I was fat. I was glad that nobody wanted to talk to me, nobody normal. When I had the wherewithal then I paid for everything and everyone was nice to me."* MS continued in this approach later in life and was willing to get into debt in order to maintain the interest of other people.

Several young homeless people were subject to bullying. Their inability to adapt or the fact that they were different could be the reason for this. This is so in the case of NP (male), who has serious schizophrenic tendencies and was in all likelihood unable to adapt to his peers during childhood. *"I was bullied from first grade onwards. It was psychological bullying. For instance, they took my baseball cap and threw it around the place. I didn't stand a chance against them and I didn't know what would work against them. It was real tyranny for me."*

MŽ (male) was also subject to bullying and attempted to deal with it by embracing the aggression displayed by his classmates. This worked, but to his detriment. *"They took me into every school* (the client changed school frequently because of problems at home)*, to third, fourth grade, and they started to bully me. There was one large class there and I was the new boy. They started to bully me. **Two held my arms, two held my legs, and the fifth started to punch me**. In later grades it was almost like a party. The class contained the stronger ones, the fighters, and then the normal lads, and then the retards. In the lower grades I was one of the normal boys and then in the upper grades, **in the eighth and ninth, I was one of the fighters**, I was always fighting. It wasn't that I was one of them, but I wanted to be one of them."* The client had experienced aggression at home and it is no wonder that he regarded it as a reasonable way of asserting himself.

Clients who had problems with peer group integration did not always come from dysfunctional families. Their inability to form and maintain at least a tolerable relationship must therefore depend on other factors and not only on the poor example set by their parents and a feeling of rejection.

2.4 SUMMARY OF THE CHILDHOOD AND ADOLESCENCE OF YOUNG HOMELESS PEOPLE

The opinions expressed by young homeless people regarding the course of their childhood and adolescence and the behaviour of their families correspond to the results of other studies. **These individuals never perceive the family in which they grew up as a calm, reliable base**. They are often, though not always, convinced that the family was comprehensively dysfunctional (the variability of the families of young homeless people and their relationships with their parents is confirmed, for instance, by Milburn et al. 2005). On the other hand many of them do not even know their own parents.

A dysfunctional family is simply one of the risk factors that can influence the social failure of young people. This is borne out by the fact that siblings who grew up in the same environment have no serious problems and develop normally. Even though we are working only with the testimony of the persons in our cohort and we do not know the opinions of other family members, it is clear that the causes of the social decline being monitored are more complex. Many families functioned at least tolerably, and yet a particular child began to act in a problematic way during adolescence.

The perception of parents as people who failed in this role is not always linked with an equally critical self-evaluation. Many young homeless people regard disagreements with their parents not as the consequence of their objectively problematic behaviour but as a problem created by their parents' unreasonable demands or lack of interest. **A lack of self-criticism and the tendency to attribute the blame to other people** can be seen as a defensive reaction that does not always suffice to maintain an acceptable self-image. An ongoing feeling of being unwanted and rejected by their parents leads to these young homeless people lacking self-esteem and on occasion to a worse self-perception and negative expectations in relation to other people.

The negative influence of the family can include genetic disadvantages. This is borne out by the higher frequency of similarly disposed individuals among relations, especially fathers and uncles. The social perception of parents as problematic people is occasionally manifested in a person's own self-evaluation. Certain clients realise that their disposition may be as unfavourable as that of their parents but do not concern themselves further with this fact. They do not look for a method of preventing a similar decline and sometimes use it as an **explanation that exonerates them** from their own social failure.

Life in a genuinely dysfunctional family or with parents who are unable to provide their children so much as a basic upbringing and acceptable model of behaviour **leads to the creation of a different normative standard**. This is manifest in relation to both strategies of conduct deployed and expectations regarding other people's behaviour, and in a different tolerance to different forms of conduct. Life on the street does not have to appear so intolerable to such individuals as to the majority of the population, because they have different assessment criteria. To a certain extent life in a dysfunctional family has deformed the way they experience and reflect upon life.

Young homeless people rate their parents very differently, surprisingly so. This may of course be due to the fact that their parents were indeed very different. The father is often perceived as being inconsiderate, someone without a positive relationship with anyone and as such rejected even by his own child. However, we also find fathers who are loved and regarded as loving, fathers who are ascribed both positive and negative properties, and fathers who are ignored. Perceptions of the mother can also be varied. In the life stories told the relationship with the mother was sometimes very deformed, damaged or even spiteful, more so than one would expect. Our cohort often expressed **insecurity and an inability to reconcile themselves to the fact that the mother had an emotional bond with someone else** (another child or partner). The level of tolerance to such a burden is visibly reduced and often accompanied by the conviction that not even other members of the family represent any security for these individuals. In some cases the relationship with the mother is only disrupted later, during adulthood, usually as a consequence of the client's own intolerable conduct. These individuals are not always willing to admit their own culpability or do not fully understand its impact because of lower social intelligence.

Not even a stepfather is always perceived as a bad person. Relationships with the stepfather were rated differently and were clearly very varied in reality. The deterioration of the relationship with a stepfather often depended on the clients themselves, who were unwilling or unable to tolerate him. The only person who is perceived positively almost universally is the **grandmother**. The people we interviewed said she was the **only source of emotional security and safety**, even though they themselves often disappointed her – in this instance they acknowledged their own culpability. The idealisation of the grandmother may be related to the fact that she is very often no longer alive, which enables the client to project whatever they wish into memories of her.

The relationship with school reflects the more general stance of young homeless people to the concept of duty and the necessity to respect basic rules of conduct. Their statements reveal that the period during which they are most sensitive to their failure in this sphere is late adolescence, when they are fully aware of the fact that they have been unable to cope with the demands made by school and that their conduct goes beyond what is regarded as ordinary. They do not view their failure as the consequence of a lack of the necessary abilities, but ascribe it to insufficient effort, lack of motivation, or random circumstances. **The significance of this educational failure is not usually given any consideration** or even processed. Their inability to discipline themselves to carry out the activities required of them and their lack of any work ethic may impact on their current situation to a greater extent than they are willing to concede. It is clear that in this sphere, too, a poor upbringing could be to blame. Their parents were unable or unwilling to compel them to meet their duties, and did not teach them that this is an essential part of life. Some young homeless people are aware of all of this but **do not think about how they might take matters into their own hands**.

Young homeless people's opinion of the **relationships they have with their contemporaries** is often of an extreme character. Our cohort included people who think that **they managed to create a certain prestige** within their group and were able to influence others. Nevertheless, **they were not among the most popular** members because they did not act in a friendly way and reacted aggressively at the slightest provocation. Their memories are characterised by insecurity and distrust, as well as possibly an inability to assess correctly the basis of their contemporaries' behaviour. They know that they were not part of the group they wanted to be part of, and if they wished to change this state of affairs they had to adapt, sometimes through aggressive behaviour. Some of our cohort **felt rejected**. They recall how the others used to hit them and harm them. Though it is clear that these feelings are not exclusive to homeless people, it may be another partial sign of reduced social adaptability.

3. THE BEGINNINGS OF HOMELESSNESS

Typical of a young homeless person is a **certain degree of social deracination, a lack of education, and behavioural problems**. Failure at school and uncompleted professional training lowers the likelihood of their finding employment and increases the risk of further social decline. The company of similarly problematic peers with the same habits also has an unfavourable impact, reinforcing these practices and discouraging the growth of whatever positive characteristics the person had to begin with. From the studies already referred to (Cauce et al., 2000; Hyde, 2005; Bearsley-Smith et al., 2008, van den Bree et al., 2009 and Mallett et al., 2010) as well as our own research it is clear that the socialisation of young homeless people tends to be impeded by the negative effects of their family. The upshot is the adoption of unsuitable ways of behaving that produce a negative reaction in the surrounding environment. Unconventional habits, opinions and conduct can impact on the direction taken by these individuals at the start of adulthood. They can more easily accept a problematic lifestyle and the company of peers who think and act in a similar way. Because of the experiences they had in their childhood this does not have to seem so unacceptable to them. However, their isolation from mainstream society further restricts their opportunity of receiving positive, corrective experiences (e.g. acceptance by another person, another lifestyle, etc.) and their deterioration continues (Rokach, 2005; Tyler, 2006; Gwadz et al., 2007; Ferguson, 2009).

Young persons have **problems managing their own lives**. They lack perseverance and a knowledge of the strategies that are necessary to achieve a set goal, and very often also lack the readiness to adapt or conform. For the most part they have never been persuaded of the efficacy of self-control and have never therefore experienced the positive feedback that desirable behaviour elicits. A premium was not placed on such qualities in their family and they did not learn to overcome the difficulties and unpleasant feelings that relate to self-control. They frequently make no effort and set themselves no targets. **They merely loaf around and survive**, doing whatever requires the least effort of them. Young homeless people have not mastered the role of an adult, a role that requires personal freedom to be compliant with a sense of responsibility for one's own actions. Sometimes they want to become independent before they are ready to, and if they somehow manage this (e.g. by running away from home), they begin to behave in a self-destructive way. These are people who lack certain important experiences and the associated competences, or in whom unpropitious traits prevail that prove a burden in life (Boydell et al., 2000).

The adoption of a homeless lifestyle may also be a poor solution to previous problems that they caused themselves (e.g. by taking on debt, stealing, taking drugs, etc.). Their decision to sleep rough may be an impulsive reaction to a subjectively intolerable situation or unmanageable conflict, as well as a sign of their having resigned themselves to not finding more effective variants. The turning point may arise as a consequence of a decision reached by someone else who is not willing to accept their approach to life and to be stressed by it. Some young homeless people did not leave home for the streets voluntarily, but were thrown out by their family, largely without reason.

Life on the streets represents an **alternative existence simplified to the maximum**, which can be stressful in many respects. Very often this existence lacks the security of being able to satisfy the most basic needs, such as safety, sleep and food. From the point of view of coping with this lifestyle it is very important how these individuals experience and evaluate their decision to sleep rough. The degree of stress depends on **what immediately gave rise to their decision**, whether they reached this decision on their own or were forced into it, and whether it was the end result of deep-seated problems or an impulsive reaction to a momentary conflict. The level of discomfort that a homeless person has to cope with is not as stressful for everyone. It depends on what experience they have, i.e. to what extent their past life differs from their current life.

Adapting to a homeless lifestyle includes not only learning how to obtain the necessities for survival and managing them (the street economy), but also the gradual **acceptance of street culture**, which is manifest in the way these individuals live, what values they profess and what rules they hold to. This might, for instance, involve all property being deemed communal, drug and alcohol use being a matter of course, the acquisition of funds through theft being regarded as legitimate, etc. J. O'Sullivan-Oliveira and P. Burke (2009) point out that homeless culture is characterised by a considerable freedom. Its values are sometimes questionable (from the point of view of the majority) and its rules not always completely consistent. The homeless community is relatively loosely structured and very changeable, and even if such a community represents a certain social capital, it is at the same time a source of many risks (drug addiction, prostitution, violence and rape, etc.).

3.1 THE DECISION TO SLEEP ROUGH AND ITS CAUSE

Young homeless people often have a history of **running away that stretches back to childhood**. Their repeated escapes can be taken as a sign of a lack of the security that home should provide, or as a manifestation of atypical socialisation and an associated inability to act in accordance with ordinary rules. Running away from home may be caused by an inability to deal with the stressful situations to which they are exposed in their family. It may also reflect a preference for a certain method of resolving problems or a tendency to employ escape strategies that are easier for the individuals concerned than expending effort on more effective solutions.

Almost a quarter of young homeless people (23.3%) say that they ran away from home, often repeatedly, which indicates that it did not represent a safe refuge for them. (It should be pointed out that sleeping rough is also not a safe option and that to begin with it is difficult to anticipate the various threats present. Mounier and Andujo, 2003). LP (male) ran away from home when his family broke up. His mother died and his father did not look after him. *"I ran away from home because of problems with my father. Mum died when I was twelve and I ran away for the first time when I was thirteen."* His adoptive father brought various men home, something the client felt tarnished the memory of his mother. As far as he was concerned his father had "died", and this is what he told his friends, even though it was not true. Saying this had a symbolic significance for him. PČ (female) ran away because **she did not feel sufficiently accepted at home.** In her opinion her mother prioritises her stepfather, who hit her frequently. *"I ran away from home and didn't go to school as a result. I didn't know how to resolve it* (the situation within the family)*, so **I tried to draw attention to the fact that something was up by the way I behaved**. They didn't know what to do with me when I ran away, so they sent me to a psychiatrist who I reckon was more of a patient than I was."* After seven years of sleeping rough she has a greater overview of her earlier behaviour. *"If I hadn't begun to run away from home and hadn't been in that young offenders' institution, I wouldn't be what I am now."* The client was a child with many behavioural problems that her mother and stepfather were unable to deal with. At present she is looking after her own child, and it is therefore quite likely that the family was not as bad as it was made out to be.

When an adolescent attains their majority, when they leave home it is usually for good. They now have the right to decide what they want to do and where they want to go, and nobody can restrict them. On the other hand, nobody is obliged

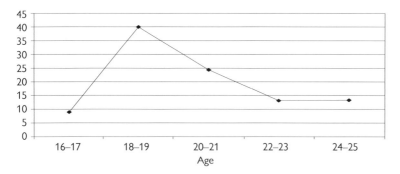

Graph 16. The age at which young homeless people find themselves on the street (the graph shows relative frequency).

to look after them any longer. **Leaving home definitively for a life on the street** has various trigger mechanisms. Sometimes it is caused by an event that does not have to be important in itself but for some reason sets off the spiral of social decline. It may be an impulsive and ill-conceived reaction or the continuation of a long-term accumulation of problems that cannot be resolved easily and the seriousness of which the client has not wanted to admit. The stories told by our clients indicate that **they are not always sufficiently responsible**, are unable or **unwilling to anticipate the possible consequences of their behaviour**, and are unable to envisage so much as the immediate future. They are focused on the present and crowd out or postpone everything that they find unpleasant. They usually realise retrospectively what their share of the blame was for their own social decline, but even then are unable to act in a more purposeful way.

The reasons why young people leave home for the street can be divided into four basic categories with a partial overlap in the case of certain clients. These categories can be viewed as life trajectories that require a different approach to both remedy and prevention.

1) Clients who opted for the street because of **excessive use of drugs or alcohol**. This resulted in failure at work and an inability to work systematically and to pay their bills. In addition, these clients faced the high cost of their alcohol and drugs. Their behaviour, unreliability and accumulated debts led not only to their being fired from their job but also being evicted from their home, apartment or hostel. Very often these are people who had other problems with adaptation and behavioural issues, sometimes starting in childhood.

2) Clients whose main problem is an **inability or unwillingness to work** that originates in their personality and that is usually apparent in childhood, above all in relation to school. These persons tend to be careless, irresponsible and lazy. They have a tendency to be parasitic upon their family and when their parents' patience runs out, they end up on the street. An unwillingness to work is not typical only of young homeless people. However, what is crucial is whether the family is willing to tolerate the laziness of their adult offspring or not. At present there exists in society a group of young people who do not work and have no intention of working and who are supported by the family. However, the question is what the future holds in store for them. In this respect drugs or alcohol are of only secondary importance. An irresponsible approach is manifest in the accumulation of debts that they make no attempt to pay off, followed by repossession of their property, after which they end up on the street.

3) Clients with a **combination of a personality disorder and an unwillingness to work** usually have not only debts but also problems of a criminal character, since they acquire funds in an unlawful way. They steal (it is common for them to steal even from relatives), cheat, and sometimes act violently and inconsiderately for no good reason. They too sometimes use drugs or alcohol.

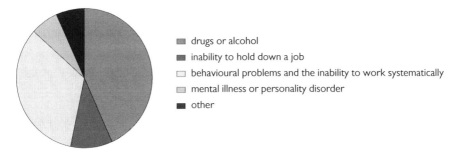

■ drugs or alcohol
■ inability to hold down a job
☐ behavioural problems and the inability to work systematically
▨ mental illness or personality disorder
■ other

Graph 17. The reasons that led young people to leave home for the street (the graph shows relative frequency).

These are usually individuals with an antisocial personality disorder that is reinforced by the negative influence of the family and the company of individuals acting in a similar way.

4) The smallest group of young homeless people are those with diagnosed **mental illnesses** (schizophrenia or schizoaffective disorder), or a disorder other than antisocial personality disorder (narcissistic, borderline or schizoid).

Other psychologists have arrived at similar conclusions. For instance, C. Martijn and L. Sharpe (2006) make a distinction according to the primary cause of homelessness, whether it was the use of drugs and alcohol that provoked conflict with parents or the breakup of the family (and that might have exacerbated a tendency to escape from problems using psychoactive substances), or more serious behavioural problems were involved, perhaps even criminal activity, which incurred the disapproval of the family, or psychological problems. Like S. Mallett, D. Rosenthal and D. Keys (2005), they discovered that drugs represent the primary cause of homelessness in the case of a quarter of people and that in other cases it was the consequence of family breakdown or protracted conflict with the parents. Many young homeless people see the root of their problems residing in the breakdown of the family, something that caused them enormous stress. Such people comprised almost two thirds of the group studied by Mallett et al. The same conclusion was reached by Rosenthal et al. (2006). Salomon-Sautel et al. (2008) also confirmed that family conflict and drug use were the most frequent reasons why young people left home for the street. The same was true of our group. As Coward-Bucher (2008) says, there are many reasons why young people leave home for a life on the street.

3.1.1 DRUG AND ALCOHOL ADDICTION

Young people who could be classified in the first group often have a realistic awareness that drugs or alcohol are the cause of their homelessness. They realise that their addiction left them unable to cope with life as they themselves would like. LB found himself on the street because of his **drug addiction**. He did not complete his schooling and was incapable of holding down employment. He moved from job to job and finally, because he used and also manufactured drugs, he lost his apartment. *"I tried working. I did holiday jobs and then found work in a warehouse. I managed six months there and then almost nine months in another warehouse. My father let me live in his apartment, but I wasn't registered there and **I had already started injecting**. So I got a **group of friends together and we began cooking crystal meth**. After a few months I had toxic psychosis. Then I came out of Bohnice. **My father threw me out of the apartment**. I lost the apartment, everything."* This client is at present completing a course of therapy and claims to have given up drugs. Unfortunately his abstinence is likely to be temporary. At present he is living in a home run by the Salvation Army.

The life story told by LC (male) is very similar, though to begin with things looked more promising for him. He completed his schooling and found a job in his field. However, he started taking time off because of drugs and was fired. When he did not have enough money to buy drugs he resorted to theft. Finally his mother ran out of patience and he lost his home. *"I'm a trained waiter and **drugs always brought me so low that I couldn't go to work. I was on painkillers**. And that's how I fucked it up. Then I worked as a labourer on various building sites and before I became homeless I found a job. But halfway through the month **I had no money** because of drugs. In order to buy drugs **I stole something**. Things got bad and I went to prison for a year. I thought about returning home, finding a job and settling down. I returned for a while, worked for two months – actually in the pizzeria where I had already worked. **Except again there was crystal meth**. I didn't go to work, I stayed in bed. So they fired me. I stayed at home, I didn't do anything, I simply did drugs. We started to argue and I had to leave."* His story involves cycles of attempts to find work and reduce his drug intake and then a return to the same problems he had before. At present we have no information on him.

IK (male) has problems caused by **alcohol**. He himself regards alcohol as being to blame for his life situation, even though it is clear from his story that he occasionally seeks to rationalise his behaviour. His family is functional, he was not neglected or tyrannised, his parents stayed together – and yet even so he ended up homeless. *"My childhood was fine. I fucked things myself. I got to know a certain crowd and **began drinking**, and things went downhill. Mum wanted to help me with everything, but I didn't want that, so I moved out so as not to cause her problems. I was a chef for two months in V, and then I moved to Prague and now I'm fucked again. **They fired me because I didn't turn up for work because of booze**. If the work wasn't so boring I wouldn't booze. I've lost everything because of alcohol and that's how I ended up here."* The client has a good relationship with his family and does not want to cause his parents problems, but seems incapable of doing more. His family would probably take him back, but he would have to restrict his consumption of alcohol, something that for the moment he is unwilling to do.

Alcohol causes absence from work and clients lose their job. A lack of funds then leads to life on the street. *"I went straight from school into work, but I lost my job because of alcohol. I got completely off my head and the second day I was completely fucked, so I called into work and told them I was sick. But somehow they guessed. And then when I returned on Monday I was fired. I've never made it beyond the probationary period." (client ZK)* As well as alcohol, this man's life is complicated by his irresponsibility and inability to manage his finances. *"I always bugger things up somehow.* **I start to have a good time, forget about everything and suddenly everything is fucked**. *I've always buggered it up somehow. I always spend all the money I have. Sometimes I think about life and say to myself that it's better to live in the present. I'm not even sure what I'm doing. All I know is I'm capable of spending a heck of a lot of money. I don't think about the consequences."* The client is still homeless and is being threatened with criminal proceedings because of failure to pay his debts. He drinks and takes drugs, but has other problems.

There is a reciprocal relationship between the use of drugs and alcohol and homelessness. People who take large quantities of these substances are more prone to sleep rough, and sleeping rough reinforces a tendency to take drugs and drink alcohol. This was the conclusion reached by K. Shelton et al. (2009), who observed that, in the USA at least, homelessness was more associated with the use of drugs than alcohol. The same is true of homeless people in the Czech Republic, more of whom are drug addicts than alcoholics, even though a considerable number consume both.

3.1.2 INABILITY AND UNWILLINGNESS TO WORK SYSTEMATICALLY

Many young homeless people are unable or unwilling to work systematically. They are **not sufficiently responsible, do not know how to manage their finances, and work up debts** that they cannot repay. They put off resolving the situation until repossession takes place. The social decline that eventually sees them sleeping rough is a gradual process the seriousness of which they are often unaware of. In the group we studied there are many people who never remained for long in a job and justify their approach in various ways. As they see it they lost their job because the work was too demanding, stressful or monotonous. They tried to find other work but without success. These people hand in their notice before finding better employment, even though the more intelligent solution would involve the opposite approach. *"For a while I did unpaid work. That was after they'd released me from my first stint in prison. I worked for two months and then I stopped turning up.* **I didn't enjoy getting up and working**, *because I knew I could always go home, where I could eat, receive some money... so why go to work? In K. I didn't bother to look for work. Perhaps if I'd looked I would have found some." (LN, male)* The client took drugs and was in prison twice. At present we have no information on him or his whereabouts.

An inability to accept various restrictions and the feeling of discomfort that any job entails feature in the story told by MH (male). In addition, in this case there appears to be a clearly egocentric focus on his own comfort and insufficient regard for other people. His unwillingness to work and the fact that he stole from his family meant he ended up on the street. *"I worked on the basis of zero-hours contracts. I worked for Tesco and then moved to a small warehouse job. Then I registered for the dole when I was expelled* (from school). *I left Tesco of my own accord because* **I couldn't deal with the drudgery**. *I stole some gold from my mum.* **I just wanted to have a good time**. *As a result mum lost all her faith in me and said, ok, you're not working, you're not at school, you're stealing from me, so I don't see any reason why I should keep you here if you're going to eat me out of house and home. I received lots of warnings, and then I stole her earrings and that was the last straw. I arrived home, she told me to put my keys on the table, take what I wanted and get lost. So I put my keys on the table, took a bag and left."* The client slept rough for two years. At present we have no information regarding him or his whereabouts.

The story recounted by client MK (male) is very similar. The only difference is that he did not steal from his mother. *"He* (his mother's partner) *didn't like the fact that I didn't go to school, that I lazed around at home for a year and a half. Mum tolerated it somehow, but then she gave me what for and chucked me out. She told me that I just came home to eat and sleep, otherwise I was out, that I didn't help around the house, I hadn't had any work for a year and a half, basically that* **all I did was laze around**. **It kind of suited me that way**. *I said to myself that I'd continue as long as I could, and then when mum got angry I'd find some work. She chucked me out of the house and paid two months' rent in a hostel for me until I found work. The problem was that I found a job in a bakery but* **I only lasted a week because I didn't enjoy myself**. *After two months they chucked me out of the hostel, so I decided I didn't give a damn and that I'd go to Prague. And that's when I became homeless."* This client still lives on the street and is occasionally in contact with his mother. However, his approach to work has not changed.

Not one of the men referred to above was able to move beyond the boundary of an unstable existence. At most they managed the occasional holiday job and spent their nights in a hostel or doss-house.

3.1.3 INABILITY TO MANAGE FINANCES AND INDEBTEDNESS

The loss of employment for whatever reason often marks the beginning of other problems that these people do not resolve but allow to accumulate until they end up penniless on the street. *"At least working in a factory I earned about CZK 13,000. I bought clothes and what have you. And now I've got nothing. We did the round of bars with the boys, we paid for girls, petrol, etc. And* **after two days the money was gone**. *I thought I'd find some work here, but there's bugger all to be had."* (JH, male) To this day the client only works occasionally. He takes temporary jobs and travels outside the country as a result, but he does not have stable accommodation and a job. He has been in prison for grievous bodily harm.

*"It was my own stupidity. I was lazy and thought that that everything would be cool, that this kind of thing couldn't happen to me. So I didn't take anything too seriously and then discovered that things were different in reality. I had the possibility of working in H, signing on the dole when I was in a hostel. But I left home, felt I was free and that was the end. I had some money saved from a holiday job or something, so I paid for the hostel and **didn't give a thought to anything else**. The reason I'm on the street is that **I didn't react in time to the situation** I found myself in." (MM, male)* The client had other problems and is a criminal recidivist who is still homeless.

Another immediate cause of homelessness can be **indebtedness and repossession**, which is often the culmination of irresponsible behaviour (maxing out a credit card, ill-thought out loans and defaulting on debts, etc.). Such an individual tends to wait for the situation to sort itself out and pushes away the thought that they should be proactive in resolving it until the problem comes to a head. Irresponsibility and an inability to consider the possible consequences is manifest in an accumulation of debts and repossession. *"Basically because **I worked up a debt** to T-Mobile and O2, a repossession order was taken out. I made an incredible number of calls and somehow didn't pay, the result being I owed more than CZK 28,000. I couldn't believe it because I had no money. **Then the bailiff came and took everything**. I've never known how to manage my finances, and finally I end up in the shit. I had been acting like a real dude, paying for everything, until this problem arrived and I didn't know what to do. By the next month I was out of my apartment. After they'd repossessed everything I hung around L for a while, where I found a Christian organisation where they offered me accommodation." (JP, male)* The client takes drugs and is at present homeless. It would be difficult to say that he has become more responsible in his habits.

An irresponsible approach to debt is not simply the domain of men. Women also very often find themselves in difficulties for this reason. *"I was already 18, I was working for Albert and one of our friends came asking **if I didn't want to take out a loan**. He said all I had to do was dress nicely. I said 'great'. At that time I had begun to take drugs, so he made me a loan and two days later he returned and offered me another. I said 'sure' and took him up on the offer. I paid four months' rent up front, but **the rest I blew on drugs and lost on slot machines**. If only I could return it. Altogether I now owe CZK 150,000." (KB, female)* At present these debts represent an impediment to the client being able to return to normal life. They total so much that the situation looks set to continue for a long time.

3.1.4 INEXPERIENCE AND AN INABILITY TO ORGANISE LIFE

When they reach 18 individuals **who spent their childhood and adolescence (or part thereof) in a children's home** often end up on the street. This happens even when they have been offered some form of basic accommodation and start-up money. It often becomes apparent that they are not capable of looking after themselves and cannot cope with their newly acquired independence (they stop going to work, are unable to manage their finances, do not pay their rent, do not respect the rules of their lodgings, etc.). They revel in their new found freedom and do not give a thought to the future. **They have become used to someone looking after them** and making sure they have something to eat and a place to sleep. IB (male) was unable to cope with independence, to work systematically and to manage his finances. He grew up in a children's home, did not finish school, and after leaving the home found accommodation that he soon, however, lost. *"When I left school, the director of the children's home said I could remain there if I wanted to. But I turned him down, and that was my mistake. **I received a lot of money from the children's home**, around CZK 15,000* (approximately USD 750). *I only managed to save a small amount, the rest I frittered away. Although I had a job, I sometimes went to work and sometimes I didn't. Sometimes it suited me and sometimes it didn't. It wasn't laziness, but say a girl wanted to go out, then I'd take her out and then get drunk, whatever, and **then maybe I wouldn't turn up for work at all**. Then I travelled to Prague and thought I'd find work quickly. I looked for a while, but then I gave up. I just thought, fuck it, I can't be bothered."* At present the client has a job and lives with a woman who also used to be homeless. They have a child together. It is possible that having had certain experiences and with the support of his partner's family he will manage to live in a more acceptable way.

BC (male) ended up sleeping rough because he was unable to take responsibility for himself and to decide what can and cannot be done. *"I finished school, found a job and they* (the children's home) *found me lodgings. Things went smoothly for six months. And then my friend was thrown out of the house by his mother and had nowhere to go, so I took him in. The problem was that **I wasn't allowed to have anyone live with me**, I could only live alone. **But I took him in anyway and it all started from there**. I had to go to work and I couldn't leave him there on his own. I gradually stopped going to work and things got worse and worse. We had a talk and moved to another apartment, except **I ran out of money and we had nowhere to go**. I simply spent all the money. So we moved and agreed to pay the rent together. So basically I went to work. But when one is going to work and two are lolling around the place it made no sense for me to do anything. In any case I wasn't enjoying myself, so I jacked in the job. We ended up on the street."* The client could not deal with the situation and spent some time in a psychiatric hospital. At present he is registered at the employment office and receives benefits. He lives in a hostel.

3.1.5 CRIMINAL ACTIVITIES

Another group comprises people who were unwilling to work and **acquired the necessary funds in an unacceptable way**. *"I found out that there were other ways* of making money and started taking out loans in other peoples' names. *The problem is those other people grew suspicious and went to the police, and I ended up with a criminal record. I started stealing when I was eighteen. I guess I had been stealing before that, but I'd made the most of it, I'd bought stuff, or I'd gone on holiday. I'd had a good time. Yeah, I worship Mammon and I wanted a good time. **My criminal past led to me to the street**. I found myself where I am because of my own inability and the fact I didn't respect the advice and opinions of other people. It all started when I discovered that I could make money without working."* (MM, male) Over the last two years this client has been prosecuted and has travelled abroad, but is still homeless.

A criminal act may in itself trigger homelessness, even though a person has various other problems and would in any event end up on the street. *"I worked for a month in a casino. I did everything, from cleaning lady to waitress, for just CZK 45 (USD 2.20) before tax per hour, and the bastards didn't even pay social security and health insurance. In addition, they behave towards you like pigs. So I decided that one day I would return to Prague. Except I couldn't go to Prague without a cent, so in the middle of a shift **I took ninety thousand crowns from the till** and walked out. They wanted to shoot me in the knees, it was touch and go. But they reported me and because I had signed for personal liability, **they did me for embezzlement**. So I lost my job."* (PČ, female) The client is a drug addict and has been sleeping rough on and off for almost five years.

The question remains as to what extent the accumulation of offences and criminal acts causes a person to opt for life on the street. M. van den Bree et al. (2009) concluded that delinquency is not so much the cause of homelessness but rather its consequence. As far as theft is concerned, this conclusion is probably sound, though generally speaking the situation is far from being that clear cut.

3.1.6 THE INFLUENCE OF A PROBLEMATIC PARTNER

In the case of women a problematic partner can represent a significant risk factor. Girls leave school to be with him, he teaches them to lounge around and take drugs, and in the end can be the reason they end up on the street. *"I fell in love just once in my life with a bloke who was in prison. **He's been in prison a year**, but I still look after him, sent him things, write to him and so on. He is the only person I have ever loved, still love, and will love for the rest of my life. I can't imagine a family life with him, because he's a terrible criminal. **He beat me. But despite that I love him**. I stood up to him, he slapped me and I punched him."* (MB, female) At the time the interview took place the client had been sleeping rough for five years. She comes from a broken home and during her childhood was often witness to domestic violence. She describes her mother thus: *"she threw a knife at her partner and hit an artery"*. Her own relationship appears modelled on that of her parents, who did so much to harm her during childhood.

PM (female) was also influenced by her first partner. Aged 18 she left home for the street and began to take drugs. *"My first boyfriend came along and **I remained on the street with him**. I fell in love and upped and left for Prague. I caught hepatitis B from this bloke* (a drug addict) *and then realised I had also caught hepatitis C. I left home incredibly quickly, without thinking about it. Some people wonder why they are leaving, but **I didn't give a damn, I didn't think about it**. I had always somehow felt that I should belong somewhere and I had always looked for that place, and eventually I found it among these squatters."* The client is still sleeping rough, her situation has not changed in any significant respect, and she still takes drugs.

The question remains as to how such men attracted these clients (and many other girls) and why the girls fell in love with them. It is difficult to say whether it was because they did not otherwise feel accepted or whether these new experiences seemed so exciting that they did not consider the consequences of their behaviour. Severed relationships with their family, the premature termination of their professional training and the drug addiction acquired have make the possibility of a return more difficult, even though they may want to and even have somewhere to go.

A life on the street often involves meeting various people who influence the individual in question and occupy an important position in their life story, be this good or bad. This is not always about the negative influence of a bad person who destroys a good person's life. Often the situation is more complex, because the **appeal of an unorthodox community arises from wishes and needs of the client** that were forged long ago. It is clear from what IH (female) says that she was not a passive victim. *"It takes place gradually. **You meet new friends** and it kicks off. It's a story in motion in which something happens to you and things are always moving, evolving. I worked for a short while. Then an insurance policy matured that my grandparents had taken out. Then I met a bloke who was working, so I didn't have to work. So I lounged around all day. I didn't split up with that guy. He escaped and then he was put in prison. Then I met a guy, we went to look at a squat together, and because that kind of life doesn't bother me **we ended up living together in that squat**. I split up with the other one after two years because he was crazy. He stopped working, had no money and started to take drugs. He went completely crazy, so I said enough is enough."* IH had a somewhat different image of her partners than the women referred to above. Her boyfriends were to look after her and provide for her, and if they began to act in an undesirable way, then she split up with them. Her behaviour may have been influenced by the fact that she had been abused by her uncle, something her family refused to believe. However, her main problem is drug addiction.

3.2 LIFE ON THE STREET

After becoming homeless every person has to get used to feelings of **social isolation**, loneliness (two thirds of homeless people feel lonely and isolated), and a loss of privacy. The feeling of loneliness relates to the lack of support, estrangement from family and friends, and an existence on the margins of society (Rew, 2000, 2003; Auerswald and Eyra, 2002; Rokach, 2005). The feeling of **complete exclusion** is not only reinforced by the recognition that one is living on the margins of society, but by disorientation within a new environment. The increased sense of **threat** ensues from the fact that a homeless person is part of public space that anyone can intrude upon and therefore cannot expect protection. Many young homeless people have nobody close to them, belong nowhere, and are not part of any community. Their world is not sufficiently stable. They migrate from place to place and keep meeting different people. This feeling of deracination is intensified by the breakdown of their daily regime, the loss of fulfilling ways of spending their time, and the boredom ensuing therefrom. All of this culminates in a tendency to assuage unpleasant feelings with alcohol and drugs. Adaptation to a homeless lifestyle is extremely demanding and requires a certain resilience (Bender et al., 2007).

The start of life on the street is very often stressful, especially the first night. A person does not know what they should do, most do not know anyone they might turn to, and they feel lonely and helpless. They somehow have to sort out their basic needs: food, a place to sleep and basic security, but do not know how to. They lack information on charities that could offer them assistance and tell them where to eat and sleep. Most people's memories of this period are not pleasant. In general, the older a person is, **the worse they are affected by the stress caused by a feeling of total abandonment**. For the sake of illustration we cite the experiences of several clients, which though different have something in common, namely insecurity and unpleasant feelings.

"Christ, that (the first night) *was hellish. **I had no idea what I should do** or where I should go. I was in Prague, so I hung around doing nothing, and this was in winter. I couldn't travel by tram because the police were looking for me, so I simply walked around Prague. Two days I was walking around when I saw Naděje. I was dead beat, I hadn't washed for three days, I was frozen stiff, worn out, unshaven, I looked a wreck." (MM, male).*

*"**I didn't know where to go** or what to do. Naděje wouldn't accept me because I was too young. Some guys wanted to sell me at Central Station. It was ghastly. I was terrified by the whole experience, I had no idea what I had got myself into." (PČ, female)* In order to feel safe, AM (male) changed his daily regime. *"I slept during the day and stayed awake during the night. I travelled by night buses. **I had to remain awake during the night**, because there was always the threat of being mugged. During the day I went to the metro and slept a bit."*

People often respond to this initial stress by resorting to **alcohol or drugs** in an attempt to eliminate their unpleasant feelings. LS (male) talks of trying to *"wipe everything out of his head"*. LB (male) tried to deal with things as follows. *"**At that precise moment I took loads of opiates** and for the first time in my life I vomited. I didn't care what happened. Maybe I lay down on the pavement. Then I recovered and* *began to function somehow."* MT (male) reacted similarly, though used alcohol to desensitise himself. *"I was simply furious, pissed off, because I knew that nobody would help me. Here I stood not knowing what I was going to do. During the first week **I hung around Central Station like a dickhead**, carrying a bottle of vodka. I thought I was going to have a heart attack. I was completely out of it and at that precise moment unable to go anywhere or do anything."*

For some clients the first night on the street was not so stressful. This was usually because they were not alone but with other, often **more experienced people**, who **advised them as to what they should do**. *"I got into conversation at Florence tram stop with some people who were homeless, and I asked them where they slept in Prague. They told me they slept on a boat called Hermes, a boat for homeless people, and that you could sleep there for twenty crowns. I ended up sleeping three months on Hermes." (VL, female)* MP (male) knew where to go thanks to his mother, who is also homeless. *"I went to the Salvation Army, because there was a time when my mum was there, and she advised me where I should go. I spent the entire winter there. It was a slap in the face to find myself at the Salvation Army, among people who until that time I had regarded as garbage. But over time I got used to it."*

As MP says, a person gradually gets used to a new situation. They learn how to survive under certain conditions, where and how to obtain food, and where to sleep safely. They also get used to other homeless people, people they had previously overlooked or sneered at. Homelessness leads to the **activation of strategies essential to survival**. This does not only refer to the satisfaction of basic requirements, but also accustoming oneself to one's own social decline and the disapproval of mainstream society. These individuals now find themselves in the position of being judged for a lifestyle perceived as a hopeless existence without any meaning, and they have to deal with this fact.

Survival on the street requires the ability to **pare down one's needs** and learn to live with limited resources while ensuring **an acceptable level of safety**. Successful adaptation requires an awareness of the main risks and the adoption of effective methods of dealing with them. A newcomer is advised by **more experienced individuals**, who teach them how to survive, what to do, and who to avoid. They usually join a group, which makes survival possible, though at the cost of having to adapt to the group and accept its rules. It goes without saying that even within the homeless community there is pressure to share certain attitudes and modes of behaviour. Good is what the group deems to be good, even though their opinions may differ from those of mainstream society. More seasoned homeless people can exploit the insecurity and inexperience of a new arrival and involve them in some kind of undesirable activity (e.g. by teaching them to steal or sell drugs). These, too, represent ways of surviving on the street and these people avail themselves of them. They do what they find manageable and what, at least to a certain extent, they find acceptable internally. The opinion of young homeless people regarding the different ways of making a living can change over time. Usually their tolerance of less acceptable possibilities increases. That which to begin with they perceived with unease becomes a matter of course after a certain time.

LP (male) remembers how an old hand taught him to survive on the street. *"Right from the start Mr H. took me to some garbage bins where I looked for cables containing copper, aluminium, anything that could be scavenged. And then we turned to junk. After that some people showed me that money could be earned simply by going and stealing something."* LL (male) tells a similar story. *"We met M. here and he showed us how to steal. Then we started doing it for ourselves. Yeah, M. is a good teacher. He really helped us a lot here."* A newly arrived girl was initiated by the more experienced MB (female). As MB herself says, *"They all know me. I taught these girls how to steal so they had some way of looking after themselves. I said to them 'Look, you decide, either you're going to eat shit or you're going to look after yourselves'."* And they proved good pupils, as EK (female), who is grateful to MB for the service she provided, confirms. *"I would thank just one girl who taught me loads of stuff. Mainly she taught me how to steal, which meant I knew that I could walk into a shop with confidence and know what I was after and what I could and couldn't take."*

Initiation into the way of life on the street is a condition of acceptance of a new arrival in the homeless community and marks the beginning of the process of their **adaptation to the rules that apply** and the lifestyle here. Alcohol and drugs are not simply a way of escaping a stressful reality but confirmation of a new identity. This identity involves allegiance to people who regard themselves as free, unrestricted by what they deem superfluous requirements. Everyone is defined by who they belong to, and the homeless constitute a socially excluded community that, as opposed to mainstream society, accepts the newcomer without reservation or criticism. It provides them with a certain support, while on the other hand encouraging the development of undesirable and sometimes risky behaviour. Under the influence of the homeless community there is a gradual, usually undesirable transformation of a person's personality, habits and feelings that these individuals, at least to begin with, are unaware of. Nevertheless, a feeling of belonging is one of the factors on which an ability to adapt depends

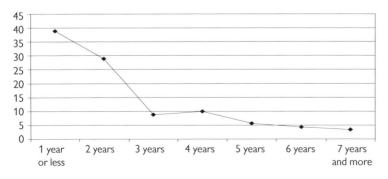

Graph 18. How long clients spent on the street (the graph shows relative frequency).

(another is the maintenance of hope: these two factors represent 50% of the variability of resilience of young homeless people. Rew et al., 2001).

From the graph it is clear that the largest group comprises people who are on the street for less than two years. This period is regarded as critical. If someone remains on the street for longer, it is very difficult for them to readapt to ordinary life and their chance of returning to society diminishes.

3.2.1 OBTAINING MEANS OF SUPPORT

Surviving on the street requires above all **food, shelter and safety**. Young homeless people have various ways of acquiring these. Charities represent one option, though they can also find the requisite items in garbage bins or among discarded goods, by begging, stealing, or as payment for sexual or other services (e.g. drug dealing). The preference for individual methods differs depending on gender and socio-cultural conditions.

The extent to which different methods are used by young homeless people to satisfy their basic requirements probably depends on the **degree of humiliation and confirmation of inferior status** involved. Begging involves immediate contact with the person from whom something is being requested. It is a direct interaction in which the homeless person demonstrates their wretchedness and dependency on the benevolence of more successful people. Though scavenging (i.e. rummaging through garbage bins) also confirms a low social standing, in this case exemplified by the fact that a person is content with the waste that another has thrown away, there is not the necessity for direct contact. A container

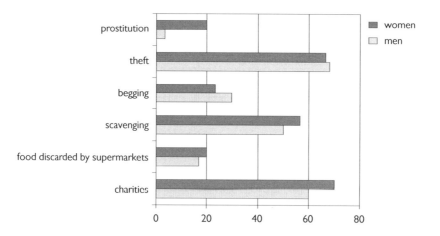

Graph 19. Frequency of the methods of obtaining sustenance used by young homeless people (the graph shows relative frequency). NB: scavenging involves rummaging through garbage cans and containers.

can be accessed at night, when nobody is around. Theft is not such an unambiguous confirmation of one's wretchedness. A thief is not the passive recipient of someone else's charity, but takes what they need. This is clearly one of the reasons why stealing is deemed more acceptable. Prostitution is a specific category. It includes selling one's intimacy and accepting a humiliating role thanks to which a person loses some of their self-respect. For this reason it is rejected by most young homeless people and regarded as an extreme variant.

S. Booth (2005) discovered that young homeless people in Adelaide, Australia, resorted most often to charities (63%), begged for money (61%) or food (44%), and scavenged (9%). The Canadian study by Dachner and Tarasuk (2002) reached similar conclusions. S. Mallett et al. (2004) found that up to 39% of young people aged up to 20 years supported themselves through stealing, 57% begged or scavenged, while only 12% engaged in prostitution. Whitbeck et al. (2000) believe that this is often the result of pressure from older, more experienced homeless people, who exploit the need of a newcomer to belong to a group as quickly as possible and can therefore be used for prostitution. Crawford and Johnson (in Whitbeck, 2009) state that 16%–18% of young homeless people steal food and 3%–13% scavenge.

According to Green et al. (1999) 28% of young homeless people support themselves through prostitution. This figure is higher than our findings, though our group contained slightly older, more experienced people who therefore did not have to resort to offering sexual services (the group examined by Green comprised individuals aged 12 to 21). Kidd and Kral (2002) state that among young homeless people 16%–46% occasionally engage in prostitution. Kidd and Shahar (2008) put the figure at 15%. Salomonsen-Sautel et al. found that 10%–30% of young homeless people occasionally resorted to prostitution. According to Tyler et al. (2004), 25% of young homeless people support themselves through prostitution. S. Zerger et al. (2008) state that almost 28% acquire the means of survival in this way. Rachlis et al. (2009) found that 11% of young homeless people engaged in prostitution. Crawford (in Whitbeck, 2009) cited similar figures: 7%–9% of young homeless girls resorted to prostitution and 5%–11% of young homeless boys (this often involved homosexual prostitution).

1. Charities

Food, shelter and clothes are provided in many charities, such as Naděje or the Salvation Army, and this offer is taken up by many people. If they turn it down, this may be because they are reluctant to come into contact with other homeless people whose appearance or behaviour is unacceptable to them (either because it offends them in some way or reminds them of their own decline). *"I don't want to go to Naděje. I went there once. But when I arrived and saw all the drug addicts, it bothered me. I didn't even wait for the soup, I simply took off immediately."* (EK, female) The client is herself a drug addict and one would not expect her to be so offended by such a situation.

Illustration 1. The Naděje Centre offers services to young homeless people (photo: Dana Kyndrová).

Illustration 2. Queuing for food (photo: Dana Kyndrová).

2. Garbage cans and containers

Food can be found in the mountain of discarded items behind many supermarkets (clients talk of *visiting Albert*), restaurants, or in containers. *"It was important to me to find an Albert as quickly as possible so I had somewhere to eat for free. They don't* throw it in the garbage, they put out three or four bags with food for me to go through and throw away the rest. **It doesn't seem embarrassing to me**. They guy who works in the warehouse is also a squatter." *(JS, male)*

"I like the fact that I don't have to steal in order to survive. Ok, I might have to go to Albert. But I know that the stuff there is fresh and that **there's nothing bad**." *(LS, male)*

"*They throw out food that is two days old, but it's still edible for a week.*" *(VS, male)* It goes without saying that on the street a person has to get used to a lower quality of food and accept whatever there is.

Some young homeless people **regard scavenging as humiliating**. ER (female) feels ambivalently about rummaging through containers. "*If I didn't know it was from garbage bins I'd be ok about it. Yeah, I've eaten food from garbage cans. But at least I knew it was proper food because everyone else was eating it. But I found it unpleasant having to rummage round a garbage bin and drag out food. I found it disgusting.*" On the other hand most acknowledge that scavenging is risk-free and provides easy access to resources. They are inhibited by the knowledge that rummaging through garbage confirms their membership of a socially excluded community. "*It was a big problem for me going round garbage bins. I literally spent two years walking around before I could bring myself to reach inside.*" *(PM, female)*

"I used to laugh at the way homeless people reached into garbage and ate what they found. And then I found myself having to do the same." *(MŽ, male)*

MH (female) was more concerned by the reaction of those around and felt **ashamed**. "*I felt terrible in front of other people*. They were walking around and looking at me rummage round in garbage bins and I said to myself that this was the end. And then somehow or other **I got used to it**. I mean, I have to live somehow, and I started to enjoy it." To begin with LP (male) also felt embarrassed. "*I would put it like this. At the start I was worried, because I didn't know how people would react. I was embarrassed. But not any longer.*" As part of the process of adapting to the homeless lifestyle, i.e. gradual desocialisation, he lost his embarrassment.

Some clients scavenge while under the influence of crystal meth, because it reduces their inhibitions and they enjoy themselves more. They feel that they have to reach down even further, that there is sure to be something interesting at the bottom of the container. "*I only used to scavenge in garbage bins when I was high. When I was really high I used to enjoy it. I always had the feeling that I'd find some money or treasure or whatever.*" *(ZŽ, female)*

3. Begging

Another way of securing the basic necessities, along with alcohol and cigarettes, is through begging. This too is unacceptable for many young homeless people, sometimes more so than scavenging. They are convinced that they would be unable to appear in the role of a loser begging for alms. There exist exceptions, individuals who know very well how to provoke sympathy. For young homeless people active begging or scrounging, i.e. addressing passersby with, "Hey, you wouldn't have ten crowns or some change, would you?", is more typical than passively waiting for charity.

MH (female) has no problem with begging. *"I'm really good at it. The last time I stood here for 10 minutes and I couldn't believe it. In 10 minutes I made CZK 150* (USD 7.50).*"* Others have big problems with begging and are unable to create the necessary impression that encourages people to give them money. *"Begging? Why not? I managed to make CZK 6. I just don't know how to do it, I'm fucking terrible at it. I always end up speaking in a way that turns people off." (JB, male)*

"When I need money I try begging, but usually people simply tell you to piss off." (JV, male)

Quite a number of young homeless people **regard begging as totally degrading** and say they would not even try it. *"I've never tried begging. It seems worse to me than stealing, because you feel completely hopeless. You're right at the end of your tether and there's nothing left for you to do other than beg." (EKr, female)* EKr no longer lives on the street and has found work and accommodation. Her desocialisation was clearly not so extreme as to prevent her from returning to society.

4. Waste picking

One of the relatively acceptable methods of obtaining the bare necessities is by **collecting anything that can be sold or used**. This often involves returnable bottles, though sometimes more valuable items can be found in garbage bins, such as clothes, utensils or electronics that can be sold to junk shops (Marek, Strnad and Hotovcová, 2012). *"Now I'm on the street I don't simply lounge around. I'm too embarrassed during the day, but in the evening I collect beer bottles. During one night I can fill two carrier bags and make CZK 200. I do this so that at least I can make ends meet." (JS, male)*

"I used to collect bottles and sometimes I would beg from people. Sometimes I would find something, a cigarette or some loose change." (MK, male) Both these clients approached the business of securing the bare necessities more actively during their life on the street. At present they have jobs, even though these are usually only temporary.

5. Theft

Theft is a fairly common way of acquiring the necessary financial resources or items. Young homeless people run the gamut of feelings regarding theft, from scruples and distaste, to complete indifference and a feeling that they are justified in acting in this way. Several individuals find their inhibitions are gradually eroded after a certain time on the street and their hierarchy of values is transformed. Others begin to steal much earlier, with almost a half of our clients having been **involved in theft even prior to starting life on the streets**, most of them as far back as childhood. This was usually in order to acquire something they could not have at home or in order to be successful within their gang. *"Yeah, I used to steal things, as far back as school. I stole a few baseball caps, **the kind you want but can't have.**" (JB, male)*

"Typical shoplifting, alcohol and that kind of stuff. We had money. But if there was an opportunity to steal, then why not? It was like that every day. They caught us, but they only gave us a fine." (MC, male) Neither of these men regard theft as something serious or reprehensible. It goes without saying that while homeless both stole.

In the population at large 43% of people admit to having stolen something at some point in their lives (Čírtková, 2009), while in the young homeless community this figure is almost twice as high. The knowledge that they might be caught does not scare them. They know that they will receive at most a fine, which in any case they will not pay. According to Fischer et al. (2008) the readiness to steal increases after a year on the street. Homelessness has a significant criminogenic potential and many researchers regard such conduct as the basic characteristic of street life and subculture (Baron and Hartnagel, 1997). Use of drugs and alcohol increases the likelihood of progressing from minor criminal acts to more serious crime (muggings and bodily harm).

The leitmotiv *"you want something, you don't have it, so you simply take it"* persists in the case of many young homeless people into adulthood and is sometimes one of the causes of their social decline. From an analysis of the interviews we conducted it seems that **life on the street increases the tendency to steal but is not its only cause**. Most young homeless people understand stealing as one of the possible ways of obtaining what they need or even as a necessity if they are to survive. Several of them did not steal in the past, but do so now because they feel they have no choice. They use the same argument – *"I haven't eaten for two days"* – when they are trying to beg money for alcohol or drugs. *"I'm a bastard. I survive through shoplifting, but **I only began on the street** so I could stand on my own two feet." (MB, female)*

"When I ran out of money I began to steal. To begin with it was awful, because I had never stolen anything in my life. And at the moment I had to deal with the fact I said to

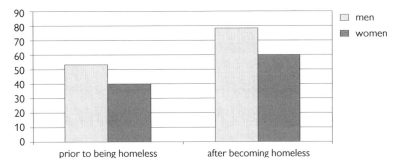

Graph 20. The number of young homeless people who admit to stealing (the graph shows relative frequency).

myself that I was simply doing it **in order to survive.**" (ER, female) It seems likely that the justification "I steal in order to survive" represents a defence mechanism explaining such conduct as essential. The same applies to another argument used by young homeless people when justifying the fact that they steal only rarely and only for their own immediate needs. "I have never stolen anything in order to have money, never. I only ever stole for myself, so that I could eat. I never wanted to steal a car so I could make two hundred thousand. I only ever stole in order to survive." (JJ, male) The sums stolen vary a lot, though they tend to be spent quickly because these people do not know how to manage their finances.

However, not all homeless people steal simply to satisfy their immediate needs. **Some sell on the items they have stolen.** This is very often true of people who need money for drugs. KB (male) is a drug addict who sold stolen goods to support his addiction. "There were two of us who worked together. We stole something and then sold it. The Vietnamese will buy anything." TŽ (female), who also uses drugs, tells the same story. "I used to steal every day, mainly chocolate, coffee and sweets. I'd steal them and then sell them to the Chinese. I got caught a lot, got given a fine and that was that."

It is clear that a **transformation in how stealing is perceived** takes place as part of the adaptation to a homeless style of life from the stories recounted by SŠ (male), who only began stealing while sleeping rough, but who gradually became used to this method of providing for himself and created his own limits. "To begin with I was really scared, but over time it came to seem quite banal. I began to steal regularly. **If it yields results it's just a matter of time.** For the most part I just stole little trinkets in order to sell them, or food and so on. It never occurred to me to start stealing cars, for instance. Yeah, they caught me, several times. I knew what that meant, that I'd have a criminal record and that was that. But I was always careful not to get beaten up if they caught me." Last year the client was sent to prison for debts. However, he is not a criminal. He acted more out of a sense of emergency and even of indolence.

Some homeless people do not only emphasise the justifiable reason for theft, but also **who their victim is**. Stealing from an anonymous shop or company is not in their opinion as reprehensible as stealing from specific people. Downplaying the importance of theft may serve as another defence mechanism eliminating possible feelings of guilt (if they are still subject to these). "**I would never steal from a person**, I only steal from the state. Yeah, they caught me. To begin with I was really scared about what would happen. But in time I realised they'd give me a thousand crown fine and tell me to bugger off. No, it wasn't degrading for me. I mean, look at how many people steal. They only ever caught me stealing a sandwich, it was only ever a sandwich." (EK, female) The client is trying to say that nothing of any great significance was involved. She was hungry and so she took the food she needed. MM (male) takes the same approach, though has committed more serious criminal activities than mere shoplifting. "**I don't steal from people**. I wouldn't be able to approach someone, tear their handbag from them and run away.

I realise they might have medicine or money for their children, whatever. But when an insurance company has enough money, then why not?" The client is still homeless, has been in prison several times, and it is difficult to imagine that he will give up theft.

However, among homeless people there are many who make no such distinction and **do not respect the rules against stealing from an acquaintance** or even a relative. For the most part these are individuals with personality disorders or drug addicts. VK (male), for instance, stole from his adoptive mother and was thrown onto the street as a consequence. *"She brought charges against me. I took her bus tickets and sold them. So what, **I needed the money. She had loads of money but didn't want to give me any**. I was almost 18 and I needed to buy cigarettes."* VK's reason was banal and indicates a certain emotional superficiality and callousness. The client returned to the street repeatedly, takes drugs, and is unable to hold down a job. LL (male) **stole from his grandparents**. *"The first time I stole CZK 73,000 (USD 3,600). It lasted me around two weeks, not even that, maybe a week. But I used it to pay for friends, buy clothes. They threw us out of work because we started to steal on a large scale, though they never proved anything. We used to steal in order to be able to buy crystal meth."* The client has not continued with his criminal activities and at present is not homeless.

Young homeless people tend to have a different yardstick for stealing. For instance, they do not think of stealing scrap iron as a criminal activity. They do not believe they are committing a criminal act when they take something they find lying around, as long as it is not locked in an apartment or car. The fact that the item belongs to someone means nothing to most of them. *"I'm pleased when I find some copper. Ok, it takes me two hours to uncover it, but it's money earned. I don't have to go and ask anyone."* (VS, male) Finding something in this case means stealing it. The boundaries of ownership are not unambiguously respected in the homeless community. *"But **it wasn't theft as such. I simply found an unlocked car**. So I took the wallet that was in it."* (ZK, male) This is a man who has been involved in credit fraud and has been living rough for four years.

Robbery as the norm in the homeless lifestyle. Life on the street demands a knowledge of the conditions and rules that have to complied with if a person is to survive. It is also necessary to accept the standards of the homeless community that are not in complete accordance with regular societal norms. One of these is tolerance of theft, i.e. its acceptance as a standard means of acquiring the basic necessities. Many homeless people are convinced that society owes them something and that they therefore have no reason to respect its norms. Theft can function as an initiation ritual confirming a sense of belonging to the socially excluded community. The longer the time spent on the street the greater the indifference to such conduct. In the end it becomes shrouded in a feeling of righteousness. For many homeless people theft becomes something ordinary, not to say desirable. *"Theft? That's became completely normal these days. Everyone's at it."* (MŽ, male) MM (male), who has been in prison many times, is of the same opinion. *"We usually take a litre or two of rum.* **I mean, we're not going to buy the stuff**, *that would be stupid. I wouldn't buy it even if I had the money."* Robbery is also a regular activity for MT (male), who recounts how he used to steal mobile telephones and sell them to traffickers. *"That suspended sentence I received was for robbery. It was this summer. I was visiting K. and* **saw a mobile telephone, so I took it**. *I reckon I nicked maybe three mobiles and immediately sold them to someone who bought them from me without needing a document. I'm simply happy they only found out about one of them and that the others weren't reported. I think I started to see the potential of this kind of theft given the way things turned out."* Stealing as such was not the problem for MT: being found out was. Both clients are still homeless and neither their behaviour nor their lifestyles have changed.

Young homeless people often steal because they need **money for alcohol or drugs**: they also steal while under the influence of these substances. *"We used to go out stealing a lot. To begin with it was for booze, because you could consume it immediately. Later it involved the kind of things you could sell in order to buy something.* **When I was plastered I didn't care what I did**." *(MK, male)* Larger robberies are often motivated by the need to acquire resources for the purchase of a much craved fix, since alcohol can be acquired a lot more easily. *"I used to steal.* **That's how I got the money for drugs**. *I started by shoplifting. Electronic goods, that kind of thing, or something worth up to, let's say, CZK 500."* *(LS, male)*

"The worst thing that happened to me was when I was twenty four and I got hepatitis C. After that I began to steal in earnest. Up until then I had only resorted to stealing on occasion, so I had something to eat, but then I went full out **so that I could buy drugs**.*" (MB, female)* There are many such people among the ranks of the homeless, whose addiction to alcohol or drugs reduces their inhibitions while increasing their need for funds.

Some young homeless people do not want to steal and if offered another possibility, will take it. This is usually because they are frightened of the consequences. *"I tried it a few times, but I was caught and since that time I haven't stolen anything.* *I tremble like a leaf." (VL, female)* Others get used to it because the proceeds make the risk worthwhile. *"Right from the start I was scared* of stealing. I used to shake, I was so afraid, but then as time passed and I got the feel of it and they catch you … it's fifty-fifty as to whether they catch you or not. But if they didn't catch me, then in half an hour I had CZK 600, I'd earned as much as if I'd worked a whole day." (LP, male)* The client is not a typical criminal and if he has the chance to earn money some other way, he does not steal. At present he has a job and lives in a hostel. His problem is that he lacks a firm base and is easily influenced.

From the perspective of young homeless people robbery is a relatively easy option with obvious advantages that is worth the risk involved. Some of them even find the pressure linked with it attractive. **Stealing becomes an adrenaline sport for such individuals.** *"When I arrived here I began to steal in earnest.* **It was a real adrenaline kick** as to whether they would catch me or not. You can earn a lot by stealing. It depends how hard you work. I used to steal clothes and every day I'd earn CZK 800* *or more." (MH, female)* The client had been stealing since her childhood, mainly for her mother, a drug addict and alcoholic, whom she tried to please in order to obtain her love. Last year she spent time in prison. Her prognosis is unclear. However, given the overall burden she carries, many complications can be anticipated.

In conclusion we should remember that, **while young people steal, they are also often stolen from**. They are both the culprits and victims. Despite its liberal tolerance of theft, the homeless community is somewhat different to other criminal groups. What tends to prevail here is passivity and resigned survival, an inability to plan and to implement whatever plan there might be. In the case of homeless people robbery is more an opportunistic activity very often conditional upon alcohol or drugs.

6. Prostitution

Prostitution is another way of acquiring the basic necessities, though relatively rarely used or at least rarely admitted to. Some of our female clients had earned money in this way before becoming homeless. Even so, for most young homeless people of both sexes prostitution is something they would only do in extremis, though sometimes this appears to be more a question of rhetoric than a genuine internal block. (For instance, KB (female) says that *"she would rather die than be a hooker".*) Prostitution entails a significant intervention in the intimate integrity of their personality, and this is associated with a loss of self-respect and a decline in social status. There are perhaps more people in the group that have made their living in this way than it seems, since not everyone is willing to admit that they have resorted to prostitution on occasion. **Prostitution is engaged in mainly by drug addicts**, above all women, because the necessary funds for basic survival can be acquired in other ways. 'Survival sex', as prostitution made necessary by the need to survive is called by M. Green et al. (1999), is not necessary for people availing themselves of the services of charity organisations.

The main reason for choosing prostitution as a means of making money is its ease and efficacy: **sufficient money can be made quickly, albeit in a demeaning way**. Even those who admit to prostitution emphasise that they only engage in it occasionally and in an emergency. *"The worst is prostitution. If it's not on a bench, then it just about tolerable as long as it is genuinely simply about money. But **it is only something I'd do in an emergency**. You'd do it with anyone for a crown or two." (KM, female)* Prostitution too has levels of acceptability: if it takes place in an apartment or nightclub, it is not regarded as being as humiliating as sex for money on some park bench.

MB (female) resorted to prostitution whenever she needed money. *"I've turned tricks ever since I was eighteen. That's five years. I put myself out for my family, and when my son was born I also turned tricks. I never did it because I needed money for myself. I only did it in nightclubs, never on the street. I wouldn't go streetwalking.* (In this respect her claims do not correspond to reality.) *It's **filthy, there's no pleasure***

Whatever happened to hope?

Nikola was wondering what to do. She looked through her handbag and found a telephone number offering payment for sex. She had no phone credit, so she found a telephone box to make the call.

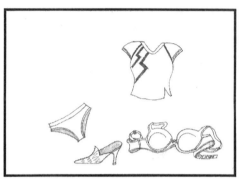

Her first job is tonight. If it goes well, at least she'll have some money. Now all she needs is some clothes. Maybe she'll find something in the squat.

She managed to put something together and looks good. The first "rendezvous" is never an easy one ... Judge for yourselves.

She received an address that she was to go to in the evening. She wouldn't normally do this, but there's the first time for everything. It was a beautiful house. In the back of her mind she wondered how anyone who lived in such a house didn't have a large family or at least a wife.

She had no idea what to say to him and how to amuse him. If only she'd known what was in store. She wanted to turn around and leave, but he appeared at the doorway. It was immediately clear to him what kind of girl this was. He invited her in. She entered and the doors closed behind her.

It didn't exactly go as planned. He asked her to take all her clothes off. He got her to light a cigarette and stand all night long by his bed. He looked at her with contempt while pleasuring himself.

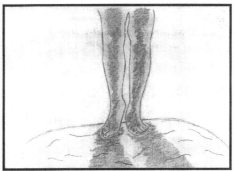

She received nothing, not a single cent. He gave her her clothes and told her to get dressed. As quickly as he'd welcomed her so he kicked her out. Her head was empty. She walked through a park, sat on a wall and put her head in her hands. She remained seated and suddenly heard the sound of water. She looked around and saw a small pond. She stood up and walked slowly to the water.

She was so ashamed she felt like abandoning herself to the water. Nobody had ever humiliated her in such a way. She undressed and slowly immersed herself in the warm water. It was a hot summer night. She wanted to wash the filth off her body. She floated on the surface like a nymph. Everything floated away. All the stress, remorse and humiliation. There was no longer anything that could torment her.

Illustration 3. Comic-strip entitled "Where did hope disappear?" (the author is one of our clients).

in it. I never want to return to it in my life. When a man looks at me, when he talks to me, I see red. I know I could kill someone. I felt disgusted by blokes. Maybe everybody experiences it differently, it depends on their personality. There are girls who would never do it because they couldn't stomach it. And then there are girls who clench their teeth and put up with it. Some do it because of drugs, others for their families. But the consequences are always the same. At the very least a lifelong trauma. I mean, how can I explain it?

*You go with a guy who's maybe 50 years older than you, who isn't remotely attractive to you, who smells. Not very pleasant, is it? I basically did what I wanted with these guys, unless it was some idiot who held you by the neck and slapped you around. In the five years I worked as a hooker **I became allergic to blokes**. I had had enough of them. I saw a guy and I wanted to puke. And if a guy spoke to me I wanted to punch him.*" The client comes from a broken home and is a drug addict. At present she is in prison. The whole of her life up till now is a story of humiliation and degradation that has impacted negatively on her self-respect. This is not only the result of traumatic experiences suffered as a prostitute.

LD (female) takes a matter-of-fact approach to prostitution and does not have a problem with it (or does not admit to one). She knows that she needs money for drugs and that it would be difficult to come by it in any other way. "*I've worked in a brothel, I've got that behind me. At least I made money there. Prostitution is better than stealing. I don't think about it. **I think about the fact that I'm going to have money** and something to eat, that I'm going to have clean things to wear. I take drugs constantly and so I turn tricks all the time.*" This is a client who was abused by her foster parents as a child and has never managed to forget this experience. She has spent most of her life in children's homes and young offenders' institutions, and this is manifest in apathy and a different attitude to generally less acceptable modes of behaviour. Recently she came out of prison and at present is registered at an employment office and living in a hostel.

KS (female), who was also **the victim of sexual abuse as a child**, learned to use sex to her advantage, taking the line that "*at least I get something from it*". (At the time it took place nobody believed she had been abused and nobody was willing to deal with the problem.) Leaving home was a reaction to this situation. Her approach to prostitution reveals a clear need to deny the basis of such behaviour and an unwillingness to admit what in reality it is about. "*I didn't even really look at it as prostitution, though it is, I suppose.*" This is a client who was one of the few we interviewed who felt the need to present herself in a better light. She was not even willing to let on that she had worked in the pornography business. At present she does not work as a prostitute but sponges off her friends. She could be described as being parasitic upon her friends.

Male homosexual prostitution seems to be relatively rare among young homeless people. However, it is of course possible that not everyone wants to admit to it. It usually involves a man with homosexual or bisexual tendencies, often very young, who cannot procure the basic necessities in any other way or is exploited by someone more experienced. "*Yeah, I tried prostitution too. It wasn't particularly pleasant, but **I had to get over it somehow**. I did it depending on what mood I was in.*" (*MO, male*) MO was adopted by a family in which his alcoholic father beat the mother. When his adoptive mother died, he was placed in a children's home. This is a person with limited mental ability who does not reflect upon his actions. At present we have no information as to his whereabouts or what he does for a living.

Homosexual prostitution played a role in the story recounted by JN (male), who is no longer homeless. *"**Not many people would own up to it**. I know which boys sell themselves, I know it one hundred percent. I was walking the streets with them at the same time. I'm not homosexual and I never have been. I'm not even excited while it's going on. My job was to satisfy others. It was hard, difficult. I felt **I had sunk as low as I could go**, I no longer wanted to live. I wanted to die as quickly as possible. That's why I started to drink more and more. I felt abused by society. **I had no problem in stealing** and doing a runner from a punter's apartment. Mind you, I stayed with some of the punters. They took me travelling around the country and to their cottages. They recommended me to others. But when I saw that there was no future in it with a particular punter and I saw a clear opportunity for a large profit, I stole from them. In C. there is an apartment where anyone can wander in off the street any time they want. They can ring the bell and they'll have somewhere to stay. However, they'll have to offer that pensioner sexual services as he wishes. But it's no problem if they take a girl with them because the pensioner likes to look. It's a degenerate place. They've even shot porno there."* The client is no longer on the street and has entered the programme T. Challenge and at present is working for other homeless people.

It seems that prostitution represents an aspect of homelessness that is currently murky and very risky, especially at the end of adolescence and the start of emerging adulthood. One of the degrading aspects of it is revealed in the story recounted in the form of a comic strip story by one client who supported herself through prostitution for a certain period of time (before becoming homeless). It reveals a knowledge of the symbolic rejection of mainstream society, even in a role that is humiliating enough in itself. The figure representing mainstream society does not want any closer contact, even though he exploits her in his own way.

7. Freeloading

Exploiting another homeless person or group is by no means exceptional. Often one person will steal or otherwise obtain food, alcohol, cigarettes, etc. and share them with the rest, either voluntarily or under the pressure of the community. This is why certain individuals are often dissatisfied, especially if they feel that they simply give and the others only take. Somewhat simpler is a similar sharing of resources within the relationship between a homeless man and his partner. Many young homeless females admit that this is how things were in their case. *"When I was going out with someone they supported me." (PČ, female)*

"R and M help me. They bring me food and they're cool about it. They're with me the whole day. We sit at A. and everything's cool." DV (female) For a woman to be dependent on her partner or other men is not as advantageous as it might seem. It is often achieved under pressure of being absolutely subordinate and sometimes coerced into prostitution.

3.2.2 ACCOMMODATION AND SLEEPING ROUGH

Homelessness is a way of life entailing fundamental restrictions on privacy and continual movement within public space. This fact acquires added significance especially at night, when a person would like somewhere to sleep securely with their personal belongings around them. During the day the elimination of private space is less stressful, because it is normal for people to move around in public temporarily. For young homeless people it is important to find some **place that can function at least symbolically as a base**. The non-existence of a more permanent place to spend the night, sleeping on public transport, benches, in a station or in a metro vestibule, carries with it a high risk of theft, as well of course as a sleep deficit. People at the start of their homeless career spend nights in this way, as well as those whose deterioration has advanced so far that they do not even look for a safer place. There are not many such people among the ranks of the young homeless.

The narrative of life on the street, including movement from place to place in search of somewhere to sleep, is more a story of the homeless community rather than of the individual. The **selection of a place to sleep or to reside for a period of time** is circumscribed on the one hand by the possibilities of young homeless people and on the other by their personal preference, i.e. by what seems acceptable to the individual in question. These conditions are usually met at least in part by some kind of closed space that a homeless person finds and

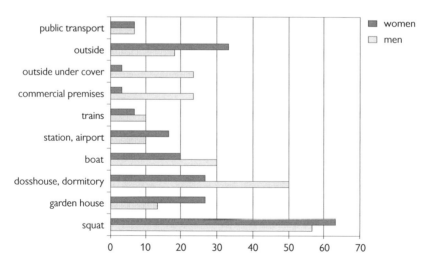

Graph 21. The places where young homeless sleep or reside.
Outside: on a bench, in a field, in a park. Outside under cover: beneath a bridge, in the sewers, in an alcove or cave. Commercial premises: in a cellar, in an attic, in a garage.

Illustration 4. The site of overnight accommodation (photo: Jakub Marek).

spends some time in unless thrown out. The knowledge that the place is not theirs and that they have no right to it influences the behaviour of these temporary residents. This can be manifest in an indifference to the place where they sleep and especially its surroundings. The character of a place where a person spends the night and to which they have a tendency to return can also provide information regarding the current state of their personality. According to Marek et al. (2012), it can be used to assess the degree of desocialisation and personality deterioration of these people.

LB (male), a drug addict, is undiscriminating. *"When I'm completely pissed **I couldn't care less where I sleep**. The important thing is to put my head down and sleep."* Two years after the interview the client is still sleeping rough and taking drugs. On the other hand LC (male) is more choosy regarding where he sleeps. *"The main thing is that **it's not too dirty**, that it doesn't smell of piss or that kind of thing. I sleep in different places. I stay as long as I can in one place, but I can't be there forever because someone would notice."* This is someone who lived on the street for only a year before finding a job and accommodation in a hostel.

1. Sleeping rough outside

Sleeping rough outside, whether this be in a public place or under cover, is usually simply a temporary solution that a person opts for **in an emergency**. *"A couple of times I felt weak and fell asleep on a park bench. I didn't have the strength to drag myself off looking for something better. This was when I suddenly ran out of money*

Illustration 5. It is possible to sleep rough in a public place (photo: Jakub Marek).

Illustration 6. A dosshouse on benches (photo: Jakub Marek).

for the hostel, we couldn't find the money for that day. We usually had the hostel paid up front, but this was an exception. I also spent a few days outside during summer, but it was warm, so that was ok, you don't mind if you fall asleep in the grass somewhere." *(IH, female)* During the summer, sleeping rough outside is not such a problem, especially if a group is involved. They can make believe that they are on holiday and that they will deal with their situation when they get home. *"Sleeping rough, it's kind of like a **lovely holiday under the stars**. We began by sleeping in the Barrandov*

Illustration 7. Living under a bridge (photo: Jakub Marek).

housing estate, but someone pinched our tent so we slept here, in the woods. It didn't seem strange to me to be living in a tent. I used to sleep in a tent even before becoming homeless. Mind you, you start to notice it when the winter arrives." (LV, female)

It is obviously impossible to sleep on the street itself because the police would not permit it. *"You can't actually sleep in the street because **the police will chase you away**. They see you on a bench, chase you away, see you sleeping in the bushes, chase you away." (SV, male)* The street is also a poor place for sleeping rough because of the cold, and a homeless individual needs to warm themselves up, most often by means of alcohol. *"You're cold on the street, so you pour a few gallons of wine down your throat." (MK, male)* Sleeping rough outdoors can also be **dangerous**. *"I'm frightened here* (in Prague). *The last place I slept was a petrol station. I was determined not to sleep in a wood or whatever, because you never know what'll leap out at you." (ZK, female)*

Sometimes the area beneath a bridge can become a base that a homeless person takes care of as though it were their home. This is not somewhere that anyone can enter. You have to be invited. *"We live under a bridge in H. We have one simple rule, which is that it has to be neat and tidy. Oh yeah, and we have to agree on things." (LP, male)*

2. Boat

The Hermes, a boat berthed in Prague, is an unusual doss-house for homeless people. A lot of people sleep on it, especially during winter. It is cheap, with one night costing CZK 20 (USD 1), though it has its rules that many homeless people are unwilling or unable to comply with. Many young homeless people regard it as an acceptable option. *"I slept on the boat. I was there almost the entire winter. You turn up, take a shower, watch TV in the canteen or go to sleep. But most of the people who go there are old people who can't look after themselves. Mind you, **there are normal people there too**." (ŠP, male)*

The requirement that a guest be acceptably sober represents a limit that more experienced clients bear in mind, and when they are drunk they do not go to the boat but look for a different solution. *"Yeah, I sleep on the boat. But then maybe I'll stay away for a week, simply in order to booze. This'll be in summer. It's not possible during winter, that's true. Right now the entire week that I wasn't there I spent boozing. I've been sleeping on the boat around two years." (MT, male)*

*"I don't go to the boat if I know I'm going to be drinking or if I've been drinking. In that case I wander around Prague, or if I've got some money, I'll continue drinking. And then **I go to the boat when I've sobered up**." (MP, male)*

For some young homeless people, especially if they take care of their appearance and personal hygiene, the **other people** on the boat, who are dirty and can be a source of various parasites, are the main problem. *"I lived for six months on the boat before **catching everything there is to catch**." (MB, female)* The relationships between people sleeping on the boat can also be problematic. Some of them can be quarrelsome or steal from the other guests, etc. *"You only have to go to the toilet and **they'll steal your food**." (JŠ, male)*

3. Doss-houses and hostels

From the point of view of young homeless people doss-houses and hostels are an attractive option. However, they tend to be more expensive, sometimes excessively so. Furthermore, in this case too the necessity of complying with rules can act as a barrier (as in the case of the Hermes). Some young people are unable to respect these rules and lose the opportunity of sleeping in a particular hostel. *"I spent the whole of winter living at the Salvation Army. But then they chucked me out and terminated my stay at that hostel, the whole-day hostel, because I had a conflict with the clients. Yeah, **I was drunk, so they chucked me out and told me to come the next day**. But I didn't pay attention and I climbed over the fence round the back. They called the police, who took me away. The next day I turned up to collect my personal belongings. It was purely down to my stupidity." (MP, male)*

JP (male) found his stay in a doss-house brought to an end because of lack of money and an inability to deal with the situation. *"I spent two months at a doss-house. Then I left, then I returned. It was all going well, I had what I needed. I always left the place when **my money ran out**. But then I started taking the piss more and more. **I refused to do the cleaning and that kind of thing**. They threatened to kick me out."* MS (male) lost his place in a doss-house because of an unpaid debt. *"I try to remain in one place, but it's not always that easy. Things haven't been so bad since Naděje opened a hostel in S. It's really great there, but I owe the place money and I can't live there until I pay off the debt."*

It is sometimes impossible to avoid unpleasant fellow residents in a doss-house. *"I first went to Central Station. I spent a week there and then I went to a Salvation Army doss-house. I stayed there for six months. It's not the regime that bothers me there, it's the filth. Human filth and filth in general. But especially the people. **Now that's what I call dirt**."* (AK, male) DV (female) does not like charity doss-houses because of the older homeless people who do not care about hygiene. *"Older people tend to stay at the Salvation Army, which means there's this **permanent stench** that I can't stand."* It is clear that doss-houses for the homeless have specific features that make them unacceptable for certain clients. Other clients would be happy to stay in them, but cannot because they have broken some rule or other. If a person is on the street for a longer period of time, they can find themselves with fewer and fewer possibilities. One such possibility is a squat.

4. Squats

A squat is normally housed in a deserted, rundown building, which homeless people occupy and use without authorisation. This is also only a stopgap measure, though often of a longer term character. A person enters a squat either by finding one for themselves or being offered a place in one. However, the accommodation is not always comfortable. The building may be cold, there may be no running water, no electricity, and there may be a lack of privacy since often several people live in the one room (in one building there are as many as several dozen people). A **squat takes some getting used to**. *"Before I got used to this squat*

Illustration 8. Living in a squat I (photo: Jakub Marek).

Illustration 9. Living in a squat II (photo: Jakub Marek).

I thought it would be better to live at home. But then I got used to it. The most difficult bit was getting used to the street and the squat... The problem is you have no privacy. There's no television or electricity." (MT, female) Nevertheless, it is a roof over one's head and a relatively stable place. A person belongs somewhere and can return there. It is better than complete homelessness. *"They offered me a place in this squat and said I could sleep in the chapel. I'm pleased I have a roof over my head and it doesn't rain on me and that I don't have to flit from one place to another outside. Right now I have a mattress, two sheets so that I can wash and change the bed linen, a sleeping bag and another blanket." (JS, male)* This client is aware that his accommodation represents one of the better options.

A person cannot always choose a squat but has to accept whatever is available. MM (male) has lived in several and can compare. *"At present I'm living in a squat in P. This is more about what opportunities there are at present rather than there being a real selection out there. **I am satisfied here** because we're quite remote and there's not many people here. I have lived in half of the squats in Prague. This is the best one. I know that there's some peace and quiet if you're here all day. The police won't chuck me out, they won't come round three times during the night and it isn't so central that I would have to worry. As long as we stay quiet they tolerate us. I don't like moving all the time. When I get used to somewhere I don't like changing."*

Some clients manage to fit out and keep clean their place in a squat. *"It wasn't so bad in U. I was there for one month on my own. That was in the room opposite P.B. and there was an incredible mess there. I began by cleaning the first half and then I discovered that the room was actually a nice one. So I cleaned up the whole of the upper floor. I stole furniture from all of the lower apartments and polished the upstairs. Every day I swept the floor." (JP, male)*

*"I live in a squat. It's a good squat. I have a couch, bed and table. **When it's cleaned up** it's cool. It used to be occupied by junkies, but now it's lived in by normal lads like me." (JH, male)* The client drinks alcohol but does not use drugs.

Untidiness and dirt can be a source of problems depending on who occupies the squat (e.g. whether they are drug addicts) and how many of them there are. Some squats are infested by mice, rats and various insects. It tends to be homeless women who complain about this, while the men are more tolerant or indifferent. *"Over the last five years I have had **lice** maybe six times. This January was the last time I had them. I was still living in P. in a squat. I have also had **fleas** after sleeping in a squat. I had to burn all of my clothes. Ok, shit happens, on the street there's nothing that doesn't happen. But it's important to go round telling everyone to check themselves." (MB, female)*

*"In some buildings it's terrible. **Rats** run riot during the night. Mind you, it's better than here on a bench." (PČ, female)*

"I used to live in squats, but not any longer. In K. it was awful, full of mice, mess and junkies. I didn't stay there long, six months maybe." (ZŽ, female)

*"I used to live in squats. I met a few people here and they took me to K. That was an awful time. K. is a squat that is not for the weak of character. The environment was simply gross. I mean, I don't know if someone would ordinarily make themselves up a bed in an attic where 40 mice, 5 rats etc. run over their head every night. **The dirt there was something…**" (IC, male)* Though not an overly sensitive person, even this client registered the discomfort of the environment. For many others it must have been far worse.

Sometimes housemates are not only problematic because of their lack of hygiene, but because they represent a risk from the point of view of possible **theft or other threat**. *"In most squats things were fine. K. was disgusting. **I arrived to find x pairs of boots**. K. is simply a junkies' den. I also lived in P. (a squat). I lived there for a long time, though as far as the inhabitants are concerned there's not much in the way of common courtesy. The good ones are outnumbered by the bad ones. Basically **I nearly died there**. Because M was stoned and drunk and in a foul mood and I was with a girl. He entered the room and it was all I could do to avoid being stabbed in the stomach and face, because M is a big motherfucker." (JP, male)*

Problems can arise in a squat for many different reasons, and some people take many risks. For instance, they might cause a **fire in the squat**. In 2010 several people died in one such fire, including one of our clients. *"Last November we started living in K. The police used to come round, but everything was fine. And then we built a fire, we cooked food, everything was cool. And then **twice the place caught fire**. We don't know who was responsible. We simply arrived back one time and there were flames everywhere." (DV, female)*

Generally speaking, **the larger the group** living in a squat, **the greater the risk** of problems arising. Ideally a few people share the space, all of whom get on well. *"I don't like it when you have sixty people in a squat. It would be best if I could be* *on my own or if there were four of us. Not a building with sixty people. I've experienced this and I don't want to ever again." (LP, male)*

*"We used to live at L. It doesn't exist anymore, it was closed. It was disgusting there, there were **too many people coming and going**. It's better when a squat isn't packed, there's simply a few people and nobody else arrives, nobody else knows where it is. Here I look after this building, I mop the floors and do the cleaning. It's cool. Only a few people know about it. To begin with there were nine of us, two old guys who've since snuffed it, and the rest we kicked out. We said to them 'show yourself here again and you get a punch in the face'. We chucked them out because they weren't fair, they didn't come with us to the collective farm. Yeah, of course there are rules. We don't take new people in and those who stay, stay. The basis is cleanliness and cooperation." (LL, male)* It is not always easy to enforce such rules.

Life in a squat is occasionally marked by pressure on the communal management methods, the sharing of resources, and participation in maintenance. For some homeless people this is unacceptable, especially if they are addicted to drugs or alcohol, in which case compromise is impossible. Such individuals tend to be expelled from the group (unless they form the majority). If the number of people living in a squat exceeds a certain limit, problems ensue and the police are eventually forced in and drive out the squatters (Marek, Strnad and Hotovcová, 2012).

Sometimes all efforts to improve an occupied place are fruitless, since a **squat is not a legal residence and homeless person can be removed at any time**. Homeless people are aware of this and most have experienced something of this kind at some point. *"We used to have a squat. The building was set to be demolished in two months, but a new owner arrived and bought it. It was well furnished, we had cleaned and tidied it, everything. We cleared up all the broken glass. We cleaned it up for her and then she called the police who turfed us out." (MK, male)* Not even a squat represents secure accommodation. It is nothing more than a temporary refuge. There is no way of meeting the need for a secure, safe base that homeless people have. This fact is deemed one of the most significant problems they face by 15.5% of young homeless people.

3.2.3 LIFE ON THE STREET HAS ITS NEGATIVE POINTS

When a person finds themselves sleeping rough, they have to learn how to survive. They have to overcome their fear of being attacked or robbed. This is commonplace on the street and most young homeless people find themselves victims, some repeatedly. Some of the homeless community are psychologically disturbed and socially deficient individuals (e.g. drug addicts, mentally ill or criminal recidivists), whose behaviour is often unpredictable. In order to survive a person has to be able to **perceive all signs of any risk** and take evasive measures if possible. Dealing with the threats, as well as with simple ostracism, can be

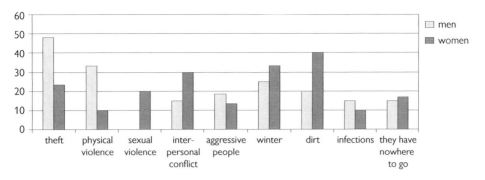

Graph 22. What young homeless people believe is worst about life on the street (the graph shows relative frequency).

demanding. It can also be difficult dealing with the negative feelings that life on the street prompts (feelings of loneliness, inferiority, helplessness, desperation, depression and anxiety).

Whitbeck, Hoyt and Bao (2000) state that 20% of young homeless people have been physically assaulted on the street and 20% have been the victim of sexual violence. (For many of these this is nothing new: 51% had been repeatedly physically assaulted even before becoming homeless.) N. Buhrich et al. discovered that 50% of women and 10% of men had been victims of violence. The results of research carried out by Adeline Nyamathi et al. (2001) were similar, with 39% of homeless women being victims of violence of some sort. They discovered that the aggressor was often a partner or someone known to the women. K. Tyler et al. (2004) write that 23% of young homeless women and 11% of homeless men are victims of sexual violence. If a woman is a victim of sexual violence, the perpetrator was more often someone she knew or even a friend, while if a man was subject to such violence the perpetrator was more often unknown. Raleigh-DuRoff (2004) says that 52% of homeless people in all have been attacked in some way on the street. A. Stewart et al. (2004) discovered that 83% young homeless people were attacked after leaving home. The group led by M. Gwadz (2007) arrived at slightly lower figures: 70% of men and 67% of women had been victims of physical violence. Women are more at risk of sexual violence, with 71% encountering some form of injury on the street (this figure is only 33% in the case of men). Whitbeck et al. (2007) offer lower figures, with 45% of men and 28% of women having been physically assaulted on the street. In this study 42% of women had been sexually assaulted but not a single man. The higher number of female victims is borne out by the study by Johnson et al. (2006). Rachlis et al. (2009) state that 48% of young homeless people have been victims of violence. K. Bender et al. (2010) found that 57% of young homeless people of the group studied had experienced some form of violence. The risk of a person being the victim of violence increases with the use of alcohol and drugs. As is clear from these results, the risk of various forms of violence is relatively high. It is encouraging to see that young homeless people based in Prague are less at threat, whatever their lifestyle.

1. Theft, physical and sexual violence

Young homeless people are very often the victims of various criminal activities. Many of them have been **attacked, beaten up or mugged on the street**. They are aware that others around them have the same experience and it is clear to them that this kind of thing is commonplace on the street. They realise that they are more vulnerable than people leading a standard lifestyle and **usually accept this fact as a given**, something they must take into account.

Homeless people who have been **attacked and mugged** view such experiences as inevitable, despite the trauma and humiliation. *"They really worked me over. I was eighteen when it happened and it was mental. Two Ukrainians came up to me and one pointed a gun at me and told me to give them everything I had on me. I told them I didn't have anything. They said I was lying and then pistol whipped me. I fell to the ground and when I woke up there were policemen and ambulance personnel standing over me. I reckon that **it could happen to anyone here in Prague**."* (MH, male)

"It's mainly at night, because that's when the criminals travel around, hordes of them. They're even willing to steal from the homeless. They don't give a damn what they take. I once saw four of them go up to one guy, kick him, rob him, piss on him and then run off." (AM, male) People who live on the street are well aware that life is not safe. However, over the course of time they get used to this risk and learn to avoid threatening situations to the best of their abilities.

The thief is not always someone from outside the homeless community. Often it is someone with whom the victim lives on the street and knows, sometimes even their partner or friend. Homeless people often steal from each other, and this usually happens in the place where they sleep. *"**They steal your things in a squat**. Maybe you leave some clean clothes out and when you return they're no longer there. They steal your bedclothes and suddenly you've nothing to sleep in. Someone who lives on the street and steals from someone else who's also on the street, that's got to be base. Instead of supporting each other they steal from each other."* (MB, female)

*"I fell asleep in L. and they **stole all my stuff**. The fact is that if you have some personal belongings you have to make sure you hang out with people who aren't going to steal them."* (KM, female) VL (female) fell prey to her partner, a drug addict. *"**My boyfriend stole everything from me**. I was incredibly hurt. We're still looking for him. But he's the kind who has stolen from loads of people."* It is clear from these stories that it makes no sense to believe in anyone on the street and that anyone is potentially a thief.

Someone living on the streets is **most at threat at night**. *"Here the nighttimes are the worst. In these squats it's a question of survival. Someone arrives, or maybe a group, or they get into your building, and immediately there's a fight. Anything can happen. Or for instance Wenceslas Square at night."* (MŽ, male)

"Say I'm sleeping here at Central Station, I'm really worried that someone could kill me. I don't know if it's true, but apparently dead bodies have been found here." (MO, male)

For JP (male), who knows life on the street very well, the biggest risk at night comes from **strange, unpredictable people**. *"The habits of these people, and fear. At night you're on the street alone and you're among these people, so what do you think? Shit, there's a junky over there shooting up. What if his hand slips and he sticks the syringe in me. That aggressive idiot, the one who's completely drunk, he'll throw a brick in your face and that's that. And often there are former convicts here who were in prison with junkies. You never know what they're going to do next, you're always at threat from them."* Life on the street is simply not safe.

JŠ (male) has been **attacked and beaten up**: *"Take a look… scars here and here… I found myself among some of our darker friends and they used me to see how sharp their knife was. One of them came up to me wanting a cigarette. I said I didn't have any, so he asked if I had any money. Again I said no. So he left and returned with another five of them. I gave them what they wanted and a fat lot of good it did me."* JS (male) was also beaten up by a gang of Roma. *"They kicked me in the head. I suffered **bruised ribs and a broken arm**. That's what they did to me. I think that's the worst thing that's ever happened to me. I reckon I was in trauma from it. When six or seven of them go for you, what can you do?"* LC (male) was attacked by a group at the other end of the spectrum: skinheads. *"**They kicked me** and left me there. Nothing was broken, but my face was a complete mess and I suffered bruised ribs."*

Homeless people are very often attacked and mugged when **drunk or under the influence of drugs** and when they cannot defend themselves or do not even know what is going on. *"Usually when you're drunk you lose all your documents. It's happened to me twice. I was boozing and had my documents stolen."* (JS, male) With JP (male) it was drugs. *"They beat me up and mugged me, yeah. They punched me in the face a few times. I said to myself, ok, in a way it's your fault."* The knowledge that he himself was responsible for a state in which he was more vulnerable than usual did not unfortunately encourage the client to think about changing his life-style. Most homeless people regard the occasional mugging or beating as part and parcel of life on the street. They defend themselves mainly by remaining in groups, even though this is no guarantee of safety. As we have already pointed out, the perpetrator is often a member of the same community.

From the life stories recounted by young homeless people it is clear that the experiences acquired sleeping rough differ from those of mainstream society. Someone who lives for a while on the street begins to view things differently. **Many homeless people** gradually found themselves in both roles: **they were both the victims and perpetrators** of various criminal activities. *"Skinheads beat me up and stole my documents. I was beaten up many times, punched in the face frequently. I was often the victim and often the attacker. I tried both roles."* (TK, male)

"They stole my documents, my wallet, they did this to me, an old timer. I was totally pissed off. I mean, I'm the biggest con man in T. and they steal from me. Yeah, of course I steal too. But I don't steal from people. I couldn't go up to someone, snatch their hand-bag and then make a dash for it, I simply couldn't do that."(MM, male) This client is a criminal recidivist.

Homeless women often have to deal with the trauma caused by **rape** or attempted rape. This trauma can often be severe. This happened to only one man from our group, who occasionally makes a living as a homosexual prostitute. Homeless women are usually the victims of sexual assault by an unknown perpetrator who does not have to belong to the socially excluded community but simply exploits its vulnerability (Čírtková, 2009). **Homeless women are aware of the risk of sexual violence** and when something like this happens they do not go to the police because they do not believe that they would receive any assistance. They are aware that in their own way they are outside the law and that either they attend to their own safety or reconcile themselves to being victims of violence. They usually resolve their situation by joining a group or finding a partner. However, this is no guarantee of safety, something the homeless community is unable to provide. It includes people who do not correspond to the norm and cannot for various reasons be relied upon (drug addicts, criminal recidivists, people with personality disorders, etc.) Reid et al. (2005) discovered that woman who have been attacked are frightened of the same thing happening to them again and do not believe that they can defend themselves effectively against this threat. This in turn leads to a feeling of helplessness that they cannot rid themselves of. This in turn unfortunately increases the risk of their being victims of further violence. The strategies they use to deal at least partially with this fact can seem strange to say the least to an independent observer. For instance, they passively accept violent behaviour and do nothing to prevent it because they regard it to be a natural part of their lives and simply wait for it to end.

TŽ (female) was raped by a group of people she knew. *"They made sure I was heavily drugged and then raped me."*

*"My drug dealer **raped me, beat me up and broke my nose**. I've got a scar here and I had bruised ribs. Plus I had my teeth knocked out by guys. That happened when I was walking along the street at night. Suddenly a guy leapt out at me. I reckon that screaming for help just excites these perverts even more to be honest. So I looked at him and said, 'ok, help yourself'. Two gave up, one didn't, unfortunately. If you look at it logically, this kind of twat likes it if you scream, he gets excited that he can hit you."* (MB, female) Sexually motivated violence became part of this client's life. This is a woman who has lived for five years on the street, is a drug addict, makes a living through prostitution, and who appears to have adapted to the circumstances she finds herself in. Another victim of violence is PČ (female). *"I've met a lot of people in my life, but I've never met such an ice-cold psychopath. It didn't matter how I acted, I tried all possible reactions, I smiled and cried, but nothing worked with this cunt. The bastard took a long metal pole, about one metre twenty, caressed me and told that if I didn't listen… I was convinced this was the last day of my life and that he was going to rape me. I didn't go **to the police** about it because nobody would have wanted to talk about it, they would simply have said that I'm a junky so what did I expect. I didn't think I'd ever get over it psychologically. For a year and a half I couldn't look at a guy."*

Victims of sexual assault find it difficult to come to terms with their trauma, even though they know that many others have experienced something similar. Sometimes they exhibit **symptoms of post-traumatic stress disorder**, such as panic, paranoia, anger, apathy, helplessness and a feeling of disgust for men, whom they regard as potential rapists. (The same conclusions were reached by Reid et al. (2005) as well as Stewart et al. (2004).) *"**For me men** – some of them, not all – are **vermin, total garbage**. So as soon as a guy starts to touch me, starts to think he's God and he can do what he lives, I immediately get nervous and put an end to it." (TŽ, female)* Very often these are women who were tyrannised and abused in childhood and whose trust in men, or indeed anyone, may have been significantly damaged.

Women on the street are often victims of all kinds of violence because they are physically weaker and more vulnerable. Another reason might be the fact that they move around public spaces, especially during the night. If a homeless woman works as a prostitute, the risk of possible contact with a sexual predator increases (Tyler et al., 2001). In addition, the actions of the perpetrator are often influenced by his conviction that when persons on the margins of society are involved it doesn't really matter. Even members of the homeless community are often disdainful of homeless women, whose social status is worse than that of the men. Perpetrators of violence against homeless women are also often their partners (Nyamathi et al. 2001).

2. Poor relationships with people

Not only violent conduct or theft is a **source of stress**. Many homeless people are troubled by the fact that there are **poor relationships in this community** and that people behave inconsiderately and aggressively to each other. *"The worst thing is the people. They're stinking, spiteful hyenas. I'm getting used to the fact there's nothing good here for a normal person. I'm here because I haven't got anything else." (MH, female)*

*"The worst thing is the relationships between people on the street. Each **envies** what the other has. You stand in a queue with them and they're screaming at each other, as though the next person shouldn't receive anything. **They argue** in such a way that they threaten to kill your family. I understand that some of them have been in prison, some for the whole of their lives, that's their character, they were changed inside. Fine, but why do people who just come for the soup or to wash have to endure it, why should they listen to such bilge? And when they say something to them, the guy who screams at them is pissed. They have knives and shit in their pockets. I've had bad experiences with this." (LS, male)* Many different kinds of people are homeless and many of them do not correspond to common expectations even given the greatest tolerance. Sometimes it is impossible to avoid them and in these cases conflict ensues.

The conduct and appearance of certain homeless people serves as a warning to others as to how they themselves might appear at present or in the future.

*"The worst thing on the street are the other homeless people, because you see that **they are exactly the same as you yourself**." (ZK, female)* They represent to the client what she is or might become, and this prompts concern. *"I have tried to talk with other homeless people, but I simply can't. I don't want to be on the street – perhaps they do. I don't want to freeze to death in winter and bang my head against a brick wall. That's why I don't want to talk to these people, because I know they would suck me under."* The client has been homeless on and off for six years. However, much as she does not want to be, two years on from our first interview she still sleeps rough.

3. Cold and filth

Hygiene is often a problem on the street. The tolerance of dirt exhibited by a homeless person indicates the degree of their social decline. TD (female) is not a hardcore homeless person. She has not been on the street long and therefore problems with hygiene cause her real grief. *"**The worst thing about life on the street is hygiene**. I mean, if you want, you can take a bath every day, but it's a real drag. You have to travel across the whole of Prague to N. and wait for a social worker before you're allocated a shower. And when you think about who was there before you... Some of these people aren't the cleanest... So that's what bothers me the most."* Men, too, are not always indifferent to questions of hygiene. *"On the street it's simply **endless, ubiquitous filth**. The whole issue of hygiene is the worst. Ok, there's Naděje whatever, but it's not the same as going home, running a bath and relaxing." (JP, male)*

Not only problems maintaining personal hygiene are stressful, but also the **dirt of other homeless people**. *"When I see it I feel sick. When I see these people... I'd rather not look at them, because it's disgusting, awful. These are people you simply can't help. The dirt on the street and on homeless people is appalling. I'm also homeless, but I don't walk around so filthy." (IH, female)*

"I slept at B. The people there are something else. I went to take a leak and there was a board covered in shit and someone was sleeping in the other toilet. I can't help feeling that these people create such a mess around them needlessly."(ZK, male) An **awareness of the degeneration of older homeless people** is stressful but unfortunately does not possess the requisite preventative impact. Young homeless people are in denial and reject the idea that they could one day end up like their older counterparts. For the moment they remain convinced that this will not take place.

Most homeless people suffer more during **winter**. *"The worst thing is you have nowhere to lay your head, and this is particularly the case in winter."(MK, male)*

"The worst is when it's cold and you've nowhere to hide. This is particularly the case on the street, when you can't sleep and you've nowhere to lie down." (BČ, male)

However, the cold is not the only problem on the street. The fact that a person has **nowhere to go and does not belong anywhere** is also highly stressful. They find themselves on the margins of society with no interest being shown in them. *"Perhaps the worst thing about the street is the fact that you have to walk somewhere all day long. When you're sick and you're always waiting for something, you can't be sure* you're going to have a place to sleep or something to eat." *(MP, male)* Unfortunately, not even these circumstances are sufficient to provoke a change of behaviour.

4. Feelings of disorientation and exclusion

Some clients **feel lost in a large city**. They do not know their way around and they are surrounded by hordes of people from whom they do not know what to expect, or in some cases know not to expect too much. *"The worst thing on the street is the flow of people, the sheer numbers that walk through Charles Square, for instance. Or finding your way around Prague in the night. And then there are these ghettoes full of Africans. It scares me." (DČ, male)* Some of these concerns may be irrational, anxieties provoked by the thought of what could happen. Many clients do not know where things are in Prague, and are capable of interpreting the prevalence of a certain type of person in a place as indicating the presence of a ghetto, even though it is nothing of the kind. Their image of the city includes only certain districts that might be quite specific in some way and differ from other districts. LB (male) speaks of the **burden involved in having to be constantly vigilant and alert for any sign of a threat**. *"On the street the worst thing is the feeling that you have nowhere to go, nowhere to lie down in private, shut the door on the world and take a break from everything. You're always here, you can't switch off."* As the interviews make clear, life on the street is stressful in many respects.

Another stress factor is being aware of the social exclusion that keeps a person on the margins of society. *"The worst thing about being on the street is that I can't talk with normal people because **they won't accept me as being one of them** and you don't have the means to make yourself one of them. You know what I mean, when you're on the street you find yourself hitching up with those who are already on the street." (JŘ, male)*

*"You're simply known as a homeless person and people look at you differently. It's the look of **people who regard you as garbage**." (SŠ, male)* Many young homeless people are convinced that the employees of various institutions, e.g. the police, also behave worse to them. *"It fucks me off the way that policemen act when they see a homeless person and a junky and the way they behave to me. It's like total contempt." (EK, female)* A homeless person is rated as belonging to a social class below which there is no other.

Taken as a whole, life on the street has nothing to commend it. *"The street is negative for me. **It gives you nothing but takes everything**. It takes your home, it takes the best a person has in himself and turns it into something bad. For instance, a person will die in winter on the street or make such an enormous mistake that when the police catch him they put him in prison. The street offers nothing but takes everything." (ER, female)*

"The street is a bitch. It's indescribable. If you're not used to it you wouldn't last a single week." (JH, male) An antipathy for the environment of the street can motivate a person to return to society. During the months following our interviews both these clients found work, and ER found accommodation.

It is only possible to survive on the street if a person learns to recognise what represents a threat and avoids conflicts that could have unpleasant consequences for them. This means exercising caution when establishing deeper relationships and giving priority to non-conflictual, superficial contact. *"Act in such a way that you never have a problem with anyone. Make sure you get on with everyone, that everyone is prepared to accept you."* *(IP, male)* In IP's opinion the best strategy is to see nothing and look after yourself only. *"Don't work, drink, do what you want and don't bother me with anything."* He believes the principle of survival is as follows. ***"Don't rely on anyone and don't believe in anyone.*** *Look after yourself, that's all you should do."* Such an attitude, while preventing a person from being disappointed, depletes them. A reliance on oneself and caution in relation to others around can operate as a source of self-confidence, as L. Rew et al. (2001) discovered. **Prudence when deciding who to trust** is an important aspect of survival on the street according to the study conducted by Kidd and Davidson (2007) and Kidd and Shahar (2008).

Young homeless people **tend not to be very satisfied with their lives**. Bearsley and Cummins (1999) discovered that young people living on the street are not satisfied with most aspects of their lives (i.e. material circumstances, health, safety, family background, society, as well as their own achievements and emotional experiences). Friends constitute an exception, by providing them at least the illusion of a certain base. One of the causes of dissatisfaction in young homeless people is the chronic stress that ensues from this lifestyle, though their opinion may have been influenced by earlier negative experiences. Many of them were exposed to huge burdens and disappointments while children, and this may have intensified their negativism and created the feeling that their lives lack

Illustration 10. The life of young homeless people is stressful (photo: Dana Kyndrová).

meaning. This stance leads to the consolidation of denial/coping strategies that are manifest in an inability to deal effectively with all the burdens they face. They feel worse and worse. Their reduced psychological resistance is then manifest in an inclination to use drugs and alcohol, emotional discomfort, and sometimes suicidal tendencies.

According to information from Sananim, an organisation that looks after drug addicts, this group of people comprises between 20% and 25% homeless people. Likewise among young homeless people approximately a quarter are drug addicts and many more use various psychoactive substances (Šupková, 2007; Marek, 2010). The number of young homeless people who have attempted to commit suicide as specified in foreign studies differs quite considerably (probably depending on cohort selection), and is something in the order of 20% to 50% (in our group this figure was nearly 15%). Kidd and Kral (2002) discovered an even higher number of suicide attempts in a group of young homeless people who had been tyrannised and abused during childhood and supported their live on the street through prostitution. Milburn et al. (2006) reached a similar conclusion: 30% to 40% of young homeless people aged up to 20 had attempted to commit suicide at least once in their lives. R. Martinez (2006) reports that 48% of girls and 27% of boys had attempted to commit suicide in a group of young homeless people. In the group studied by Kidd and Carroll (2007) this figure was 46%. However, this last case also confirmed that experience of tyranny and abuse and a lack of belief in a better future increased the tendency to resolve problems through suicide.

The feeling of having more control over life, either by finding better conditions or adapting to the current situation, makes for improvements to the quality of life. People who manage this usually feel better. In the case of young homeless people this involves, for instance, the question of whether to learn how to avoid the various dangers that threaten them on the street. If they become convinced that it is not possible to control this, they have to adapt and accept an increased level of risk as a natural part of life. This also happens a lot. The subjective interpretation of the significance of intractable events is very important and can make it easier to accept these events. People who have experienced trauma, been beaten up, raped or mugged, often create their own version of what happened. This helps them to deal with the event (Ensign, 2004). (If they are unable to process the traumatic experience acceptably, they may develop post-traumatic stress disorder.)

3.2.4 POSITIVE ASPECTS TO LIFE ON THE STREET

For many people, life on the street is something that they would fervently wish to avoid. They would be hard pushed to find anything positive about it. However, the opinions of young homeless people are not so clear cut. Some of them are convinced that there is nothing good to be found on the street. Others appreciate the freedom and latitude it offers. It suits them not having to take matters into their own hands and not having any duties. For these individuals the fulfilment of duties represents such a large burden that they attempt to avoid it at all cost, even with an awareness of the consequences, which include the loss of previous relationships, their own deterioration, and social exclusion. Men believe life on the street is more acceptable (60%), while women are more sceptical, perhaps because homelessness is far more demanding and destructive for them.

The possible benefits of life on the street as rated by young homeless people can be divided into three categories:

You learn something new, you are more resilient, and you learn to take care of yourself.

*"It's the **experience**, the experience of looking after yourself."* (ŠP, male)

*"I think it's because you learn how to take care of yourself with nothing. If someone else found themselves on the street, they wouldn't have a clue as to what and how. **You learn an awful lot here**."* (PM, female)

*"The street teaches you a heck of a lot. You either learn **how to look after yourself** or the street will force you to."* (ZŽ, female)

You have freedom and latitude, you can do what you want and nobody is bossing you around.

*"To tell you the truth, I'm starting to enjoy this way of life. **You can do whatever you want**. And I'm the kind of guy who gets used to things really quickly. I'm already used to this lifestyle. It's great in that **nobody bosses me around**. The street doesn't argue with me, the way I see it, it calms me down. Yeah, I suppose you could say it's like being on holiday for me."* (JŠ, male)

*"The freedom, the fact **I don't have to pay anyone for anything**, I don't have to do anything."* (IC, male)

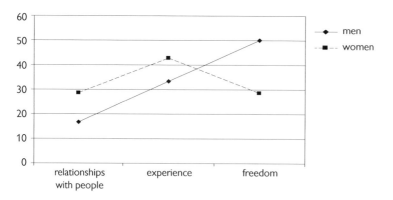

Graph 23. How the benefits of life on the street are rated (the graph shows relative frequency).

Illustration 11. You can spend life on the street as you want (photo: Dana Kyndrová).

*"It's a kind of holiday. I'm free of problems, **I have no obligations**, the only obligation I have is to look after myself." (LP, male)*

*"What I really like is that **everything is one big holiday**. Street people are clever in their own way. They have everything free, without effort. If a normal person wants something, they have to go to work and earn money, don't they? Street people have it all without money and without work." (KS, female)*

Some clients believe one of the merits of the homeless way of life is the problem-free acceptance of other people and a willingness to share food, accommodation, drugs, etc.

"The fact that these people accept you and that you deal with things." (ŠŽ, female)

"Because people here take me for who I am and not what I have or how I look or what I own. They accepted me with all the shit I was carrying, they simply took me warts and all." (KB, female)

This opinion is slightly at odds with the rating accorded relationships between homeless people (see the following sections). Nevertheless, it is possible that some of these people had such bad experiences in their former lives that even superficial, unreliable relationships seem good to them in comparison. Furthermore, we cannot exclude the possibility that there is an element of bluster to these declarations, an attempt to justify why these individuals remain on the street even though their words do not correspond fully to reality.

3.2.5 CHANGE OF VALUES AND NORMS

For most young homeless people the first days on the street were a very traumatic reminder that apparently easy solutions to problems have their negative sides. It took them a while to orient themselves and learn to survive without too much stress. However, they managed this and after a while began to feel better. Their gradual adaptation to the homeless lifestyle and their inclusion within a group of people with a similar fate offered them many new experiences, though was also manifest in a different approach to generally valid norms and a change to their hierarchy of values. This change was to a certain extent caused by the necessity to **adopt the moral code of the street** in order to survive. The gradual adaptation to these norms sometimes leads to a shift in moral considerations, which in many respects differ from the standard moral standpoints of adult people. On the street it is above all necessary to look after yourself and not pay too much attention to others. Duplicity and danger are par for the course and conduct is tolerated that would not be accepted in mainstream society. The gradual adaptation to the life of a homeless person can be seen as a **specific form of socialisation** that is essential under the circumstances but that complicates a return to society. (It can also be viewed the other way round, i.e. as a process of gradual desocialisation and feralisation.)

Managing the often stressful experiences of life on the street requires an **ideology of homelessness** that includes some rather illusory ideas that can be summarised in several points (Ayerst, 1999):
1. Homeless people share a sense of exclusion and are rejected and disdained by mainstream society.
2. Homeless people are the victims of infelicitous fate, be this real or assumed.
3. Homeless people are free and independent and do not have to deal with the pressure of various duties. They do not have to do anything they not want to. Poverty and existence on the margins of society is presented as an advantage, as liberating, albeit associated with certain problems.
4. Homeless people have a magical faith in the good fortune of outsiders who manage to survive in the face of infelicitous fate.

Street ideology **serves to confirm the value of life on the street**. Despite the many stresses and disappointments it offers young people the illusion that there is something positive and meaningful about it. They need to feel that opting for the life of a homeless person is acceptable despite that fact it is not acknowledged by the majority. The ideology offers young people the chance to reject their marginalisation and lays emphasis on the positive exceptionalism of the identity of the outsider. It downplays the loss of social status and former contacts. Indeed, it regards members of mainstream society as enslaved and imprisoned. It has its own norms that allow for various ways of satisfying needs and rationalises the acceptability and legitimacy of parasitizing off society (be this through theft, fraud, begging, or some other means). The influence of the homeless ideology contributes to maintaining acceptable levels of self-confidence, while at the same time preventing people from returning to society.

3.3 RELATIONSHIPS WITH PEOPLE ON THE STREET

Leaving home **weakens links with other members of the family**, always supposing these existed. On the other hand, it speeds up the process of orientation among one's peers, including incorporation within this specific and often risky community. Generally speaking, the less support relatives or former friends offer young people, the greater the likelihood that they will associate with people on the street. Most are unable to judge the potential risk involved in such an association. Life on the street can generate a certain social capital that will not impact favourably on the future course of the individual and will prevent a fundamental change of their lives.

R. Martinez (2006) states that homeless youth create new relationships on the street, but that after a certain time they discover that they are not as good as they appeared at the outset and that they come with various risks attached, e.g. inclusion within a group of drug addicts. Despite all of these risks, other homeless people represent a community that serves as a source of a certain security. Even this kind of social network reduces feelings of stress and negative emotions such as anxiety and depression (Johnson et al., 2005). Bao, Whitbeck and Hoyt (2000) remind us that on the street only other homeless people can provide support, be this genuine or illusory, but that they can at the same time be a source of threat. Even so, the acquisition of new friends and acquaintances is deemed a positive strategy (Rew and Horner, 2003). This community helps a young homeless person acquire the necessary experience and supports the acceptance of their new lifestyle. However, a homeless person must learn how to distinguish who they can make use of and who might represent a threat to them. As Rew and Horner (2003) point out, it is important that a homeless person present themselves assertively and does not reveal any weakness that someone else could abuse.

The social network of homeless youth comprises mainly their contemporaries on the street. The number of people belonging to such a network tends to be relatively small, averaging from two to five people (Marek, Strnad, Hotovcová, 2012). A group will be homogenous in terms of age and include individuals of both sexes. These contemporaries can provide the feeling of a certain base, though **they do not usually make for more permanent relationships**. This is often more an illusion that something of this kind exists than a genuine source of support. A couple or group can feel safer, but even the homeless themselves concede that these are not deep relationships and they do not usually expect much from them. Many say that you have to be cautious on the street and not trust everyone you meet. Excessive trust in another could be dangerous. The need to form a relationship quickly, i.e. to form it at all cost, sometimes leads to subordination to more powerful and experienced people. When young people were asked by van der Ploeg et al. (1991 – in Johnson et al., 2005) to say whether they had at least one real friend, 80% replied in the negative.

Snow and Anderson (1993 – in Auerswald and Eyere, 2002) confirm that **easy sociability, but also superficiality and instability**, are characteristic for homeless youth, often ensuing from the effects of drugs and alcohol. Sociability is often associated with caution, which is particularly necessary in contact with strangers who could be dangerous in some way. A feeling of belonging can be acquired in a homeless community, but it is impossible to avoid experiencing unreliability and inconsiderateness. As a result many homeless people prefer not to invest too much in relationships with people. They are afraid of being disappointed again or are unable to (our group contains a number of people with experience of early emotional deprivation). They can easily feel an internal solitariness, even though they live in a group and are almost never physically on their own.

K. Johnson et al. (2005) found that, **despite negative experiences, a significant number of homeless youth** (60%) **said that friends were important to them**. They help them survive, forget their problems, and alleviate their feelings of loneliness, even if this involves simply the illusion of friendship. Young people have a need to stick together because it is easier to survive this way under the circumstances, even though relationships do not have to take the standard form. The character of homeless people's relationships is influenced above all by their orientation on the present. At any given moment they may be intense. However, nobody relies on this continuing into the more distant future (Unger et al., 1998; Bao et al., 2000; Whitbeck et al., 2000; Miller et al., 2004; Taylor-Seehafer et al., 2007)

3.3.1 INTERPERSONAL RELATIONSHIPS WITHIN THE FRAMEWORK OF THE HOMELESS COMMUNITY

Relationships with people on the street have their specific features and risks. The **necessity to live in contact with various problematic persons** from whom nothing good can be expected represents a considerable burden. It is not easy to accustom yourself to the fact that not only considerate and helpful individuals live on the streets, but also criminal recidivists, people with personality disorders, and people under the influence of drugs and alcohol, and it can take a long time. The problem of homeless youth resides in the fact that they are dependent on others. Under the circumstances in which they find themselves **it would be difficult to survive alone**, and they are only in a position to choose with whom they associate within the given community. They hold various opinions regarding the group in which they live and differ in terms of whether they create more stable smaller groups or accept almost anyone they meet.

An extreme, albeit infrequent, variant is the **conviction or illusion of a cohesive group** that can operate as a family. *"I lived with people who mattered to me and as you can see, we still meet now. We are a kind of close-knit family and we don't allow others to join us. I've found loads of friends, mainly among the young people, not so much among the older ones. I've also met good people, though I know loads of bastards who robbed me. But these are the people who are my family." (MB, female)* The client has lived on the street for five years and the homeless community genuinely represents her social base. Indeed, she has no other. Her idealisation of the group is probably a certain form of defence mechanism in a situation in which she had

Illustrations 12 and 13. Relationships between young homeless people can be good (photo: Dana Kyndrová).

Illustration 14. Life in a squat does not offer much in the way of privacy (photo: Dana Kyndrová).

to come to terms with the breakup of several partnerships, being infected by hepatitis C, and the loss of her original family, including her own child.

The need to find more secure and permanent relationships is sometimes manifest in the creation of a **group that shares accommodation and certain items for a period of time.** The more ravaged people tend not to belong to such groups because it is impossible to live with them in acceptable relationships. *"Things are good among the people I live with in this squat. We share everything – food, drugs, whatever. What I like about them is that they are open and receptive, they're people who look after themselves, wash their clothes, and wash when they come in from outside."* *(PČ, female)* It is almost like being at home. Again, this is a woman who appreciates good relationships. She is an experienced client who has lived on the street for three years and has no other base.

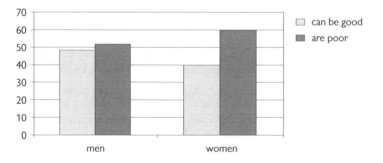

Graph 24. Relationships with other homeless people (the graph shows relative frequency)
NB: Relationships with people are always more important for women, and this is true of homeless women, who are also more aware of both the positive and negative aspects of interpersonal relations.

Sometimes what is important is not a relationship but simply the advantages of the existence of a group, the **symbiosis that makes life on the street easier**. People wait together for food, exchange information, offer a bed for the night, etc., though they do not have any strong links to each other. They are basically unconcerned as to who arrives, as long as they behave in an acceptable way and do not interfere in their habits. The opinion prevails that **relationships among homeless people are poor** in a group.

A better understanding of the opinions and experiences of homeless youth can be acquired by addressing two fundamental questions: can assistance be expected from other homeless people or simply deceit? Do rules apply between them, perhaps different from mainstream rules?

1. Assistance or deceit? Both

Most young homeless people have the experience of being cheated or harassed on the street, as well as being helped. Either way the experience is likely to be intensified by the fact that a person is more dependent on others and is in almost constant contact with them on the street. They have no privacy and hardly any personal belongings. The idea of sharing absolutely everything sometimes leads to behaviour that does not respect any boundaries. However, the homeless also have a need for privacy and the maintenance of at least a minimum of personal space (including ownership), and when this is disturbed it is experienced negatively. Though aware that that they have to take such possibilities into account, this does not mean that they are not frustrated when it happens. It is very difficult to resolve such problems, because a homeless person cannot afford to provoke more serious conflict or move elsewhere. It is clear to these people that, wherever they might move, things will always be the same. Insecurity and inconsiderateness towards life belong to the street and the homeless are helpless in this respect. This is why they do not overreact to such incidents, even though they had not anticipated them to begin with.

PČ (female) speaks of the unreliability and inconsiderateness of other homeless people. *"It's happened to me many times. But I forgive and forget. They think that when they cheat you it represents a personal victory and that you're a fool. I couldn't give a fuck, **I ignore things**. It's not that it doesn't bother me. But the fact is you'll never explain to that kind of person, they've sunk so low, they've become degenerated by life. And **above all you shouldn't punish them** by beating them up. You do that and you hurt yourself, it's just not worth it."* The client has been living on the street with short breaks for three years and though she has plenty of experience with other homeless people she clings onto certain illusions (see her previous description of the group she belongs to).

Many other clients recount similar experiences. *"Yeah, **you have to assume it's going to happen** when you're living on the street. Some people simply cheat, it's as simple as that. I let it go, though I remember it."* (IC, male)

Illustration 15. Relationships between people on the street can be conflictual (photo: Dana Kyndrová).

"I've been cheated by loads of people. It always made me feel bad, because I had hopes in several people, I taught them about life on the street and then they go and let me down. But the pain always goes away. No, I don't want revenge. Life itself will give these people what they deserve." (TK, male)

The behaviour of people on the streets surprised many clients, who were not used to anything like it. *"I wasn't used to such behaviour. I had never seen people taking such liberties with others. For instance, someone's talking to you and suddenly they take everything you have on you. They don't give a shit and the next day they carry on talking to you as though nothing had happened. I have never experienced this and it shocked me. People on the street do exactly what they want, they seem to have no scruples or limits." (LN, male) "They always cheat you on the street.* **You don't find many good people on the street.** *I don't know how many times I've been disappointed by someone's actions. You'd never think it of them. I've never done them any harm. On the contrary I've always obliged them. And then one of them goes and takes my mobile telephone. No good deed goes unpunished, I guess." (JŘ, male)* (This type of conduct is very often the result of drug addiction, which eliminates any kind of consideration.) LN and JŘ are very different individuals, but their opinion of relationships among homeless people is similar and can be summarised as follows: on the street **you cannot trust anyone a hundred percent** and this has little to do with how you behave yourself. This means that the rule "if I behave well towards other people they will behave well towards me" does not apply.

Though homeless people are unreliable, **they can also be helpful on occasion.** Sometimes there is the problem of not being able to assess how a particular individual will react, whether solidarity with the rest will predominate (perhaps supported by the realisation that next time it might be they themselves who need help) or the need to satisfy a need (e.g. by obtaining a fix). *"People on the street don't know each other, they simply hang out together. This is a bad thing when they're people who are only interested in exploiting you. This is a feature of the street, because everyone needs money and when someone hasn't got any, they exploit the rest. This kind of cheating is part and parcel of the street. But sometimes you get a positive feeling. For instance, when **someone does something for you even though you don't know them.**" (ES, female)*

Many young people have received assistance from someone, though they have also been cheated many times. A willingness to help is always a source of pleasure. *"Not many people ever helped me out. But **you feel happy when someone comes and helps you**. It changes everything, but unfortunately it isn't often." (JŘ, male)*

"Yeah, someone helped me out. I hadn't actually asked him for help, but he just offered it himself." (LS, male)

JŠ (male) is more sceptical. *"I reckon that **all this helping each other out is a kind of barter**. There's no such thing as a free lunch."*

In many homeless communities it is taken for granted that individuals will share what they have with the rest. Very often the individual is not permitted to keep anything for themselves. This approach can of course be demotivating, because it hinders any kind of individual endeavours. Most young homeless people claim that they are willing to help, at least in some way, and that they will share their food, alcohol, accommodation, etc. *"If I have it, I share it. When I go looking for food at Albert I might find loads of salami and sausages, and if I've got a full bag and I can't eat it all myself, then I walk around distributing it. I'm not a miser. **If I have it, I share it.**" (JS, male)* To be more precise, if he has a surplus, then he shares it. This is a positive approach because it is linked with the expectation of reciprocity.

Sometimes assistance is conditional upon the willingness of the other to offer something in return. *"Yeah, of course I'd help someone. But I would want to feel that they are going to try to help me too. If they start the ball rolling, then I'll join in." (MŽ, male)*

*"Of course I share things. I help people I know will help me in some way. **When I know they have something to offer**, then I help them." (ŠP, male)* On the street assistance is regarded as a kind of loan and in an emergency the lender can demand repayment. A homeless person might well take the line that if someone has nothing to offer during such an emergency, that this in itself is a form of deceit.

MB (female) is willing to help anyone. *"Yeah, **I help everyone** who asks. If I could, I'd take everyone home. Either I'm too nice or too stupid."*

*"Whenever I have anything, I share it. I think **I must be a bit of a simpleton.**"LB, female)* It is interesting that many homeless people in a position to provide assistance think that this is a sign of their own stupidity, which will sooner or later be abused by others. This may well be their experience, but while it reinforces their pessimistic expectations, it does not weaken their willingness to help.

Assistance may take many forms and **has a certain limit**. *"You have to establish some kind of limit so you don't offer so much help that you end up with nothing yourself."* *(PM, female)* Sometimes this limit may involve one's personal space being invaded, personal effects taken, and one's sleeping space used by another (which is not always only a bed). PM is against this. *"I don't approve of people taking things from their roommates and it is also unpleasant to find someone else lying in your bed."* There should be limits and they must be maintained. The problem is that everyone sets different limits and this can be a source of conflict.

Most homeless people are willing to offer someone food, a cigarette, somewhere to sleep or some loose change. This involves helping out with the **basic requirements for survival, but no more**. This is clear from interviews with various clients:

*"I don't provide financial assistance because I know I wouldn't have enough for myself. But I help out by sharing **food** or offering a tip as to where someone can **spend the night**." (LC, male)*

*"I definitely help. If I see someone begging, then I tell them I'm in exactly the same position and offer them a few crowns. Or if we have a fair bit of food and some others don't even know where they should go for food, then I give them some. Food and **loose change** at most." (LL, male)*

*"Yeah, of course, a **cigarette** or some change if I have it. Maybe five or ten crowns. Mind you, I don't usually have any money myself." (LN, male)*

Assistance is not always of a material character. It may take the form of **advice or psychological support**. *"Yeah, I offer help. For instance, by helping someone arrange something at an office, that kind of thing." (LM, male)* MM (male) offers psychological support. *"I try to offer assistance, but not financial, I don't have enough for that, but more through humour or a bit of fun so as to take their mind off things."*

Among homeless people there are many who **feel they offer more assistance** than others. *"I always try to help. I'm always helping people out and nobody gives a shit about me." (TŽ, female)* A willingness to help out is highly prized in this community, but is also regarded as something that should not be relied on. The conviction arises that a person should be more cautious: *"If I am too considerate then I simply become a fool that everyone exploits."*

Some homeless people openly state that **they do not want to help anyone**. There can be many reasons for this, for instance negative experiences, a current shortage, or priority being given to their own needs, which are often linked with drug addiction. *"I don't help anyone because nobody helps me, so why should I help others? I have enough problems of my own without looking after other people's." (PK, male)*

"I sometimes think about helping out, but I always end up thinking they have to look after themselves. I'm more interested in junk." (LB, male) Both of these clients are long-term drug addicts with all of the ensuing consequences, including a lack of consideration for others. IK (female) is also unwilling to help others. She does not take drugs but **feels that homeless people are too ready to leech off**

others, and disapproves. *"No, I don't help others. Look after yourself, because I look after myself."*

2. Are there any rules that apply among homeless people?

Some homeless people are not willing to respect the norms of mainstream society and act in accordance with them. The very fact they leave home and opt to sleep rough represents their rejection of accepted rules. Moreover, the attitude of young homeless people to various rules changes under the influence of the street. Survival is not easy under such circumstances. They have to adapt to the situation as they find it and to various people who are not always helpful or considerate. This is manifest in a change of customs, opinions and attitudes. Many young homeless people are convinced that the **normal rules do not apply on the street**. *"It seems to me that if you're living on the street you couldn't give a fuck if there's laws or not. A person with a normal job has to behave in accordance with the rules, but **here nobody gives a toss**."* (KM, female) At the time she was interviewed the client had been living on the street for three years and her adaptation was manifest in the scepticism she exhibited and the fact she had become resigned to change. Life on the street is different and demands different behaviour. *"When I was still living at home, I tried to play by the rules. But when I ended up on the street it was a different ballgame entirely. You have to give things a go. When I need money, for instance, then I know what I'm doing is illegal but **I simply take the risk**."* (TM, male) This client is more interested in justifying his own behaviour.

When young homeless people reflect on the need to abide by generally valid rules, e.g. laws, **their considerations are dominated by the need to avoid being punished**. They are not so much interested in the content of their actions as in how not to be caught and how to avoid problems. MM (male) is a criminal recidivist. *"I haven't changed my opinion of the law. You should respect the law or break it in such a way that nobody catches you."*

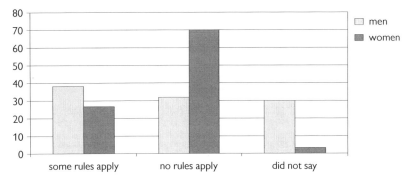

Graph 25. The rules that apply among homeless people (the graph shows relative frequency).

"Basically I couldn't give a shit about the law. But I'm always aware of doing something wrong and then I get worried about being punished." (JJ, male) JJ suffers problems ensuing from a lack of self-control and drug use. At present he is not living on the street.

The relationship to generally valid rules that prevails among young homeless people corresponds to the ethics of a schoolchild. They do not accept responsibility for their own conduct and do not manifest any need to act in accordance with given standards, but simply want to avoid problems and not to be punished. Their scepticism regarding the expected behaviour of other people is also significant.

The rules of the homeless community, such as they exist, differ from those of mainstream society. They can often be **boiled down to the principle of reciprocity**: "You scratch my back, I'll scratch yours". *"The commonest rule – not so much a rule, but something they say among themselves – is, **don't thank, remember**." (KM, female)* However, the reciprocity rule has not only a positive side but a negative side too. *"Fuck with me and I'll fuck with you. But twice over." (TN, male)*

"If someone behaves nicely to me, I'll be nice back. But if someone acts like a cunt, I'm going to be more of a cunt to them. You have to create respect on the street." (LP, male) This introduces another rule of homeless conduct: the **need to secure the necessary position** in which threats are minimised because nobody would dare take you on.

It goes without saying that very often life on the street is about the survival of the fittest. *"It's not a rule, but overall I would say it's about the law of the jingle, survival of the fittest. Like it or not, you have no option on the street. If you want a certain status, you simply have to deserve it." (PČ, female)*

*"There are definitely some rules. **It's usually the stronger who boss the weaker around and set the rules**." (ES, female)*

"The rules of homelessness are such that the strongest wins. That's how it seems to me recently." (TK, male)

Some young homeless people perceive an overall shift in their relationship to certain norms and believe that **no rules apply whatsoever in their own community**. *"When I look around I don't see any rules. Most homeless people lose any sense of structure." (IB, male)* Some believe that at some point in the past the community **had its own principles, which it has since lost**. It is not clear what gives rise to this idealisation of the homeless community. Perhaps it is simply the fulfilment of a wish that things be this way, because then life would be better and the homeless themselves would ensure greater security and safety. *"There used to be one rule: a homeless person doesn't steal from another homeless person. This rule no longer exists. These days the rule between homeless people is: "steal as much as you can and **don't give a fuck about anyone else**." (LP, male)*

"People used to help each other out and now they fight each other. These days one person takes everything and doesn't give a fuck about the fact that the others around are hungry." (LB, female)

"The law here is: the earlier you arrive, the more you eat." (JS, male) Though the system as outlined here is reminiscent of that of a pack of animals, in reality it does not always have to be this ruthless.

It is clear from the interviews that the rules of homelessness, such as they are, lay an emphasis on reciprocity and the rights of the more powerful (or perhaps the more ruthless). This is the only way to survive life on the street, and the question arises as to what extent this experience is an obstacle to a return to society.

3.3.2 THE OPINIONS OF HOMELESS YOUTH REGARDING FRIENDSHIP AND PARTNERSHIPS

Most young homeless people would like a friend or partner on whom they could rely. However, most feel this is impossible while sleeping rough. Some of them admit that they would be the ones who would find it difficult to maintain such a relationship, though a sizeable number have been left by someone close. It is unclear as to whether their relationships fail because they repeatedly choose unsuitable friends or partners (the choice is limited on the street) or because they are unable to behave in such a way as to be acceptable to another person. Both factors most likely play a part.

Friendship is manifest in the form of mutual trust (which, as we have seen, is not very frequent in this community) and a willingness to support and assist the other. On the street this more often involves the basic necessities for survival, such as food and shelter, and so a friend is a person who shares and helps when necessary. Repeated negative experiences led many homeless people to conclude that it was **impossible to find real friends among people on the street**. Those around are simply interchangeable acquaintances who cannot be relied on. In addition, some of them come from an environment in which poor relationships predominated or have never encountered an alternative. The street then merely serves to confirm their prejudices.

Many young homeless people think that friendly relationships cannot last on the street. Under these conditions they quickly break up and so a more experienced person will take care before believing that someone is their friend. *"Don't believe everyone you meet. Yeah, and above all, as I say, I have no friends on the street." (LP, male)*

"I'll accept anyone as a friend who can be trusted, to whom I can turn. But I'm afraid that here that isn't possible." (MH, male)

*"Yeah, we chat together like normal people, but for some reason **I don't form any stronger links with anyone here**." (ZK, male)* These are very different types of people, but their opinions of friendship are the same. The accumulation of poor experiences of life on the street has led them to generalised negative expectations. They have a problem in that they do not have much of a choice. Their friends will be from the homeless community and there are risks involved in this.

Illustration 16. A dog is a good companion (photo: Dana Kyndrová).

The opinion that **friends can be found on the street, albeit not always**, is heard less frequently. *"Of course you can find friends on the street. You're walking along, you meet someone and fall into conversation with them and you discover they're a great guy, that they're not someone who would rob their friends. Mind you, there's not many such people." (IH, female)* Homeless people tend to be sceptical and realise that **instability and unreliability** characterise friendships on the street. *"Relationships are incredibly difficult on the street. You only have to brush past someone the wrong way and everything changes. Everyone is protecting their own turf. So when you find someone you can be friends with, you can be together a couple weeks, a month or six months. But in the end you argue and become worst enemies. You make friends incredibly quickly and you lose friends just as quickly." (JJ, male)* The client whose words these are was not a typical homeless person and at present does not live on the street. His description of the instability of friendships between homeless people is very accurate.

As far as drug addicts and alcoholics are concerned, more lasting friendships are out. *"There's no problem finding friends among people who don't take drugs. But **wherever there's drugs** and so on, **friendship simply doesn't exist**. That's my opinion." (SP, male)*

"Yeah, that's happened to me. When my friend was going cold turkey and wanted to steal my mobile. He punched me. That's when I realised that these people change and they're no longer your friends."(EK, female)

An awareness of the instability and unreliability of relationships with other homeless people results in an ongoing and sometimes deeper feeling of solitariness. One reaction to the unsatisfactory state of interpersonal relationships involves a preference for an animal as companion, usually a dog (Rew, 2000). A dog will not disappoint its owner but will remain with them and do what they want. It is difficult to expect this from a person.

A **partnership** is a more complicated and delicate relationship than friendship even under normal circumstances, and this is especially so in the homeless community. The partners of homeless people are usually members of the same social group. The likelihood of meeting someone else is small, and it is not at all certain that someone from mainstream society would accept a homeless person as a lover. It tends to be **women who look for more lasting partnerships**, since survival on the street is more difficult for them than it is for men and so they try to find at least something positive even in a problematic relationship. *"Right now our relationship is better. It used to be a lot worse. He was nasty and nervous when he needed a drink, and when he was on drugs he became aggressive. I love him and I do everything for him. After everything he's done to me, **if I didn't love him I would have left ages ago**. But I matter to him. I can tell that he makes the effort to do things because of me."* *(MH, female)* This client has mainly negative experiences with people. She was tyrannised and neglected during childhood and perhaps has little idea of what a normal partnership is like. This makes it unlikely that future partners will behave any better to her.

Men can also entertain illusions of partnership. They too can fall in love, though usually the relationships ends quickly and a new couple forms that is as unstable as the previous one. *"M. and I are together, we have a relationships together. She's pregnant with that black-haired idiot. M. is the only person on the street for me. We click. I opened my heart to her, I love her. I haven't had relationships on the street. But now M. is the only one on the street for me. **She loves me. I mean, she had to fight to win me**. She was already pregnant, but she got me in the end."* *(JJ, male)* A year later the relationship ended, the child was put up for adoption, and the woman in question found another boyfriend. JJ lives with a new girlfriend and has found a job. Even from his description of the problems associated with partnership it is clear that he is interested in a good relationship and was able to establish one (though whether or not he will manage to maintain it is another matter).

Partnerships on the street are unlikely to be successful. There are many young homeless people who would like to have a lasting, deeper relationship, but who realise how difficult it is to find a partner on the street. Partnerships are difficult to sustain for the same reasons as friendships: **unreliability, lack of trust and promiscuity**. *"For the most part it's not sex I'm after but love. But it's obvious that with love comes sex. Recently I've suffered the consequences. I've found a girl, but then she's gone off with someone else, or was sly with money, or a junky. I've never found anyone normal."* *(MŽ, male)*

*"Yeah, I tried having a relationship. But since them **I don't pin my hopes on homeless girls**. When I learned that that girl was working as a prostitute I decided I didn't want any relationship while living on the street."* *(LS, male)*

IC (male) is another who does not want a girlfriend from the street. *"Things are difficult when you're living on the street.* **You have to find a normal girl, not the slags you see around here.** *If you have somewhere to live and you're not on the street, then things are different. You have everything. But on the street you simply don't have these possibilities."*

"To begin with I was attracted by the idea. But when I saw what slags these girls are it was a right turn off, disgusting. I started to feel sorry for them. It's far worse for girls here than it is for blokes." (SŠ, male)

Several women also feel mistrustful regarding potential partnerships with homeless men. *"You never know what you'll catch. If you imagine that the blokes here dip their wicks into every other girl, you quickly lose the desire." (PČ, female)* This woman's partners, though not homeless, were far from reliable.

Several homeless people have **doubts about themselves** and the possibilities that life on the street offers them. Some men are aware that they are not ideal for more acceptable girls. *"I've realised that I just don't have what it takes for a more serious relationship. Right now, in this situation, I wouldn't appeal to a nice girl." (ZK, male)*

"If a girl is normal then great, she'll be my friend, and if she falls in love with me, then why not? But this has never happened on the street. **I can't afford to go out with a fucking nutcase.** *It's hard enough looking after myself, let alone a girl." (JH, male)* When a person is pleased just to be surviving, a partnership is a luxury too far.

Drugs and alcohol represent a fundamental impediment to maintaining a good partnership. *"When I was 16 it was true love. We were together for a long time and then we split up shortly before my 18th birthday. Because of him I stopped going to school and I got a job. That was love." (IH, female)* Her partner abandoned her and shortly afterwards was sent to prison. Now she has no interest in a relationship. She is aware that this is a difficult matter for a drug addict. *"I went from one bloke to another to another. Right now I'm not interested in a relationship, I need to relax. When you're on crystal meth a relationship is impossible. The drugs destroy everything. It was always the same:* **the drugs broke things up.** *And that's why I no longer want a relationship."* Her last boyfriend committed suicide under the influence of drugs and we have no up-to-date information regarding the client.

An awareness of the destructive influence of drugs on any relationship is also clear in the interview given by ES (female): *"It was* **typical junky love.** *We weren't particularly faithful to each other but we were together. Typical for junkies. Normal people don't have that kind of relationship. I've never had normal relationships, only druggy relationships. To begin with the relationship was good. After three years my boyfriend was aggressive while on drugs."* The client has a new boyfriend and continues to take drugs.

Someone who takes drugs will find it hard to find someone who does not take them. Or perhaps they do not even want to find such a person. *"All my boyfriends have been junkies. I don't know why, I seem to attract them. If a bloke hasn't experienced what I have gone through, I'm not interested. And anyway, as soon as you tell them what you've been up to they simply judge you for it. I don't want a normal bloke.* **When he finds out about my past he'll judge me for it.***" (LB, female)* The client is in prison at present for drug dealing.

Young homeless people have often had bad experiences and **do not want to be disappointed again**. Not only homeless people worry about being disappointed: members of mainstream society have similar problems. However, on the street the creation of a stable partnership is far more difficult and the associated risks far greater. *"I'd prefer not to have a relationship.* ***Every relationship I have turns me upside down and inside out*** *and I'm a wreck. I fall in love incredibly quickly and it's really difficult to fall out of love." (TK, female)*

"What happened was that I got pregnant and had an abortion in the second month. Then we started to row, I began to drink and I became depressed. He slapped me around and called me a whore. I couldn't take it psychologically anymore. In the end I finished it, it was unnecessary. On the street I couldn't really care less who I'm with. ***I try to avoid STDs. And*** *not to have sex." (KM, female)* Two years after the interview the client had a new relationship with someone who was not homeless, but that too has ended.

MS (male) is another who is not interested in a longer term relationship, though for different reasons. *"I like peace and quiet. I don't want a woman around all the time because I wouldn't have any privacy. I like being single, I like the quiet life.* ***I definitely don't miss*** *a relationship. For the most part I've simply shagged a woman then beat a hasty retreat."* It is clear from what he says that he would not be capable of having a deeper relationship even if he had a normal lifestyle. People with personality disorders involving emotional detachment are to be found on the street in greater numbers.

Sex outside of a relationship often features on the street. Even such a superficial act is lacking in any selectiveness, and some homeless people are indifferent as to who their current sexual partner is. *"I've been with everything that looks remotely like a woman. But I've taken precautions, thank God. I wouldn't stick it in something like that without protection, and certainly not with the girls here on the street." (JP, male)* Several men admitted they had **lowered their sights** and that their girlfriends were women they would not previously have accepted. Here too their personal decline is manifest, and they are aware of this. *"I haven't really made any change to my sexual conduct. All I've done is reduce my demands as far as partners are concerned. For instance, if someone had said to me two and half years ago that I would have something with someone in this environment, I'd have told them to fuck off. Now it seems completely normal, which I reckon is negative." (MM, male)* The client had a longer term relationship on the street, but this has come to an end.

Not all young homeless people are promiscuous. Some are scared of casual sex and avoid it. (Their concerns are legitimate: there is a high frequency of sexually transmitted diseases in the homeless community.) *"If what I've heard is true and most of these homeless people, these junkies, have hepatitis or whatever, then I'm afraid of that and I'd rather not have anything to do with it." (PV, male)* Of course, it is not certain that he will always act with such restraint and not end up like those whom he criticises.

3.4 RELATIONSHIPS WITH PEOPLE OUTSIDE THE HOMELESS COMMUNITY

Johnson, Whitbeck and Hoyt (2005) discovered that many young homeless people are in contact with someone from their family or with former friends. Twelve percent of them believe that their parents would help them in an emergency, a third would expect assistance from other relatives, and 61% would rely on former friends. A third of those questioned think that one of their parents might provide emotional support, 40% would expect it from another relative, and 50% from old friends. Similar conclusions were reached by Noom et al. (2008): 47% of young homeless people are in contact with someone from their family and 28% with former friends. The different ratios of relationships retained with family and friends may be down to age. Trina Rose and K. Johnson (in Whitbeck, 2009) found that 23% of homeless youth see their parents as a source of possible emotional support, 23% other relatives and 33% friends. However, only 7% of them are convinced that their parents would genuinely help them and more place their trust in other relatives (19%) or friends (51%). It is interesting that former friends (66%) were more likely to be perceived as a source of possible assistance or support in this group than other homeless people (38%). Even though former relationships have been weakened and perceptions of them distorted in various ways, this bears witness to the survival of important links.

Some homeless people are **in contact with someone from their family**. To what extent a relationship is preserved depends on the reason a young person left home and the location of their former address. It is a lot easier when a person's relatives live in or near the same town. A third of young homeless people maintain contact with their mother and somewhat fewer are in contact with siblings

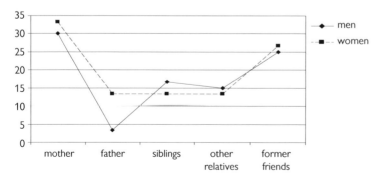

Graph 26. Contacts with people who are not homeless (the graph shows relative frequency).

or other relatives. We can assume that the preservation of a relationship with a person who lives a normal lifestyle is important in terms of a homeless person returning to mainstream society. These contacts can help them. The family can accept them back, friends can offer them temporary accommodation, find them work, etc. Young homeless people who have broken off all contact and associate with only members of the same community are unable to draw on such support.

In this respect **people who grew up in a children's home** and have nobody to reconnect with are at a disadvantage. Sometimes they do not even know where their parents live or discover that they have no interest in them even as adults. PK (male) lived in a children's home from the age of three. *"I used to tell myself that I'd go back to my mum. A couple of times I rang on the doorbell and my stepfather came out and said she wasn't at home, even though I could hear her through the open window. I could also hear my sister and brother. But I said ok and left. Yeah, of course, I wanted to run through and hurl myself off the balcony, but instead I said to myself that I wouldn't create unnecessary problems. I tried a few times, but after that I gave up."*

*"The last time I met my mother was when I was 18. What did we talk about? We said that, though mother and daughter, we simply didn't click. And with my brother? I spent a few years in the children's home with him. What kind of relationships do we have? None when we aren't together. **I don't have a relationship with anyone from my family.**"* (ZŽ, female) Such people do not have much chance of obtaining the sympathy of a person from mainstream society and creating a relationship with them. Given the change to their personality resulting from their early emotional deprivation the chances of this being possible with anyone are slim.

Another variant is a breakup of the relationship with parents, be they biological or foster. LR (male) has no relationship with his parents, even though he was adopted as a baby and his adoptive family looked after him very well. *"I'm in contact with them occasionally when I need something, but otherwise not. **I don't miss my parents** much, I'm kind of satisfied with the way things are."* The client uses drugs, has never worked, and is involved in criminal activities. Other members of his family operate in the standard way.

Sometimes relationships with the parents are so poor that there is no interest in even occasional contact. However, at other times this tends to be a **manifestation of a negative attitude on the part of the client** that could be changed if the parents demonstrated greater interest. However, they no longer have such an interest. There can be various reasons for this: disappointment, scepticism regarding the possibility of improvement, the need to protect themselves against further conflict and problems that contact could cause, etc. *"I don't have any relationship with her, none whatsoever. I can't remember anything nice, just stupid things. The idea that mum and I would go for a coffee together... it just wouldn't happen. The idea that **she'd invite me to dinner or lunch**... forget it. The idea that **she'd come up to me** and say 'here you are, here's a hundred crowns, buy yourself something nice'... **never in a million years.**"* (ZK, female) The client has been living on the street for six years, uses drugs and has a very problematic relationship with her family.

"I wanted to return to my mum. I was there on Saturday and I wanted to go home. But she told me that I'd chosen this path myself and that I should remain in K. and give up the idea of Prague. She said it was my choice to live this way and that I should sort myself out. **Now I'm not in contact with anyone** *(from the family)." (SP, male)* This is a client who has long-term problems with drugs and the behaviour they provoke. This was one of the reasons his mother rejected him.

A significant number of young homeless people **maintain contact with their mother or another relative**. Quite often these are people who do not want to admit to themselves or others that they are sleeping rough and play down the negative aspects of their life. *"When I moved into this squat* **I told mum it was a hostel**, *because my parents would have freaked if I'd told them I was sleeping rough. Finally I told mum and of course I had to calm her down and tell her that things weren't as bad as they seem in the news." (TD, female)* The relationship with the family had not been so impaired that the mother rejected her when she returned home with a child that she had had with another homeless person, a drug addict. PP (male) maintains contact with his mother and grandmother. *"Things changed after I stopped visiting. Then when I did, mum would ask me where I was living, and* **I lied to her**, *I'm constantly lying to her. I tell her* **I have a place to stay and a job.** *I was afraid she'd see me leaving Naděje."* The client has been involved in criminal activities and two years on since our interview is still sleeping rough.

The relationship between young homeless people and their mothers can go through several phases in which one party attempts to maintain it and the other rejects their efforts, and vice versa. *"Mum used to visit me in hospital every Friday saying she'd wash my clothes and bring me some coffee and biscuits. But in fact she wanted to argue. She used to arrive and start complaining about things I'd done three years previously. So I stopped contacting her and only got in touch around Christmas. She ended up be telling me it would have be better if I died.* **I would like to show my mum** *and myself that* **I'm not simply a loser.** *" (TM, male)* The client has been diagnosed as suffering depression and borderline personality disorder. At present his relationship with his mother is improving. He is in contact with her, lives in sheltered housing, and has a job.

3.5 YOUNG HOMELESS PEOPLE AND PARENTHOOD

Parenthood, if we are not to speak of it as simply the biological consequence of the sexual act, is an extremely demanding role. It requires prioritisation of the needs of the child and the acceptance of responsibility for its development. A parent ceases to be free and this is a burden that is difficult for most homeless people to tolerate. It is precisely the latitude and rejection of all obligations that makes life on the street so appealing to certain people. Children are born here in an unplanned way, as the consequence of unprotected sex between more stable or completely random couples. Inadequate responsibility and an inability to

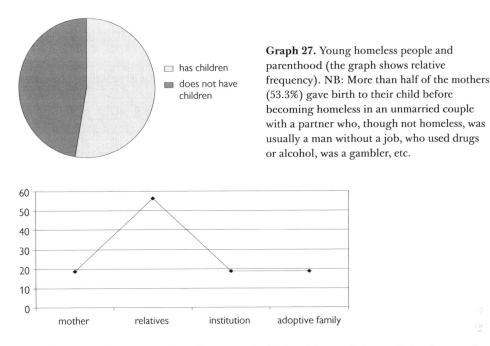

Graph 27. Young homeless people and parenthood (the graph shows relative frequency). NB: More than half of the mothers (53.3%) gave birth to their child before becoming homeless in an unmarried couple with a partner who, though not homeless, was usually a man without a job, who used drugs or alcohol, was a gambler, etc.

has children

does not have children

mother   relatives   institution   adoptive family

Graph 28. The primary carer of homeless women's children (the graph shows relative frequency) NB: A mother sometimes looks after one of her children while the rest, usually the older children, are in the care of someone else. We can assume that the youngest of the siblings will at some point meet the same fate. The results of foreign studies differ. According to Crawford (in Whitbeck, 2009), only 7% of the children of young homeless women were adopted, while 25% are looked after by the grandparents or other relatives.

take on such complex duties is manifest in an **inability to deal with parenthood**. This is especially clear in the case of homeless women: men tend to be laxer at the best of times.

As is clear from the graph, **most homeless women do not take care of their children**. (The children are placed in a children's home, a Klokánek[5], adopted or looked after by relatives, most often grandparents.) They do not visit them often and do not show much interest in them. *"I last saw my children about three months ago. They're in a pretty poor way." (VL, female)* Last year six women from our group (20%) became pregnant. The fate of their offspring will probably be the same. They will either be set aside immediately after birth or the women will look after them for a certain period of time before discovering that they are unable to cope with the burden and abandoning the child or having it taken from them. These women find it difficult even respecting the regularity of the daily regime in a refuge, and in addition are very often drug addicts, miss their freedom, etc. Their failure as parents is often exacerbated by the **lack of interest on the part of the**

---

5 Klokánek (*kangaroo*) is an institution offering temporary foster care.

father, who refuses to look after the child or is only interested for a short time. *"I gave him up for adoption. My boyfriend and I were junkies and he didn't want the child. I don't regret doing what I did." (ES, female)* This client had psychological problems even as a child. She has attempted to commit suicide on a number of occasions, is a long-term drug taker, and lives in a similarly oriented group. She has been sleeping rough for six years and it is difficult to see her managing to make any fundamental changes to her lifestyle.

It would not be true to say that these women had been uninterested in their children from the start. Three mothers (10% of the group monitored) found themselves on the street because they were trying to provide for their family after their partner stopped working. Unfortunately they opted for prostitution and when their partner or a relative found out they were forced out of the family and the children ended up being cared for by someone else. These women were not bad mothers as such. They were simply unable to resolve a difficult situation in an effective way. Failure as a mother is also often caused by drug use, either previous or subsequent, or infection with hepatitis C. Under these circumstances a women is incapable of being a mother regardless of where she lives.

Both the existence and loss of a **child is an important part of the life story** of many homeless women and it is interesting how the women in our study interpreted it. Their stories indicate that objective problems caused their failure as mothers: a lack of money, poor accommodation, a lack of support, etc. **They made every effort, but things did not work out**. Others around them did not trust them and failed to help them in some way. PČ explains how her daughter ended up being looked after by her grandparents. *"I was living here in P and then I lost my flat. They took my daughter from me and I found myself on the street. I left my parents because they were simply intolerable. They were constantly bossing me around. Then I lived with a couple of friends in a sublet. The problem was that the girl, his whore, was jealous of me, so one night she threw me and my daughter out onto the streets. At that time when I had nowhere to stay I went to Naděje. They called around all the sheltered housing and either everywhere was full or they didn't accept people from outside Prague and said that the only thing to do was put my daughter into an infant care centre. But they completely cheated me. When I went there the next day they told me that she was showing signs of being tyrannised. My world collapsed. I thought I was going to attack the centre. So I started going to work and sent my daughter some money every month."* The client does not mention her child later. She continues to sleep rough, takes drugs, and has spent time in prison. Fortunately she has not yet had another child.

TŽ (female) lived with an unsuitable partner and made money through prostitution. She ended up on the street and her child in an infant care centre. *"I wanted her to have a good life, to get somewhere. I had to give her to an infant care centre. What else could I do when my entire family gave up on me? I didn't have anyone. The worst thing is that I deal with things by using drugs instead of picking myself up, dusting myself down and having my daughter with me. I stopped thinking of her,*

I started to think of drugs and how I could be better off." The client is certainly self-critical, but has not managed to change anything about her conduct towards her
child.

MT (female) lost both her children over time. *"One of my kids is with my parents and my aunt adopted the other because the social services took it away from me. My
brother sent a letter to the court saying I was a junky and a whore. The court took my
little one away from me and said they'd give it to my parents.* **I wanted to look after
it but mum didn't give me the opportunity,** *which is why they took it away from me.
The second kid was born while I was living at my friend's. It was a premature birth in
the seventh month, so they put it in an incubator in Prague. But then the social services
stuck their noses in and that was that. Now it's with my aunt. She couldn't have children
so she took it."* The client sometimes visits her parents and her son. She has given
birth to another child that is currently in a Klokánek. It seems highly likely that
the story will be played out once again.

It is clear from the stories we heard that it is often those **women who were
very critical of their own mothers** and regarded them as the cause of their own
lack of success in life that end up on the streets. Perhaps this is also because
they were unable to forge a strong, secure bond with their mother, for whatever reason. The lack of basic security can be manifest negatively in an inability
to manage other relationships, including the relationship with their own child.
We do not know whether these mothers, now grandmothers, were poor carers.
However, it is often they who are willing to look after the child of their homeless
daughter (and often drug addict). We do not know if they are good substitute
mothers to their grandchildren. A positive signal might be the fact that only
one of their (often two) children was problematic, while the second dealt with
emerging adulthood without difficulty.

3.6 THE MENTAL HEALTH OF YOUNG
HOMELESS PEOPLE

Mental disorders are more prevalent among young homeless people than in the
population at large and may be linked to the loss of a home. **Mood disorders**,
especially depression, **increase the risk of social decline** and promote suicidal
tendencies because of the sufferer's inability to deal actively with difficulties or
at least seek help from someone. The number of people suffering depression is
significantly higher within the homeless community than in the population at
large. Signs of depression are visible in 15% to 80% of homeless youth, while a
third of homeless people suffer a major depressive disorder. Women are more
prone to depression (39%) than men (26%) (Sleegers et al., 1998; Cauce et al.,
2000; Goering et al., 2002; Votta and Manion, 2004; Whitbeck et al., 2004; Clatts
et al., 2005; Chen et al., 2006; Rosenthal et al., 2007; Aichhorn et al., 2008; Merscham et al., 2009).

The **aetiology of depression** is varied. Negative family experiences can exacerbate a tendency to mood disorders. Persons who were tyrannised or abused in childhood are more often depressive (at r=0.27 the correlation between both factors is not high but is not insignificant). The greater frequency and seriousness of the negative life events that they had to cope with may play a part. Insufficient social support may be another factor. Longer term or repeated experience of homelessness leads to a feeling of hopelessness and acquired helplessness. People who suffer depression are not able to deal with the burden of returning to mainstream society and so remain on the street. Depression is linked to suicidal thoughts and is often associated with a tendency to use psychoactive substances or a dependency on such substances; this is so in the case of 18% to 28% of young homeless people suffering depression (Sleegers et al., 1998; Smart and Walsh, 1993; Ayerst, 1999; Whitbeck et al., 2000).

Homelessness may be related in a similar way to the development of **anxiety disorders**. The necessary vigilance and alertness, anxiety and worry, which lead to increased caution, while effective in terms of adapting to life on the street, also increase the overall feeling of discomfort or stimulate the development of anxiety disorders. Some form of anxiety disorder is suffered by 17% to 22% of homeless youth, and a similar figure (23.3%) is cited by Dragomirecká et al. (2004) in the case of homeless people of adult age in Prague. Like depression, increased levels of anxiety exacerbate the tendency to use psychoactive substances, which in the case of young homeless people involves mainly non-alcohol drugs. Thirty-two percent of persons suffering anxiety disorder have an inclination to use drugs on a more frequent basis, in this case as a form of self-medication aimed at eliminating unpleasant feelings of stress and anxiety (Sleegers et al., 1998; Whitbeck et al., 2004; Slesnick and Prestopnik, 2005; Rosenthal et al., 2007; Aichhorn et al., 2008).

Given the incidence of depression among young homeless people it is not surprising to find they suffer **suicidal tendencies** far more often. The frequency of attempted suicides cited in different studies is fairly dissimilar: something in the region of 20% to 50% (the Australian study by G. Kamieniecki (2001) puts the figures as high as 40% to 80%). Most people make more than one attempt at suicide. The number of those who have thus far only considered the possibility is of course higher (Goering et al., 2002; Kidd and Kral, 2002; Reid et al., 2005; Martinez, 2006; Milburn et al., 2006; Kidd and Carroll, 2007; Yoder et al., 2008; Zerger et al., 2008; Merscham et al., 2009).

In the case of young people **suicidal thoughts and attempts** are often a reaction to negative life events, the instability and unreliability of the family background, feelings of isolation, rejection and betrayal by those close to them, or an inability to take control of their own lives. Low self-respect and a feeling of worthlessness, which relate to unfavourable anamnesis and social marginalisation, are deemed important triggers of suicidal conduct among homeless youth. These suicidal thoughts also often result from a feeling of helplessness relating to dissatisfaction with the life they lead and which they do not know how to deal with. They are often a reaction to physical or sexual abuse in the family. In addition, the experience of young homeless people of the various kinds of violence to which they are exposed on the street is not without significance. Young people who have attempted suicide were tyrannised (52%) and abused (44%) in childhood more frequently than their contemporaries in the homeless community who have not attempted suicide (Rew et al., 2001; Votta and Manion, 2004; Kidd and Shahar, 2008).

A **risky and self-destructive lifestyle** can be one of the manifestations of a suicidal tendency, or at least indifference to such a possibility. Prostitution and the use of drugs or alcohol can function as a method of slow self-liquidation, while overdosing sometimes reflects a conscious or unconscious need to end life. Twenty percent of young homeless people realise that using ever greater amounts of drugs increases the possibility of an overdose and that this is a process leading to self-destruction. Several studies reveal that 25% to 50% of young homeless people who overdosed had suicidal intentions over the longer term and were not concerned about what would happen to them (Best et al., 2000; Neale, 2000; Rohde et al., 2001; Kidd and Kral, 2002; Kidd, 2003).

Young homeless people face a **greater threat of violence**, be this within their original family, in various groups, or from other members of the homeless community. Eighty percent of young homeless people say that they have been victims of violence at least once in their lives, though usually repeatedly, with 50% having been beaten up, 15% to 20% victims of a sexual attack, and 20% mugged. Women are more often the targets of sexual violence, and a third of them have been attacked at least once during their time on the street. The perpetrator was most often someone they knew (40%) or even their boyfriend (25%). The need to survive forces them to select risky strategies that increase the threat by making contact with a potential attacker more likely. The risk increases with the duration of their time on the street and ensues from indiscriminate relationships with various people, insufficient caution, and risky conduct (Tyler et al., 2004; Kidd and Shahar, 2008; Shelton et al., 2009).

Traumatic experiences, usually repeated, are **far more frequent** in the homeless community than in the population at large and as a consequence there is a far higher occurrence of **post-traumatic stress disorder** (10% to 35% of homeless youth suffer PTSD). Post-traumatic stress disorder affects three times as many homeless women as men, and 20% to 60% of women and 15% to 24% of men sleeping rough suffer at least one symptom. This usually involves excessive irritability (46%), and less often is manifest as evasive conduct (27%) or emotional apathy (23%). The risk factors leading to homelessness are the same as those leading to PTSD (Buhrich et al., 2000; Tyler et al., 2003; Johnson et al., 2005; Thompson et al., 2007; Yoder et al., 2008).

PTSD rarely appears in isolation, but rather in combination with other psychological disorders, above all depression, anxiety disorder, the excessive use of psychoactive substances, and behavioural disorders. A fairly high percentage of homeless people (40%) would be deemed according to official criteria as abusing psychoactive substances and suffering PTSD. Half of those who suffer PTSD also suffer depression, and the same people often say that they have suicidal thoughts. Almost all men and two thirds of women who suffer PTSD have behavioural problems, and these are often problems that contribute to the continuation or intensification of their psychological problems (Morgan and Cauce, 1999; Buhrich et al., 2000; Tyler et al., 2003; Stewart et al., 2004; Gwadz et al., 2007; Thompson et al., 2007; Whitbeck et al., 2007; Merscham et al., 2009; Bender et al., 2010).

The incidence of **schizophrenia** does not change across various different communities, and therefore its significantly higher rate among homeless young people would seem to confirm the fact that these people are not able to exist without help from others and are prone to social failure. If they lack the necessary backup they end up on the street very easily. Here they are at greater threat of various forms of violence against which they are not always able to defend themselves. On the other hand, there is also a greater risk that they themselves will behave unreasonably or violently. They are often incapable of acting in a more acceptable and effective way, especially if they are not receiving treatment, which tends to be true of homeless people. On average 13% of young homeless people suffer schizophrenia or another psychotic disorder. This figure is at least ten times higher than in the population at large. The psychological state of these people is negatively influenced by the fact that they are not treated while on the street (in the case of the chronic homeless this figure was 18%). (Caton et al., 1995; Sleegers et al., 1998; Cauce et al., 2000; Kamieniecki, 2001; Folsom and Jeste, 2002; Cougnard et al., 2006; Fischer et al., 2008; Merscham et al., 2009).

3.6.1 MENTAL HEALTH DISORDERS AND YOUNG HOMELESS PEOPLE

When assessing the mental health of our cohort of young homeless people we were unable to rely purely on the data provided by the in-depth interviews, because no psychiatric diagnostic interview schema were used in them and our colleagues who conducted the interviews were not trained in the clinical assessment of the mental state of the subjects. We based this section on the questionnaire part of the research, in which we have information from 75 subjects.

In order to assess the mental health of our subjects we used the Brief Symptom Inventory [BSI] (Derogatis, 1983). The BSI is a short version of the SCL–R-90 checklist (Derogatis, 1977), the validity of which has been confirmed in both psychiatric research and clinical practice. The BSI has 53 items that acquire information on the level of eight subscales: somatisation, obsessive-compulsive symptoms, interpersonal sensitivity, depression, anxiety, anger-hostility, phobic anxiety, paranoid ideation and psychoticism. The BSI also includes three scales of which the most significant is the Global Severity Index (GSI), which is essentially the mean of all the subscale scores.

A **profile of young homeless people** on BSI scales is shown in graph 29. Given that we do not have national normative data at our disposal for BSI, we used data from two studies in order to compare the profile of our subjects with a population norm and a set of psychiatric patients in out-patient care. As normative data we used values acquired by measuring the German population (N=600) (Endermann, 2005). The values for psychiatric patients being treated on an out-patient basis (N=1002) are derived from the work done by Derogatis and Melisaratos (1983). It is clear from the graph that the mean scores on BSI scales are significantly higher than in the population at large and approximate to the profile of the group of psychiatric patients being treated on an out-patient basis.

Young homeless people score more highly in all subscales. When comparing the mean values of men and women in our sample we discovered an exceptionally high correspondence. The mean scores did not statistically deviate between men and women in any of the eight subscales. Our study therefore did not confirm that women suffer symptoms of depression far more than men (Blazer et

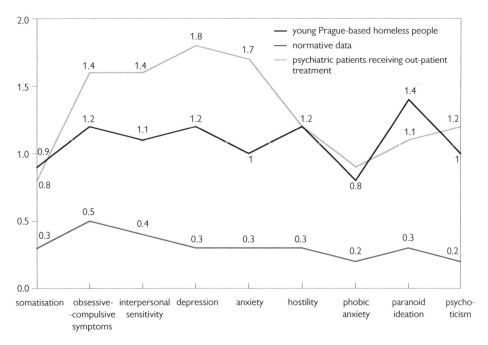

Graph 29. Mean values on the Brief Symptom Inventory scales of the psychiatric symptoms of a group of Prague-based homeless people, a normative group (N=600), and a group of psychiatric patients being treated on an out-patient basis (N=1002).

al., 1994). A correlation analysis indicated a high correspondence between the values of individual subscales. This would indicate that **psychiatric comorbidity will be a relatively frequent phenomenon in the case of young homeless people**. The accumulation of psychiatric symptoms from various different domains is a circumstance that significantly limits the ability of homeless young people to adapt to demands that are commonplace for the mainstream, well integrated population.

Young homeless people are not a homogenous group. Various circumstances have influenced their development. As well as genetic factors the environment, especially family socialisation, and individual psychological characteristics have played a part. On the basis of in-depth interviews it was possible to create a **typology of young homeless people based on their developmental trajectory**. In the case of our sample, we were able to assign 69 of 75 subjects (see table 1) to the three types that we defined. It will be interesting to see whether these three types differ with regard to the seriousness of psychiatric symptoms.

Table 1. Distribution of cohort according to developmental types and gender

	Type A	Type B	Type C	Unassigned	Total
Men	16 (32.7%)	13 (26.5%)	15 (30.6%)	5 (10.2%)	49 (100.0%)
Women	13 (50.0%)	3 (11.5%)	9 (34.6%)	1 (3.8%)	26 (100.0%)

Three types of developmental trajectory of young homeless people:
Type A – Pathological family – This group contains homeless people who come from families that were problematic and highly disturbed from the start. These families feature frequent conflicts between the parents, domestic violence, and alcohol or drug abuse in the case of the father or both parents. The conflicts lead to the breakup of the family and the child then alternates between different environments and people. They often have conflicts with the father or, as is more likely, with their stepfather. Behavioural problems appear in prepubescence and are incontrovertible in puberty. The child experiments with alcohol and drugs, plays truant, runs away from home, and steals. In adolescence the child is often placed in a youth detention centre, alternates between environments (latent homelessness), and finally runs away from or is thrown out of their home. They lack education, qualifications, and basic life and work habits. Drug taking and dealing is routine, as is criminal conduct (theft and fraud).
Type B – Institutional care from early childhood – The child is removed from its family or abandoned immediately after birth or during early childhood. It is placed in an institution or in foster care. Adoption or foster care fails for some reason. The child begins to act problematically and leaves (or is forced to leave) the family for an institution, usually during puberty. After periods spent in youth detention centres or juvenile homes there is usually a short

period of latent homelessness (the child has no safe home), and the child ends up on the street.

Type C – Long-term conflictual relationship within the family, behavioural disorders – The family breaks up later in the child's life when they are an adolescent. Conflicts ensue with the parents or stepfather, environments alternate, and the child eventually opts for or is thrown onto the street. This type also features experimentation with alcohol and drugs. Girls often experience domestic violence and sometimes abuse. The absence of support and a non-functioning maternal role model is often resolved by the child repeatedly running away or self-harming. Personality disorders appear in boys that lead to inappropriate behaviour, usually from school age, as well as to truancy and experimentation with alcohol and drugs. The child leaves the family or is thrown out of their home because of their intolerable conduct. During adolescence and emerging adulthood the likelihood of criminal conduct increases.

The profiles of individual types are statistically significantly different in BSI dimensions (graph 30). In terms of the seriousness of psychiatric symptomatology type B is in first place. Type B values overlap completely with those of psychiatric patients receiving treatment. Compared with types A and C the values are significantly higher in all subscales. Persons belonging to type B are extremely hostile and exhibit symptoms of depression, paranoid ideation and psychoticism. In light of the **developmental trajectory one would look to the consequences** of long-term psychological deprivation that is typical for development outside the family. The accumulation of psychological problems indicates that the effect of institutional care may be worse than the effect of a family, however dysfunctional it may be. Type B most often requires expert psychiatric assistance or treatment, without which successful social reintegration is difficult to imagine.

Of the three types type C comes out the best relatively speaking. Compared to types A and B it features a lower level of somatisation as well as anxiety, depression and psychoticism. Type C individuals often display behavioural disorders, but lived for longer in a family that, though over time stopped functioning and became conflictual, nevertheless offered more than the type A pathological family from the point of view of developmental needs. More favourable developmental characteristics and a lower overall seriousness of psychopathological symptoms create better conditions for type C individuals in terms of a return to society.

As opposed to type C, type A individuals display higher levels of depression and obsessive-compulsive tendencies, as well as more frequent paranoid feelings. The pattern of symptoms in the case of type A can be linked to a significant extent with **extensive exposure to the parents' pathological behaviour** (violence, abuse, alcoholism, etc.). The absence of safety and a positive child-parent relationship, the constant changing of homes, and an ongoing anxiety regarding the future led these children to leave their family early for a group of similarly problematic individuals in which, though they felt better, their socialisation was now impeded. Without qualifications and suitable habits these adolescents have nothing to offer on the jobs market and have no inclination to do so. They are able to survive on the street through drug dealing or minor street crime, but their resources are not sufficient for them to escape from homelessness.

The values of the Global Severity Index (GSI) are as follows for individual types: type A = 1.05 (SD = 0.7), type B = 1.48 (SD = 0.6), type C = 0.8 (SD = 0.5). The differences between types are statistically significant (F=5.18, P<0.01) and closely reflect what was specified regarding the profile on BSI subscales. We also compared the three types from the point of view of other characteristics. The distribution of the incidence of psychiatric hospitalisation, treatment for drug addiction and suicide attempts did not differ. A significant fact is that 39% of young homeless people have never been in contact with a psychiatrist or psychiatric hospital, and 20% only once. Of the remaining 41%, 14 (18.7 %) have been hospitalised.

We have selected examples of how young homeless people speak of their psychological problems from the semi-structured interviews.

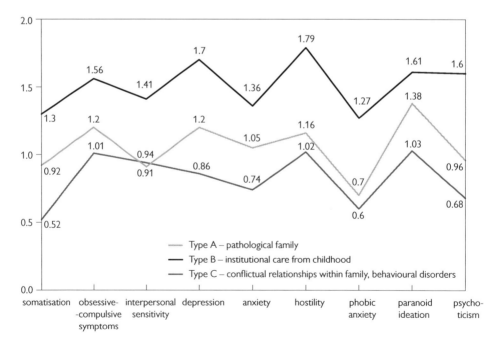

Graph 30. Mean values on the Brief Symptom Inventory subscales correlated with developmental trajectory types.

LD, 20-year-old female, sleeping rough for a prolonged period of time, in a children's home from childhood, placed in foster care and then returned to the children's home because of sexual abuse. **Symptoms of anxiety and depression** predominate, repeated psychiatric hospitalisation, including for drug use. LD has been taking drugs since the age of 13.

"I was placed in a children's home when I was still a baby. When I was three years old I was placed with foster parents, but they weren't good people because they abused me when I was only three. You know what I mean, don't you?"

[Interviewer] It was really difficult for you to deal with. In what way?

"I suffered psychological trauma and my childhood was destroyed. I was afraid I would be traumatised, but I dealt with it. I didn't dwell on it, I tried to forget it, not think about it. But it's always with me."

[Interviewer] How is it manifest psychologically?

"Nightmares, I couldn't sleep, I was afraid of the dark and I still to this day experience trauma sometimes. I get frightened, depressed, the whole bit."

[Interviewer] And have you spoken of this with a psychologist?

"I have seen a psychiatrist. I don't want to because they don't know how to help. They give you tablets to calm you down. They say that antidepressants will help. And then you have sleeping pills, they make you dopey and put you to sleep so that they can get rid of you. They way they are isn't fair, they behave horribly to people with real disabilities and they're friendly to junkies. That's not fair."

TN, 23-year-old male, repeatedly treated for depressive disorder:

"I've been diagnosed with depressive syndrome and borderline personality disorder. I have helped out people and then when I need help, they're nowhere to be seen. They don't have the time, they're off boozing somewhere, they simply don't have any time for me."

[Interviewer] How was this depressive syndrome manifest?

"It was pretty horrible, because I had no idea what it was. I closed in on myself completely and then I closed off from my surroundings. I simply shut myself away at home. I didn't set foot outside. I pretended I wasn't at home. In the end I didn't even go to the toilet. I wanted to die."

[Interviewer] What persuaded to you see a doctor?

"That was thanks to my mother."

[Interviewer] Were you hospitalised?

"Yes, several times."

[Interviewer] How long for?

"Mostly for a month or so. It wasn't for prolonged periods of time."

[Interviewer] I see. So it was of a cyclical character?

"Yes. My mood is up and down like a yoyo. Right now I don't have money for my prescription drugs so I only got hold of them yesterday, so I have to wait until they take effect. But without the drugs I can't function, especially in the situation I'm in now. It doesn't really make for a good mood, does it?"

OP, 24-year-old male, suffers psychotic disorder of the schizophrenic type

"When you sit in front of a computer half of your brain closes down for a really long time. I got used to that, I really liked switching off half of my brain. I managed it and it took me a year or two before I sorted myself out and now I know how these problems work and it's far worse. Imagine you're sitting in front of a computer and then you sell it and you no longer have it. You have the DTs. Experiences play a large role. You think about them, analyse them and compare various addictions. When you sit at the computer only the analytical logical part operates and the emotional part is switched off. The longer you sit at the computer the more you train the analytical part of the brain and then you end up resolving everything without any emotion. You become like a robot that is connected to the computer. It's like sex with a computer. This is how everyone experiences it."

PV, 21-year-old male, hospitalised in a psychiatric ward for children and youths, **personality disorder, difficulty in controlling rage, violent conduct**

[Interviewer] From early childhood you spent time in various psychiatric clinics. What happened?

"Yeah, it was like a rehab for pills. They gave me pills to supply blood to the brain, and to calm me down they gave me chlorprothixen and piracetam. The piracetam was for increasing blood flow in the brain and the chloroprothixen was to calm me down. That's because I got incredibly nervous when someone said something to me. Or rather when my father said something I would start on at him and for three or four hours I was on edge with anyone who saw me. So I launched myself at him and began to hit him, maybe even without reason."

The timely diagnosis of mental disorder and appropriate treatment is a very important part of the process of social reintegration of young homeless people. Efforts at re-socialisation, whatever their intensity, are not always successful unless they resolve the psychological or psychiatric problems of young homeless people.

3.6.2 THE USE OF ADDICTIVE SUBSTANCES AMONG YOUNG HOMELESS PEOPLE

Young homeless people **use addictive substances very often**. In a survey of 29 studies carried out in the West, Fazelová et al. (2008) cite alcohol and drug addiction as the most frequently occurring mental disorder among homeless people. The level of dependency ranges from 8.1% to 59% in the case of alcohol and 4.5% to 54% in the case of other drugs (Rew et al., 2001, Rosenthal et al., 2007).

The excessive use of addictive substances is cited as **one of the reasons a person ends up on the street**. Usually it is not the single reason, but part of a broad spectrum of characteristics (personality disorders) that result in a young person leaving their apprenticeship or education prematurely and being unable to find or hold onto a job without qualifications. The inability to work and earn money systematically, combined with the necessity to pay life expenses, leads to debts which an individual is unable to repay. They then lose their accommodation and find themselves on the street. The abuse of addictive substances does not have to be the primary cause of homelessness. However, even in cases in which it is not the cause, the abuse of alcohol or other drugs appears in connection with the acceptance of a homeless lifestyle (Stein et al., 2008).

For many young homeless people the **use of addictive substances is one form of protest against** societal norms. Psychoactive substances also allow an individual to eliminate unpleasant feelings and traumatic memories and to shut out the pressure of various stresses, and are a way of ameliorating feelings of insecurity and the absence of safety (Martijn and Sharpe, 2006). The excessive use of alcohol and drugs is part of the risky lifestyle of young homeless people and has a close relationship with risky sexual conduct and manifestations of antisocial behaviour, including criminal behaviour.

There is **often a comorbidity of psychoactive substance abuse and other psychological disorders** among young homeless people. This was the finding of various studies in the case of 35% to 60% of homeless youth. Psychological discomfort increases the necessity to use psychoactive substances, which can subdue or eliminate it in some way, though the long-term abuse of these substances causes a deterioration of the psychological state of the user. The excessive use of drugs increases both directly and indirectly the likelihood of criminal conduct and the risk of victimisation – both are increased in the group of young homeless people (Rew et al., 2001;. Rosenthal and Rotheram-Borus, 2005; Slesnick and Prestopnik, 2005; Rosenthal et al., 2007).

In order to acquire information we used data gathered from the questionnaire-based survey that supplements findings from the semi-structured interviews. We ascertained alcohol use using the shortened version of the AUDIT questionnaire (Alcohol Use Disorder Identification Test, Babor, Higgins, 2010). As far as the use of illegal drugs was concerned, we asked an open question and we were interested in current use (over the last six months).

After evaluating the AUDIT we divided the group being monitored into **three categories**. The first comprised individuals who **are not consuming alcohol at present**. There were thirteen (17%) such individuals in our group. The second group comprised individuals who drink alcohol but whose **drinking cannot be deemed problematic**. There were 44 (59%) such individuals in our group. The last group comprises individuals who **drink frequently and to excess**. This group contained 18 (24%) homeless people. These people consume alcohol every day or almost every day and drink five or more glasses corresponding to a consumption of 80 grams of ethanol or more during each episode. In a normal healthy person this level of consumption would result in mild to medium drunkenness. There were more problematic drinkers among the men than among the women (31% : 12%). It is likely that several problematic drinkers meet the diagnostic criteria for alcohol addiction.

MP, 22-year-old male, a problematic drinker
[Interviewer] … And alcohol? At what age?
"Alcohol at 15."
[Interviewer] At 15. So you would say that alcohol is perhaps your biggest problem, would you?
"I don't see it as a problem."
[Interviewer] But you drink a lot?
"It's my worst indulgence."
[Interviewer] Indulgence? Do you feel you have alcohol under control?
"Uh, maybe not."
[Interviewer] Have you received treatment because of it?
"No."
[Interviewer] And did you use to drink more or less?
"I used to drink less. I've been drinking more since being on the street."
[Interviewer] Would you say that when you start drinking you can't stop for several days, or that you feel you need to drink, say, five beers a day?
"Sometimes I have five beers and then nothing for a week. But sometimes I knock back 30 beers and I'm boozing for a week."
[Interviewer] Yes. Would you call yourself an alcoholic?
"I guess so."
[Interviewer] Yes?
"I think I'm an alcoholic."

A **total of 61% of those questioned** used some kind of illegal drug. The most frequently used substance was **crystal meth** (commonly known in the Czech Republic as pervitin) (29 of those questioned, i.e. 39% of the cohort). Marihuana is also often used (19 individuals). With the exception of Subutex (buprenorphine) (8 individuals) other drugs were only used sporadically (heroin in the case of two people and cocaine in the case of one). Subutex is a substitute drug used to treat opioid addiction, which is often used for non-medical reasons. The use of drugs by young homeless people differs from figures applying to the general population, where marihuana is the most common drug. Young homeless people often use marihuana in combination with another drug, most frequently with crystal meth. Given the seriousness of the consequences of using crystal meth, we will restrict our examination to this drug. As in the case of alcohol we did not record differences in usage based on gender.

We examined whether the developmental trajectory of homelessness (the types described in the previous section) are related to the incidence of problematic drinking or the abuse of crystal meth. A statistical evaluation did not reveal any differences in terms of representation by type. We can therefore conclude that developmental determinants do not influence in a decisive way the use of addictive substances by young homeless people. Current consumption is more influenced by an individual's previous experience with a psychoactive substance, their current situation, and the referential group with whose norms and conduct the individual identifies.

Table 2. Problematic drinking and use of crystal meth according to developmental trajectories (types A to C)

	Type A (N=29)	Type B (N= 16)	Type C (N=24)
Problematic drinking	27.6 %	18.8 %	20.8 %
Use of crystal meth	41.4%	31.2%	45.8 %

Profile of psychiatric symptoms among crystal meth users

The use of crystal meth (methamphetamine) has a significant influence on the functioning of the central nervous system. Sekine et al. (2001) monitored the density of the dopamine transmitters in three regions of the brain using positron emission tomography scans of users of methamphetamine and control subjects. They discovered a significant reduction in the density of dopamine transmitters in the group of methamphetamine users and a sharp increase in psychiatric symptoms among drug users as against the control group. There was a direct relationship between the total time spent using the drug and the seriousness of psychiatric symptoms. In research into the treatment of methamphetamine users Zweben et al. (2004) analysed which psychiatric symptoms are more expressed in patients. It was shown that there was an increase in the frequency of symptoms of depression (and suicide attempts), anxiety and psychoticism. Methamphetamine users also had difficulty in managing anger and violent conduct.

The following example well illustrates the use of drugs, attempts at giving up and depressive episodes in the case of one young homeless person. PJ (a 20-year-old man) users crystal meth and has tried other drugs. He also consumes alcohol, but denies he has a problem. He spent time in a juvenile home and has experienced several young offender institutions.

PJ on the effects of drugs and the cycle of drug use
"It's a way of unwinding. It's not that you're a different person on drugs, or at least that's how I see it. It's as though you're suddenly filled with testosterone, as though everyone suddenly likes you. I was able to be pleasant and accommodating to people. Yeah, of course, it was a laugh. You don't think about anything, you simply walk around with a smile on your face. You want to do something, create something, learn something new. And then it fades and the comedown begins. You simply sit and again you can't stand anything. You feel shit, and even though the cold turkey is really bad you decide not to take more drugs but to sleep it off, in which case it's still manageable. As soon as you starting looking for

more and more so as not to get over the comedown but postpone it, the worst it gets. Try it from the beginning: yeah, I'll take some, so I take some and I feel shit, so I take some more, then some more... The problem is that after a week or two the drugs have gone. Then you realise how long you've been putting back things. Everything adds up and all you can do is lie there curled up tightly. You feel unbelievably shit and you know you simply can't move a finger. You're tired, exhausted, drained of all strength, your face is completely deformed, completely different to how it usually is. You've got sunken cheeks, your teeth are visible, your whole jaw is visible, everything's creeping out. Your eyeballs protrude, and your eyelids are drawn back. You look like a disgusting cadaver, your nose changes and you simply lie there. You have big black stains around your mouth, your mouth is dry, you can't stop chewing your lips. It's disgusting, your skin is rotten. You're dehydrated, which is why your mouth is black, your breath stinks like a dead body, you're disgusting."

PJ on how he attempted to stop taking drugs
"I've never drunk alcohol and my relationship to drugs changed after I decided that no way would I end up a junky, even though I already was one. So I decided enough was enough and that I'd fucked up my brain enough and that I was going to work on myself. I'm pretty stupid. I've lost a lot of my vocabulary. So I decided to give up drugs but I refused detox, like everyone else goes to, because it's shit. Everyone who comes back from detox carries on doing drugs and even though it's not that long ago, I haven't been doing drugs for three months, so officially I'm clean for three months, there's no trace of it in my blood or my urine."

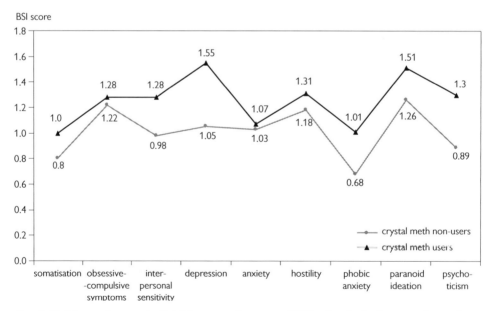

Graph 31. Mean values on the Brief Symptom Inventory (BSI) subscales in the case of crystal meth users and non-users from the cohort of young Prague-based homeless people.

PJ describes his bouts of depression
"I don't know if depression is the right word. It was as if the light had been switched off. But the light wants to continue at all costs for another five minutes. But I don't do anything, I just sit, scowl at people and even though I don't mean it from their faces you see them wondering what they've done to you."

The BSI profile of crystal meth users does not differ greatly from that of non-users in the spheres in which we expected it to on the basis of research findings and clinical practice. It is clear from graph 31 that **crystal meth users have higher depression and psychoticism scores**. This chimes with clinical experience, demonstrating that the use of crystal meth is accompanied by psychotic symptoms and often by paranoia (see the increased paranoid value).

The profile of psychiatric symptoms complements data on personality trait differences from the Eysenck personality questionnaire. **Crystal meth users have higher values of psychoticism** (which accounts for their problems controlling aggression and anger) **and neuroticism** (indicating a higher level of psychological instability and anxiety).

Table 3. Eysenck's personality traits in crystal meth users and non-users.

	Non-user [Mean (SD)]	Crystal meth user [Mean (SD)]	t	p
Extraversion	9.27 (2.7)	8.64 (2.6)	0.96	ns
Psychoticism	4.09 (2.0)	5.25 (2.1)	2.36	0.02
Neuroticism	6.11 (3.2)	7.61 (2.7)	2.07	0.04
Lie score	3.80 (2.1)	3.18 (2.4)	1018	ns

Thirteen percent of those questioned admitted to having attempted suicide. This is a lower figure than that cited in specialist literature. Our group is too small to make it possible to test the relationship between suicidal tendencies and the use of alcohol or drugs. Six people said they had been treated for addiction. Given the incidence and seriousness of psychiatric symptoms and the extent to which alcohol and illegal drugs are used by young people, these medical interventions were insufficient. It attests to a failure to diagnose and treat psychiatric illnesses and an availability of specialist healthcare services that fails to meet the needs of these people.

3.7 LEAVING HOME TO SLEEP ROUGH – A SUMMARY

Leaving home for the street is usually the **result of an accumulation of problems** that the individual in question is unable to deal with or which they have created for themselves. Very often these are people who already suffered many different problems, whether these were caused by defective personality development or insufficient socialisation caused by a poor upbringing. The same problems that are manifest in an inability and unwillingness to accept responsibility for life and the restrictions ensuing therefrom see a person end up on the street and become homeless over a longer-term period. **Adaptation to life on the street** results in an increase in uncommon attitudes and ways of thinking and behaving. Such changes can be useful for the purposes of survival, but prevent an individual returning to society. Limited contact with members of mainstream society and the all-encompassing influence of the homeless community are adverse factors.

Young homeless people often regard leaving home for life on the street as a **manifestation of their own inability to resolve anything**. Very often this involved an ill-conceived, impulsive reaction that brought further difficulties they had not foreseen and that catch them unawares. Most of them know that prudence and foresight are not their strong points, but are not troubled by this fact. Some would like to return home, and if they could turn the clock back would not opt for life on the street. However, **they are not able to accept restrictions** and act in accordance with society's demands. Although they acquire skills on the street, the nature of these skills is such that they do not help them in normal life but are more likely to act as a barrier. Knowing how to shoplift or which supermarkets are good for discarded goods are not competences that are highly appreciated in mainstream society. A **parasitical lifestyle** and the ongoing assumption that someone else will take care of their problems is another serious obstacle.

Young homeless people suffer various **different psychological problems** that can be both the cause and effect of their unusual lifestyle. Increased levels of depression and anxiety are the most frequent psychological problem and often remain undiagnosed or untreated. A negative outlook, pessimism and excessive concerns can place a significant block on the resocialisation process, above all the motivation to exert greater effort and overcome various obstacles.

The **use of drugs and alcohol** is both the cause and effect of many problems suffered by young homeless people. The regular use of psychoactive substances intensifies the deterioration of the personality and contributes to a further reduction in their social capital. It can also lead to various psychological problems, above all increased anxiety, depression and suicidal tendencies. These appear in people who regularly use crystal meth. Problems regulating negative emotions and controlling aggression are also significant. All of this leads to other difficulties, sometimes of a criminal character. People addicted to psychoactive substances often end up on the street without much chance of returning. Many of them know this, but are unable to modify their conduct. Resolving their situation would involve overcoming their addition, the seriousness of which they are not always ready to admit. Passivity and the acceptance of simple survival form a strong blocking mechanism. There are many such people among the ranks of the homeless.

The **transformation or loss of interpersonal relationships**, especially close relationships, is another consequence of homelessness. Young homeless people display a certain ambivalence in relationships with other people that might relate to their unconventional life. This includes both a knowledge of mutual dependencies and therefore the necessity for a certain solidarity, as well as a lack of trust and caution. Young homeless people often say that they try to help other people because it is necessary on the street, but that they do not trust them much because they have been repeatedly let down. **They form both friendships and partnerships quickly but lose them just as quickly**. It seems that the homeless are not always sufficiently empathetic and react disproportionately even to banal differences of opinion because of increased mistrustfulness. Such conflicts seem more significant within the context of their lives because they are dependent on others to a greater extent than they would be under normal circumstances.

People who live on the street are sometimes afraid of close relationships and steer clear of them. They tend to have good reason for their **caution, distrust and suspicion**. They have bad experiences and many have never encountered any model of a balanced, reliable relationship. They often come from broken, dysfunctional families where nothing of this kind existed. The inability to deal with parenthood, which is more demanding than maintaining a relationship with an adult from the point of view of responsibility and the extent of duties, is another sign of the problematic development of their personality. In many cases this is the consequence of a total breakdown caused by the regular use of alcohol and drugs.

4. THE OPINION YOUNG HOMELESS PEOPLE HAVE OF THEMSELVES AND THEIR TRANSFORMATION

4.1 THE PERSONALITY OF YOUNG HOMELESS PEOPLE

Several personality traits change over time on the street, and there is a concomitant transformation in the way their significance is perceived. This is caused by a change of lifestyle and social context that puts pressure on the value and normative system. What was previously deemed desirable may now be insignificant, and vice versa. Asserting one's presence within the homeless community or even simply surviving on the street requires other priorities. This kind of life is far harsher while being at the same time more tolerant.

Above all young homeless people have to **react in some way to their marginalisation**. The inferior social status that mainstream society assigns them is difficult to accept, and so they look for a way of dealing with this fact and use various strategies to this end. Either they deny that they are part of the homeless community and that they have changed in any way, or they highlight the advantages of said community, which, they believe, balance out the negative attributes. An idealised concept of homelessness includes, for instance, an emphasis on freedom, altruism, a willingness to share and to provide assistance, as well as strength and independence, even though this is more often a case of wish-fulfilment than reality. Homeless people deny that they are dishonest, unreliable, lazy and incompetent, which is how they are perceived by mainstream society. And although many of them possess these properties, they have others that the mainstream population overlooks. The simplified image of the homeless that includes only inferior characteristics and undesirable properties does not correspond to reality because **these people are not all the same**.

The fact of being homeless is inevitably reflected in the **self-identity** (or self-concept) of the individual in question. Each person is defined by what they do and by the group to which they belong or feel they belong, and this membership becomes part of their identity. The **transformation of identity** depends on the **extent to which an individual identifies with street subculture** and with the people who are part of it. Usually people who began life on the street early and have been homeless for some time identify more with the homeless community. Limiting one's contact to members of this social group leads to a faster transformation in identity, while, on the contrary, ongoing links to people or institutions that are part of mainstream society contribute to the maintenance of its original form. In the case of young people who have lived on the street since adolescence the **development of identity is suspended** more than it is transformed. In these cases there is no loss of social professional status, because such a status never existed in the first place.

K. Boydell et al. (2000) speak of the "devalued self", and it would be possible to speak of the **lost and deracinated self**, etc. Adams et al. (in Vott and Manion, 2003) say that 80% of homeless people admit to having failed, 63% say they are not proud of themselves, and 53% feel they are useless. The feeling that one's own personality has been devalued is reinforced by the behaviour of members of mainstream society whom the homeless person meets, as well as the accumulation of negative experiences. Such people have to deal with being ignored, scorned, and sometimes subject to violence. From the point of view of the majority a homeless person is someone who has elected to exclude themselves from society and therefore is not deserving of their consideration (Chamberlain and MacKenzie, 1994). A homeless person's self-confidence can sometimes be boosted by reminding them of past successes (e.g. in sport) or at least of conditions that could be recreated. These represent a certain kind of security, even if things have now changed. A sense of social decline can be intensified by, for instance, the loss of documents, which operate as the symbolic deletion of a person's existence from society.

The inability to deal with emerging adulthood depends not only on social context but the personality of a young person. Homeless people make up a diverse group that differs in respect of its abilities, personality traits, experiences and reasons for sleeping rough. Their social failure is **only rarely the consequence of insufficient abilities**, but is more likely to be a **manifestation of a disadvantageous constellation of personality traits**. Although people with a lower level of intellectual ability regularly feature among homeless people, the intellectual level of most of them is broadly average. This means that the **problem resides more in how the intellect is used** and often arises because of the insufficient development of regulatory abilities, an inability to work systematically, and inadequate self-control. Rohde et al. (1999) examined whether the overall level of intelligence also influences the ability to survive successfully on the street and a possible return to society. Unsurprisingly they discovered that only 20% was dependent on intellectual ability, while the remaining 80% was influenced by non-intellectual factors, mainly personality traits and resistance to stress. Votta and Manion (2003) found that young homeless people tend not to resolve their problems and avoid anything they would find unpleasant. A manifestation of an avoidance strategy is passivity and opting for escape routes (including denial). On the whole this kind of approach does not have the sought-after effect. Low self-esteem and a preference for non-engagement are regarded as signs of a risk of an increase in psychological maladaptation (Votta and Manion, 2003).

One of the basic personality dimensions is extraversion-introversion. This includes **properties that influence the relationship to people and the surrounding world**, as well as the level of active involvement. In the case of young homeless people we can expect extraversion to predominate, which is manifest in greater openness, sociability, the ability to strike up superficial relationships easily, and a tendency to react impulsively. This is bound up with their freer relationship with norms, lower self-control and reduced reliability. These people allow themselves to be attracted easily and influenced by anything new that occupies their attention at any particular moment (Vágnerová, 2010).

A significant personality trait is a **tendency to experience things in an emotional way** that is manifest in almost everything a person does and influences their way of thinking about and evaluating everything. Young homeless people often have more negative emotional experiences and feel less satisfied overall. This is partly because homelessness in itself intensifies emotional distress. Heightened neuroticism can be manifest both in anxiety and depression, as well as a predisposition to be annoyed or angry. Depression is not only linked with pessimism, but with an unwillingness to do anything that would require any greater effort to be exerted. Life on the street can be relatively acceptable to such people because nobody is forcing them to do anything or expecting anything from them. They can spend days doing nothing and nobody will mind. Bearsley-Smith et al. (2008) say that up to 40% of young people suffered symptoms of depression. Whitbeck et al. (2000) found that a third of homeless adolescents showed signs of depression. This figure was approximately a fifth in the group examined by Cauce et al. (2000) and 25% in the group studied by Ayerst (1999).

Another important personality dimension is **social adaptability** and its opposite, which Eysenck terms psychoticism (in the Big Five model this is divided into conscientiousness and agreeableness). This is a complex of traits that are manifest in the management of relationships with people and the surrounding world and the **ability to take on duties and limitations and subordinate oneself to valid rules**. We can expect young homeless people to possess a lower level of social adaptability. It is clear from their behaviour that they are indifferent to conventions and tend to ignore social norms. Their approach to people is more complex. Homeless people are not always considerate. Sometimes they can be hostile and aggressive. They are incapable of maintaining or sometimes even forming long lasting, deeper relationships. They may also be lacking in empathy and be less sensitive to others. They approach mundane conflicts in a radical way without regard for the other. They tend to be people it is difficult to trust and who do not trust other people, usually because of bad experiences. On the other hand, certain moral rules continue to apply, e.g. the requirement to provide assistance when someone from the homeless community needs it. It would appear that this is a norm facilitating survival under the difficult circumstances that life on the street undeniably involves. The asocial tendencies of homeless people are often a manifestation of various personality disorders and can be intensified by the long-term use of alcohol and other drugs, something that is commonplace in this community. Many other studies have reached the same results. Zerger et al. (2008) found that up to 97% of young homeless people used alcohol and drugs.

Although this figure was only 70% in the group studied by Martijn and Sharp (2006), it is still high. Cranford (in Whitbeck, 2009) says that 44% of homeless adolescents drank to excess and 40% regularly took drugs.

An important precondition of acceptable social adaptation is the **ability to orient oneself within one's own feelings and the experiences of other people** and to control one's emotions. The unconventional behaviour of young homeless people may relate to the fact that they have not had the opportunity to acquire sufficient experience in distinguishing between different emotional signals. Their parents did not teach them to differentiate between individual emotions or to control their own feelings, because they themselves were unable to. A lower level of emotional intelligence is apparent in various problems with adaptation, an inability to function normally in society and the social failure ensuing therefrom. Homelessness is only one of the possible variants of such failure.

4.1.1 HOW YOUNG HOMELESS PEOPLE EVALUATE THEIR OWN PERSONALITY

A comparison of the results of self-evaluation using the EPQ/S questionnaire of a group of young homeless people and a group of similarly aged young people

Table 4. Mean values and standard deviations in EPQ/S among a group of young homeless people and the t value ensuing from a comparison with the control group.

	men			women		
	mean	SD	t-value; p	mean	SD	t-value; p
E	9.17	2.66	3.04 p<0.01	8.72	2.73	1.35 insignificant
N	6.09	3.13	4.59 p<0.01	7.68	2.70	5.11 p<0.01
P	4.57	2.17	4.17 p<0.01	4.48	2.02	4.27 p<0.01
L	3.38	2.20	2.87 p<0.01	3.92	2.20	2.16 p<0.05

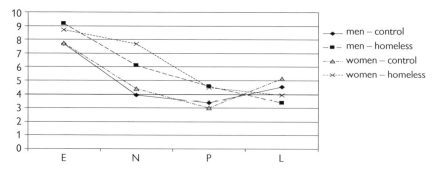

Graph 32. Mean values of EPQ/S among a group of young homeless people and a control group.

applying for university (Kožený, 1999) shows that young homeless people attribute different personality traits to themselves than their peers who are part of mainstream society (Vágnerová, Csémy, Marek, 2012).

Young homeless people have significantly higher mean values of extraversion (only the men), neuroticism and psychoticism, but a lower lie score than the group of university applicants. The **differences between men and women** are greater in the group of young homeless people, and homeless women score significantly higher in neuroticism (t=2.35, p≤0.05) and have a slightly higher lie score, facts that bear witness to their greater vulnerability as well as conformism. The reason for this may be the fact that the homeless lifestyle is more stressful for women and they do not cope with it as well as men. There is a similar ratio of mean values in the control group, though the differences are markedly lower. It should be pointed out that this is an exercise in self-evaluation, i.e. this is how the people concerned see themselves: in reality they might give a different impression.

- The **high extraversion value** measured in the group of young homeless people corresponds to the expectation that these are mainly individuals who regard themselves as social and are convinced that they strike up friendships easily. They maintain relationships with many people, though these relationships tend to be superficial and fluctuate frequently. This kind of behaviour meets the needs of life on the street, where a person is in constant contact with various people who are forever changing and it is difficult or even inappropriate to establish a deeper relationship for many reasons. Homeless youth regard themselves as active, sometimes impulsive people who like change. One consequence of this high level of extraversion is poorly developed internal self-control.

- The significantly **higher level of neuroticism** is indicative of the fact that young homeless people are often individuals who have a tendency to behave erratically and emotionally and to have unpleasant experiences of different types. They admit that they are unable to control their feelings sufficiently and it seems that they are more vulnerable that might appear to an observer.

- The **increased level of psychoticism** indicates a certain inability to adapt and a tendency to ignore societal norms. Such people often engage in risky, sometimes asocial activities. They do not regard themselves as being very empathetic or attentive to the feelings of others, and are quick to react aggressively and inconsiderately.

- The **low lie score**, as well as confirming the validity of the results obtained, indicates a minimum effort being made on the part of young homeless people to present themselves in a better light. This fact can also be interpreted as a manifestation of indifference to mainstream opinion and an unwillingness to subordinate themselves to the expectations of society. They would argue that *"I am the way I am and there is no reason why I should change"*. They regard an almost callous openness and honesty as a positive characteristic. They are not particularly concerned at what people think of them, perhaps because they encounter negative reactions on the whole and have become immune to them.

Table 5. EPQ/S items with which young homeless people most often agree (the table shows the statements with which more than 80% clients agree).

Men	I'm a lively character
	I like meeting new people
	I do things the way I want to and not according to custom
	I am able to unwind and have fun in pleasant company
	I can be the life and soul of the party
	I have sometimes taken things that do not belong to me
	I have broken or lost something that belonged to someone else
	I have said something negative or spiteful about someone
Women	My moods often alternate between good and bad
	Sometimes I feel bad without knowing why
	I don't like it when people are afraid of me
	I'm a talkative person
	I like meeting new people
	I like being among people
	I think that looking good and presenting a positive image are important
	I feel sad when I find out I've made mistakes in my work

From the table it is clear that young homeless men are different from women, or at least rate themselves differently. The men emphasise a superficial sociability, the need to have fun, and indifference to mainstream rules. Women display greater anxiety, self-criticism and a need to be found at least acceptable. Women are not as indifferent to the opinions of other people (see graph 32).

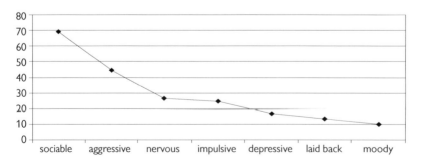

Graph 33. Personality traits corresponding to dimensions E and N that young homeless people cited in their stories (the graph shows relative frequency).

If we compare the results obtained by the EPQ/S questionnaire with the characteristics the clients used to describe themselves in the interview, it is clear that there is concordance. Young homeless people more often regard themselves as extraverts who **enjoy company**, are gregarious and **strike up contact easily**, even though not all of them speak this way of themselves. (*"I like company..." "I'm someone who searches out people and things to do."*) Their **relationships** are characterised more by quantity than depth and are more **superficial and changeable**. (*"It only takes me an hour to find new friends, I don't have a problem with that."*) They feel carefree and admit that they like to make the most of this regardless of the consequences. (*"I like having fun and don't think about the future much."*) Most say that they are active, often impulsive, and that they do not think of the consequences of their actions.

The young homeless are people who **tend to be erratic and emotional**. In their interviews they frequently say that they are emotionally unstable, unbalanced, and that they are unable to exert much self-control. (*"I'm incredibly sensitive." "I'm really nervous."*) However, there are also individuals who describe themselves as being completely different. (*"I'm phlegmatic, laid back, I put it all behind me."*) Poor self-esteem and insufficient self-confidence give rise to anxiety. (*"I simply don't trust myself at all... when I see the way I am."*) The increased level of neuroticism may be both the cause and the effect of life on the street, where a homeless person has to deal with various stresses and traumas that do not always serve to bolster their psychological comfort (Whitbeck, Hoyt and Bao, 2000).

The increased levels of neuroticism relate to a predisposition to negative emotional experiences and a greater readiness to react to insignificant stimuli with anger and annoyance. Young homeless people speak of their **exasperation and anger** more frequently than anxiety and fear. They realise that they allow themselves to be easily wound up by trivial matters. (*"There's anger inside me. I can be easily provoked." "I get pissed off easily and then go for the person who's pissed me off."*) The homeless community includes people who tend to be pessimistic and depressed, though there are not many of them. (*"I'm basically a pessimist in outlook.*

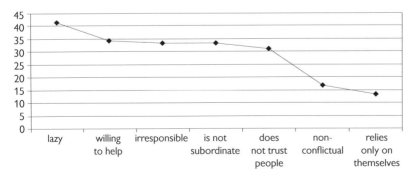

Graph 34. Personality characteristics corresponding to dimension P, which young homeless people spontaneously used in their stories (the graph shows relative frequency).

As though someone's switched off the light.") These are tendencies that are given by a person's disposition, though they can be exacerbated by external influences. They relate to the course of a person's life and above all to the long-term use of psychoactive substances.

The higher level of psychoticism in the EPQ/S questionnaire indicates **lower sociability, less ability to adapt**, and an indifference to conventions. The same is true of the lower lie score. A person's relationship with duties and their willingness to respect the rules of a situation is one of the dimensions of social adaptability, which also includes the level of their self-control and their ability to resist disturbing influences. (The Big Five model terms the complex of such properties conscientiousness, made up of the categories diligence and self-discipline). If anything the opposite tendency is visible in young homeless people. They often recognise that they are **lazy, irresponsible and undisciplined**. They know that they tend to react without thinking on the basis of their current preferences and momentary mood and that they focus on the present and immediate satisfaction and do not think of the consequences of their actions. A lack of self-discipline and self-control manifests itself in a greater tendency to alcohol and drug abuse.

Young homeless people often say that **they do not like being subordinate to someone or something**. This results in their being less likely to respect social conventions. This is perhaps the personality trait that most frequently appears in their stories. From their point of view this is a positive characteristic that is an important part of their self-identity: if they abided by rules, they would lose their identity. (*"If I decided to fit in, it just wouldn't be me." "I need my freedom. I have to be able to do what I want, how I want."*)

Young homeless people admit **that they have never met their obligations** and that they remain unable to force themselves to even now. (*"I have never met my obligations or done what I was supposed to." "I'm unable to force myself to do something I'm supposed to and I'm always putting everything off."*) They are aware that they are lazy and irresponsible, that they would prefer to laze around doing nothing than to do something useful. (*"I'm lazy and incredibly irresponsible."*)

4.1.2 A TENDENCY TO AGGRESSIVE BEHAVIOUR

Many young homeless people admit that they have a **tendency to react aggressively**. Even an insignificant event can provoke such a reaction and the intensity of their aggression may be heightened or unreasonable. In the case of some their attitude toward aggression has changed under the influence of life on the street, while others have been influenced by their experience of domestic violence during childhood. The group also contains people with antisocial personality disorder and people whose personality has changed as a consequence of the long-term use of psychoactive substances.

It is clear from the graph that men have a greater tendency to react aggressively. This corresponds to the situation in the population at large, where men are generally more aggressive.

An interesting finding is the **subjective conviction that their tendency to act aggressively went down after beginning to sleep rough**, a feeling expressed mainly by men. It is possible that this is the result of the elimination of certain stressful factors and the triggers of aggression, which may include the demands of family and employers. On the other hand, they are exposed to other stress factors that most people would regard as more serious. This might be the consequence of the different feedback received from members of mainstream society and other homeless people. The pressure to comply with rules may be less on the street and therefore does not provoke such disproportionate reactions. There may also have been a simple shift in the evaluation of certain modes of conduct, including aggression. What is important is the difference in the cause of aggressive behaviour. Among homeless people the bad moods and impaired self-control caused by the long-term use of drugs and alcohol may be playing more and more of a role.

In order to understand the basis of aggression among young homeless people it is important to know what stimuli provoke such reactions, i.e. what most often induces a person to act in such a way. A **heightened readiness to react aggressively may be one of the consequences of life on the street**, when a person is at greater threat and must defend themselves. Some young homeless people react in such a way upon simply a hint of a threat. At other times this may in fact be simply a demonstration of their readiness to act in such a way and is intended to serve as a preventative defence. *"I don't have a problem with aggression, I just kick everyone in sight. The truth is I'm not at all aggressive and people who know me from when I was fifteen know that actually I'm a bit of a wimp. But the longer I'm here the more I've learned that **you can't afford to display fear on the street**." (LC, female)* This client is an experienced homeless woman who is not essentially aggressive

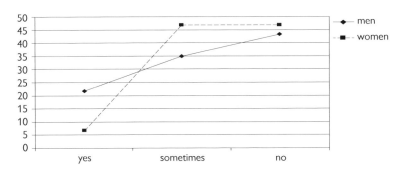

Graph 35. The opinion of young homeless people regarding their tendency to act aggressively (the graph shows relative frequency).

but actually quite accommodating. However, she uses aggression for demonstrative purposes, and this works under the circumstances.

The trigger for aggression is often the **unpleasant or belligerent behaviour of other people**. Homeless youth are easily irritated by the smallest thing. This tendency is then reinforced by the lack of privacy and the constant contact with people that they did not choose to be with and whose behaviour is sometimes difficult to tolerate. This is how client PK (M) explains his behaviour. *"If someone gets at me, I can be aggressive. **If they're getting on my nerves or provoking me**, well… I'll let myself take the first blow, but after that I see red and I couldn't give a fuck what I do." (PK, male)* The client spent his childhood in institutions, first in a children's home and later a young offender's institute. The influence of emotional deprivation can be assumed. He uses drugs and has spent time in prison. He has been living rough for three years.

MŽ (male) takes a similar line. *"I'm a calm person. But **if someone fucks me off then I don't care** whether I punch him in his face or his stomach, I simply go for him full on. If some bloody lunatic or dickhead comes at me and pisses me off, then I find it difficult to keep calm."* The client has been prosecuted for gross bodily harm, fraud and unpaid debts. He was thrown out of his family because of the threat of repossession. He uses drugs and alcohol.

In the case of JP (male) aggression is provoked by **tension and the need to take his mind of things**. *"I made the most of the fact that people are so fucking thick. I can use them with my intelligence and hone my mind with them. I couldn't stand them (other homeless people). I would never have dreamt that I'd end up like this and I used to despise people in this situation. For me they were outcasts. **I would have poured petrol over them and set them alight**. And I still have this compulsion, even though I'm now one of them. I'm nothing. But they're even bigger losers than me."* JP's aggression is aimed at those who reflect back at him his own undesirable form. JP is a drug addict with a probable personality disorder whose social adaptability is so disturbed that he would find it difficult to deal with the demands of ordinary life.

MM (male) maintains that his tendency to act aggressively is caused by frustration. *"I'm dissatisfied with myself. **I'm pissed off with myself and I take it out on other people**."* The client has been involved in many criminal activities, was prosecuted for grievous bodily harm as an adolescent, and has spent spells in prison for burglary. He was the victim of domestic violence as a child and was often beaten by his father. He has been sleeping rough for four years.

A common problem of young homeless people is a lack of self-control and the absence of judgement, or indifference to the consequences of their own conduct. This can lead to various problems, the least serious of which are complaining and breaking things. *"Yeah, I have problems with aggression. I bottle things up for a long time inside, and then suddenly I crack. Rage, everything. **I can't calm down**. I explode and do terrible things. When they locked me in a cell and I wanted to get out I started banging my head against the wall." (MS, female)* The client has been sleeping rough for three years and has a range of problems she has been unable to resolve. She uses drugs and as a child was frequently subject to corporal punishment. At school she was the victim of bullying. She has committed credit card fraud several times and has unpaid debts. PC (female) has similar problems. *"Sometimes I just can't control myself. If someone catches me unawares or surprises me, I explode.* **I can't control myself** *and I reckon that's because of the drugs."* The client has been dependent on heroin for a long time. She comes from a broken home where she was often witness to domestic violence. She has been on the street for four years.

Aggression, or rather a tendency to unregulated impulsive reactions, is exacerbated by **alcohol and drugs**. Many clients are aware of this link and understand that they should regulate their intake of psychoactive substances. *"I had problems with aggression when I was boozing, but not anymore. It was only when I was drinking." (KB, female)*

"I have problem with aggression, but only when I drink. Otherwise I don't." (LB, male)

"I sometimes have problems with aggression. **When I'm in a bad state** *nobody has to say anything to me, I just start to be aggressive. I'd shoot someone if I could. I get rid of my frustration by beating someone up and I feel better." (LB, male)* In this case too aggression serves as a way of forgetting unpleasant feelings and the client is unconcerned at the thought he might harm someone else. He is dependent on drugs, specifically crystal meth, and has experienced toxic psychosis several times. It is therefore no wonder that he does not react in the standard fashion. MB (female) also suffers fits of uncontrolled aggression. *"I don't know if there's some psychological reason for it, but sometimes* **some switch goes off in me and I don't know what I'm doing**. *I wouldn't even know if I killed someone. Then I come around and learn what I've done. But it's as though the blinds come down over my eyes and I can't see and I do things without thinking of the consequences."* In MB's case too this is the result of the long-term use of drugs. She has been sleeping rough for five years, supports herself through prostitution and has often been the victim of different forms of violence.

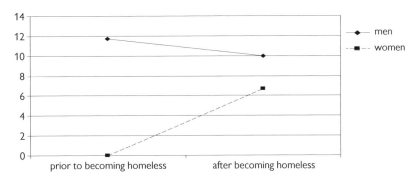

Graph 36. Young homeless people often commit GBH (the graph shows relative frequency).

Assault and battery and even grievous bodily harm are not unusual in the homeless community. This can be the result of an **ongoing tendency to violent conduct** that is one of the manifestations of antisocial personality disorder, but also of the tense conditions of life on the street and the effect of psychoactive substances. In the case of JH (male) aggression is probably not the result of the environment but more deep-seated personality traits. *"I popped into a pub that my father used to go to and one bloke, one of my father's enemies, started saying I was a bastard just like my father. So I beat him up and broke his jaw. He reported me to the police and I spent 15 months in Leopoldov Prison. I also punched my mum's boyfriend. He was behaving badly to mum and I flew off the handle and beat him up.* **I've given almost everyone a thrashing and I've never felt bad about it.***"* It is likely that in this case the client's negative inherited disposition was exacerbated by his recurring experience with violence as the norm and excessive drinking. His father beat and terrorised the entire family and also acted under the influence of alcohol. The client has been sleeping rough for three years.

As is clear from the stories they recount, many of the clients displayed **aggressive tendencies as far back as childhood**. *"I've been really aggressive every since I was a child. Personally I think that's because my stepfather was that way to me. I picked it up from him. At school I had problems and the police were called in to calm me down. I fought a lot in the children's home.* **It didn't take much to get me punching someone when I was young.** *I simply didn't realise at that time what I was doing. I still have it in me when the occasion demands. Several times the occasion did demand, but then I remembered that I'm on a conditional discharge* (for grievous bodily harm), *so I thought better of it." (TM, male)* This is a client who was neither an alcoholic nor a drug addict. His aggression has other causes. He comes from a family in which domestic violence was commonplace and associates with similarly oriented people (a gang that attacks the homeless). He has been sleeping rough for four years.

Aggression may be selective and may be aimed against a certain group of people. In this case it is associated to a certain extent with a client's life experience up till now. In the case of homeless women who support themselves through prostitution or have experience of violence, men can provoke aggression. Sometimes this involves a certain type of man, but can apply to all men. *"I was aggressive to blokes. As soon as a bloke started to touch me I yelled. And loudly." (TŽ, female)* TŽ has been raped several times and has many unpleasant experiences from the time she worked as a prostitute.

"When a man looked at me or spoke to me, I opened my penknife. I know that I could kill someone. I was repulsed by men." (MB, female)

Women who sleep rough are often at threat of sexual or other violence and can only defend themselves to a certain extent. VL (female) was given a suspended sentence for aggressive defence. *"I was given two years suspended for GBH. I beat up a guy. I kicked him between the legs because he tried to rape me."* Under these circumstances it is impossible to speak of a general tendency to be aggressive.

4.1.3 THE NEEDS, FEARS AND WISHES OF YOUNG HOMELESS PEOPLE

In order to evaluate the needs and wishes of young homeless people we used three pictures from the TAT test created by H. Murray and C. Morgan, along with two others, similarly indeterminate, that we had drawn for this purpose. The ambiguous pictures were used by clients to create a story that would reflect how they saw the surrounding world, other people, and their own position in the world, as well as what was expected from them. The assumption is that a client will identify with a character in the picture and project onto it their feelings and needs. We were worried as to whether young homeless people would be willing and able to interpret such indefinite events. However, they had no problem with the task. The findings are interesting.

The first picture shows one person standing behind a fence and another in front of a building. They may be neighbours, friends, members of the same family or completely unfamiliar to each other. The likelihood is that a young homeless person will identify with the person standing outside, though this does not have to be the case.

The need for material benefit. The topic of **burglary** sometimes crops up. *"The person standing behind the fence can see something valuable, maybe copper or a bike. And he is waiting until there's an opportunity to take them. The person inside thinks he's got a problem. It all ends up ok, he doesn't take anything." (IB, male)* The topic of burglary is typical of this particular man, and a thief forms the main character in other of his stories. This is a client with similar experiences, even though the hero of this particular story does not in the end steal anything.

The need for help. AK (female) sees the person behind the fence as being homeless, and in this she is joined by ZŽ (female), even though she does not express this opinion explicitly. *"**Perhaps they are thirsty and hungry**. They expect*

Illustration 17. A person behind a fence (drawing: Anna Pospíšilová).

to receive something. The other one is saying that they need something. I don't know how things turn out in the end." The need for help appears in the story told by MO (male). "*Maybe he needs help but expects to be turned away. The person in front of the house thinks he's a thief, but **helps him in the end**.*" A similar story told by LS (male) has an interesting outcome. "*The person behind the fence is definitely hungry. He rings the bell and asks whether he could have some food. He doesn't know what to expect in the way of a reaction. The person in front of the house is thinking that it is not often that a stranger rings the bell in order to beg. He feels sorry for him and they reach an agreement: I'll give you food but you have to promise to make something of your life.*" During his interview this client said he would like to quit the homeless life. He had not managed to so far, but "*I believe that things will get better.*" In the story recounted by KB (male) the homeless person does not receive anything. "*He's begging and expects to be given something. But the man in front of the house is saying to himself 'go find a job and stop bugging me'. **He doesn't receive anything**.*" The client is still on the street, takes drugs and has no work.

The need for revenge. SŠ (male) used his story to work through his own experiences and their possible culmination. He had been deceived by a friend and had to take responsibility for the latter's debts. This was one of the reasons

people who do not know each other
acquaintances
friends
family

Graph 37. Who are the people in the picture? (the graph shows the relative frequency).

They came for a visit, they are waiting for the other person
They are waiting for someone to open the gate
They need something
They need assistance
They are returning home
Something else

Graph 38. What is the person behind the fence doing? (the graph shows the relative frequency).
NB They need something = to discuss something, to ask a question, to do a job.
They need assistance = they are thirsty or hungry, they are begging or need a place to stay and to sleep.

he fetched up on the street and was finally put in prison. His story is a fictional continuation of real events. *"He is visiting an old friend. He is waiting for him to agree to the conditions they agreed on in the past. But the person standing by the house is saying to himself that all of that is in the past and no longer applies. The person by the fence wants to lynch the other one but it will be to his own detriment."* As far as we know the client did not in reality lynch the friend who had swindled him, though it is very likely he wanted to.

The need for a sense of belonging and the acceptance of other people. In the stories prompted by this picture a return home does not appear often. RB (male) is an exception. *"He wants to return home on a visit. He doesn't know what will happen and has no expectations. He is waiting for a response. **It'll all go wrong and they won't accept him**."* This is in fact the case in reality. The client has no family background. ŠZ (female) reads the future more optimistically. *"He wants to go home and is waiting for the person by the door to let him in. And **in the end he takes** the person standing by the fence **into his home**."* ŠZ's own life story is similarly hopeful. Despite all her problems and the fact she was thrown out of home, she is now in contact with her mother.

The story told by VK (male) is that of a family that does not in reality exist. *"This person is looking to see whether his wife locked their house up properly. Nothing will happen and she in turn simply stares stupidly at him, at how disgusting he is. He is thinking that they could have a better house. And it will end up like every other day."* The story is far from idyllic, and neither was the client's life in his foster family, above all because of his own problematic behaviour. The critical person who *"simply stares stupidly"* was in reality his adoptive mother, i.e. also a woman. The *"better house"* could be a symbol of a better home.

Far more frequently the stories feature an **encounter between two friends or acquaintances**. *"This man came to visit his friend, whom he hadn't seen for a long time. His friend goes to open the gate, but says to himself: **I don't have time today. He could have come another time**. The two eventually agree that he will visit next week and they'll go for a coffee."* (KM, female) The person being visited is unenthusiastic but does not reject his friend and agrees on a future meeting. The expectation that a person will not be completely rejected by his former friends is fulfilled.

Negative expectations and an awareness of not being accepted by members of mainstream society feature in the story told by VL (female). *"The person wants to walk through the gate and is waiting for the other to open it. The problem is that the other one is thinking "what the fuck does this prick want?" However, he forces himself to open the gate."* This client does not have good experience with people and does not except them to act receptively. MK (male) tells a similar story. *"He is waiting in front of the house for someone to open the gate. He is waiting for the other guy to open the gate in invite him in. But the other is thinking **"who the fuck is this bothering me and what do they want?"** The person by the house discovers that the other one is selling vacuum cleaners and sends him away."* This clear rejection corresponds to reality. The client is still sleeping rough on the very margins of society.

The people in the picture are mostly regarded as knowing each other, sometimes as friends, and young homeless people are optimistic in relation to them and usually expect that the person inside the building will open the gate for the other or meet them somewhere else. The need for acceptance, even when a person is in a socially excluded status, is manifest in how the story ends, which is mostly happily. The picture is rarely about the family, and the theme of family relationships appears more often in reaction to the other pictures.

The second picture shows a person looking over a fence and through a window into an apartment where three people are sitting at a table. It evokes the theme of the family and home life, though it could be about something completely different. It is also likely that young homeless people will identify with the person who is standing outside and might like to enter the building.

The need for material gain The theme of **theft** appears here too. *"That person is watching the people in the house. He is planning to burgle them, though in the end he walks away. The people are a family."* (SP, female) The client does not steal herself, but is surrounded by people who do. Theft is an everyday occurrence for her. The burglar as the main figure appears in other stories. *"He is standing there because he would like to steal something. He is waiting for them to switch off the light and go to bed. But they are having dinner. It is a family with a child. They don't go to bed but help*

- Who is it and what do they want?
- A visitor
- A homeless person
- A thief
- What are they gawping at me and bothering me for?
- Nothing
- Something else

Graph 39. What is the person standing by the house thinking? (the graph shows relative frequency).
NB: It is interesting to note the relatively high number of people who expect the person by the house to display no enthusiasm or even suspect the other person of malicious intent.

- The person in the house opens the door and invites the other in
- They meet elsewhere
- They call the police
- Something else

Graph 40. The story's outcome (the graph shows relative frequency).

Picture 18. A person standing in front of a building in which other people are sitting at a table (drawing: Anna Pospíšilová).

themselves to more food, and so in the end he doesn't steal anything." (VK, male) This client does not steal on a regular basis, even though he has experience of doing so during emerging adulthood. It is interesting that in both cases the burglary does not in the end take place even though the main figure had such a plan in mind.

The need for assistance. The theme of homelessness appears less frequently, though is repeated in the story recounted by AK (female). *"The person is standing there because he is hungry. He is waiting until the people leave the building so as to talk to them. He doesn't know them. But in the end they invite him inside and **give him something to eat**."* The client experienced a particularly uncomfortable life on the street. At present she lives at home. In the story told by LR (male) the main figure is a beggar and is successful. *"He is looking into the building and waiting to be given something. Inside there is a happy family and in the end **he receives money from them**."* LR has a similar relationship with his adopted family. He expects nothing but money from them and usually receives it. Leaving aside the problems that his family has with their adopted homeless son who is a drug addict, this is a happy family too.

The typical **problems and needs of the homeless** appear in many other stories. The story told by TŽ (female) reflects her long-standing dependency on

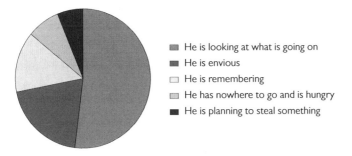

- He is looking at what is going on
- He is envious
- He is remembering
- He has nowhere to go and is hungry
- He is planning to steal something

Graph 41. What is the person by the fence doing? (the graph shows relative frequency).

crystal meth and the personality changes that are associated. *"He is standing there because he's bored and he's staring at the people in the room. Nothing will happen, he's just a bit out of it.* **The people at the table are dealers**. *In the end he leaves and goes off looking for money in order to buy some drugs called good mood."* The mafia features in the story told by MŽ (male). *"He is watching them, monitoring them, and expects them to spot him. The people at the table belong to the mafia. In the end they see the guy standing outside."* The client doesn't say what happens next. He himself feels threatened and during his interview said that *"anything can happen on the street, especially at night"*. However, his conduct is also problematic. He is aggressive and has been handed down a suspended sentence for actual bodily harm.

The need to belong and to be accepted by other people. The theme of the family is commonest among women. Some of them are convinced that the person looking at a happy family will be jealous, because he himself has nothing. *"He is thinking back to the past. He would like to return home. The people inside are his family. But in the end he* **simply walks away sadly**.*" (LB, female)* He doesn't dare ring the bell and wait to see if he is invited in. LB lost her family because of the way she was behaving and her use of drugs. She is not happy about the fact but is unable to change and put right the damaged relationships. The story told by MM (male) ends with an unambiguous rejection that corresponds to reality. *"He is observing events in the house. He is waiting to be allowed in. The people inside are his family that he lost. But* **they don't allow him inside**.*"* The client is a criminal recidivist who has been sleeping rough for four years. It is sometimes unclear as to whether it is his family or someone unknown in the picture. The same is true of the story told by VS (male). *"He sees something that interests him and perhaps he thinks back to his home. Perhaps he's waiting for a miracle to take place. But he doesn't know the people inside the building and* **in the end they call the police**.*"* Everything was an illusion and he must reconcile himself to the fact that he has no family.

Memories of a previous home appear in the story told by JJ (male). *"He used to live there. He isn't even sure himself what he wants. The people at the table are his family. How things end up* **all depend on him**.*"* The client sums up his own situation well. His family would be willing to help him and take him back if he could change his behaviour. The story told by SŠ (male) has a happy ending. *"He wants*

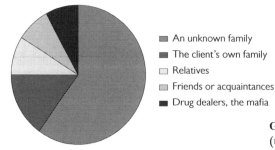

- An unknown family
- The client's own family
- Relatives
- Friends or acquaintances
- Drug dealers, the mafia

Graph 42. Who are the people at the table? (the graph shows relative frequency).

to remind himself of how things used to be around the family table. *The people inside are his family and he is waiting for them to notice him.* **They notice him and invite him** *to sit down at the table as before. At least, that's what he'd like."* The client still lives on the street. He has spent time in prison for non-payment of debts, but his family have not rejected him completely.

The way the subject matter is processed may represent a fictitious **fulfilment of the need for a family**, even though none exists in reality. *"He is looking at a family. They are happy and he would like to have such a family. But he doesn't know the people sitting at the table.* **In the end they invite him in and accept him as one of the family.**" (JV, male) The client comes from a broken home and spent some of his life in a children's home. The only person close to him was his grandmother. He feels rejected and misunderstood and it is clear that he would like to feel he had some kind of base. However, the question is whether he himself would manage to behave in such a way as to be accepted by someone else.

The people at the table can be friends, relatives, or complete strangers. In the story told by KM (female) it is her brother's family. *"The person outside is looking at the people inside. He is looking for his brother and expects him to see him. The people at the table are his brother, his wife and their son. They call the police, because they think he's some kind of pervert."* They do not recognise their relative and call the police. KM herself has two younger, more successful brothers who are not homeless, but she is not in touch with them. She may be scared of rejection or some kind of negative experience. Relatives play a role in the story told by ŠZ (female). *"He feels lonely and is wondering whether they will invite him in. They're his relatives. But* **in the end he remains outside.**" The client was thrown out of her home because she was trying to support her family through prostitution, though it is clear that she misses home. She is not a typical homeless person and it is likely that she would manage to reintegrate into normal life. She is not indifferent or apathetic, and relationships with friends are important to her. **Feelings of loneliness and deracination** feature in the story told by MK (male). *"He is curious. He will look through the window and nothing will happen. A family is sitting at*

■ The people inside open the door and gives the watcher what they want
■ Perhaps they open the door
☐ He makes no further attempt and leaves
▨ They reject him
■ Nothing happens
▨ Don't know

Graph 43. The story's outcome (the graph shows the relative frequency).
NB: An unhappy end to the story sometimes features in which not only do the people inside the house not invite him in, but call the police.

the table. He goes away and is sad that he does not have a home and friends." It is clear that life on the street does not suit the client. However, he has so far been unable to change things.

The story told by ES (female) concerns a **problem-free meeting with friends**. *"This person has a meeting with the people in the house. He rings the doorbell and they come to open the door. In the end **they sit down to dinner together**."* In reality the client has problems in relationships with everyone around her. She feels unaccepted, is depressed and has made repeated attempts at suicide. The story told by TM (male) is similar, though in his case it may correspond to reality. *"This person is waiting for a friend. The friend arrives. Inside the building is his friend's family. He and his friend greet the family and then **go off somewhere together**."* The client has several old friends on the street, though one has to ask whether they are simply more for his own convenience. The theme of the family, sadness over its loss and the need to return appears relatively often. The homeless people we interviewed would like to belong somewhere but very often do not even wait to see whether they will be accepted but prefer to leave. Only a small number of stories feature a theme other than the family. Sometimes an awareness of their own exclusion and abandonment appears in a story. Identification with a homeless lifestyle is manifest in the themes of theft and drug dealing.

The third picture, which is part of the TAT test, shows a child sitting in the doorway of a log cabin. The picture may evoke memories of childhood as well as current needs and problems. There is only one figure in the picture and so the client must identify with it or distance themselves from it.

The need for emotional security and safety. A recurring theme is the desire for a calm, safe base, which either the child does not have or is problematic. LC (female) projects the arguments her parents used to have into her story. *"The boy is **thinking about problems at home**. He would like his parents to stop arguing. He goes home, nothing changes, and they continue arguing."* The boy is also often perceived as being at threat. *"The child has escaped and is hiding. **He is frightened** and hopes that nobody finds him. He wants his mum. In the end they catch him." (EK, female)* It is

Picture 19. A boy in a log cabin.

– 166 –

not clear why the child has escaped, but he feels threatened and it is his mother who could help him. However, in the end they catch him and nothing more is said about his mother. We do not know whether she could have come or did not want to. EK's mother died suddenly, which caused a fundamental deterioration in her life. The mother represents security that can be easily lost. In AM's (male) story the child is waiting to be beaten. *"He is sad. **He is waiting to be beaten**. He is thinking about life and what will take place in the future. I don't know how things work out."* The client comes from a broken home. His father used to beat him and he ended up in a youth detention centre.

The child is running away from home because he is being abused, according to TŽ (female). *"He is sitting there because he has run away from home. Perhaps someone is abusing him. He is frightened and wondering what will happen. Why has he ended up here? He would like to feel happy and not to be alone, but he doesn't want to be abused. He will either carry on sitting there or find some people."* The client herself would like to feel happy and not be alone. However, she has been a victim of violence both at home and on the street.

The need for assistance and support. Running away from home can be a cry for help. *"The child has been grounded or is being tyrannised. **He is waiting for someone to come who will liberate him from this hell**. He is wondering why he has still not run away from home and what would happen to him. He would like to have a peace-*

Graph 44. What the boy is doing in the picture? (the graph shows relative frequency).

- Waiting and thinking
- He has nowhere to go and is lonely and sad
- He is bored
- He is sulking
- Something else

- A home, an apartment and parents
- An apartment and friends
- Not to be alone
- A game, ice cream
- To make good a bad situation
- A better life
- Something else

Graph 45. What does the child want? (the graph shows relative frequency).

ful childhood like other children. In the end he is put in a children's home and when he grows up he will be grateful that he was in the home and was not tyrannised." (PP, male) The client spent several years in a children's home. His stepfather ended up in prison for grievous bodily harm and his mother was incapable of looking after her children. In his interview PP is grateful for what the institution did for him.

The stories told by several young homeless people express not only the need for assistance, but support and reassurance. *"He is sulking. He is waiting until someone takes pity on him. He thinks that everyone hates him and **he would like someone to reassure him**. He will continue to sulk until someone arrives." (ES, female)* The client behaves similarly in real life. She draws attention to herself through self-harm and attempts at suicide. She is convinced that her father hates her and that her mother, though kind, is too weak. In her interview she said *"I wanted to draw attention to myself so that they took notice of me. I wanted someone to take pity on me".* However, this did not happen.

The need to belong and to be accepted by other people. *"He is waiting for someone, for his mum or dad. He is waiting for someone to arrive. He is wondering what to play with. He would like not to be alone. In the end someone comes for him and takes him home." (TD, female)* The return home is important. The client herself managed it and the story of the fictitious child also ends positively. The problem of loneliness is the main theme of the story told by JH (male). *"He is sitting there because he has nowhere else to go. He is waiting for someone to help him and he is thinking about the fact that he is alone. **He would like not to be alone**, but perhaps that is how he will remain."* The client himself remained alone. He could not get on with his mother, has no relationship with his brother and has nobody else. His problem is alcoholism and a tendency to react aggressively.

The **home left by the client** may have been happy and is not **idealised**. *"He is sitting and looking at his mother as she returns from work. Then both of them go to buy some ice cream. He is thinking about what bus she will arrive on. He would like an ice cream. It all ends happily, they go off together for the ice cream." (JJ, male)* Things appear to be going well for this client. With the support of his family he managed to quit life on the street. His relationship with his mother was not seriously damaged, though there was a great deal of conflict between the two for a certain period of time.

Graph 46. The story's outcome (the graph shows relative frequency).

- Happy
- Sad
- He goes home to play
- He remains where he is
- Doesn't know

During childhood, **friends and acceptance by one's peer group** is important. *"He's there because he's waiting. He is waiting for someone to come and play. He would like to play with his friends. **His friends arrive** and they all play."* (DČ, male) However, SP (male) sees things differently. *"He is waiting for his friends to arrive. He is wondering why they're so late. He would like them to arrive. **His friends don't turn up** and he goes home disappointed."* The client did not have problems with interpersonal relationships as a child. He found himself on the street later than most. He has no friends here, does not trust other homeless people and has lost touch with his former friends.

The need to go back in time and receive another chance. *"He did something and is now thinking about it. He is thinking about the punishment he might receive from his parents. He is thinking about the mess he's in. He would like to go back in time to before he did this thing. If he's a little boy, then the parents will spank his bottom at most. But if he's an adolescent, they may throw him out."* (AK, male) The client himself would like to go back in time. He is aware of where his conduct has brought him but is incapable of resolving his situation. Previous mistakes can be the cause of something important being lost. VK (male) views the child as being responsible for the death of his grandfather. *"He is grieving because his grandfather was buried beneath grain. Then a large bus arrives with the social services. He is wondering whether he will find new friends there* (in DD). *He would like to turn the clock back** and not play with the levers for grinding corn. It ends up with him being taken away by a social worker."* (VK, male) The client was adopted and when his father died, whom he loved, his mother was incapable of bringing him up and he was placed in a youth detention centre. His father was an older man and may appear in this story as the grandfather.

The stories told by clients about the child sitting in the doorway of the log cabin frequently feature solitariness and an attempt to deal with the lack of interest or even abuse that they themselves experienced in their childhood. Other stories reflect their feelings of guilt for the way they have behaved, memories of their lost home, and the desire to turn back the clock and behave differently. There is a need for support, assistance and reassurance. Not every story ends happily, though in many of them there is a hope expressed that things will work out well in the end.

The fourth picture is part of the TAT test. It shows the silhouette of a person sitting at a window and can be interpreted in many different ways. The open window may evoke ideas of the future or the need to escape from current problems and fulfil subjectively important requirements.

Basic biological needs. The basis of the stories told by several young homeless people is the satisfaction of biological needs. In the story told by RB (male) this involves **sex**. *"This person likes nice views and is looking outside. He is waiting for his friend to arrive so that they can go looking for women. He is thinking of how to make the most of it and how he'll pull a beautiful chick. He would like this **because it has been a long time since he had a woman**. How things turn out is in the stars."* The

Picture 19. A person sitting by an open window.

client does not seem to be suffering at present and his needs are relatively limited. Attaining sexual satisfaction is also the main theme of the story told by TŽ (female). *"He is being jerked off and waiting to see how long it will take. He is thinking about how beautiful it is. He no longer needs anything but peace. He's going to feel satisfied. Hurrah."* It is not clear who will satisfy whom, though there is no mention of a girl/boyfriend. It is someone anonymous and so insignificant that they are not worth a mention. The concept of the story may be informed by the fact that for a long time the client made a living through prostitution and something approximating the content of the story was part of her work. The figure in the story told by MS has similarly basic needs. *"I don't know … he wants to go out and he goes out. He wants a beer. He leaves and goes to the pub."* The focus on a basic need and the simplified formulation of the story corresponds to the client's competences. His real life follows a similar pattern.

The need for material gain. The open window may give the impression that there is something worth stealing inside. *"He's a burglar. He's thinking about what to steal. Maybe he needs* **money***. It all ends happily and they don't catch him."* (MS, female) The client herself steals on the street and has been involved in credit fraud. The need not to be caught is clearly close to her heart. In the story RL (male) tells the thief is caught and put in prison. *"Maybe he's sneaking into the building.*

- Looking at the stars
- Sitting and thinking
- Preparing to jump
- Preparing to commit burglary
- Something else

Graph 47. What the person is doing by the window (the graph shows relative frequency).

He is waiting until there's nobody there and is thinking about what to take. He would like to find **something valuable** *so he can sell it. They catch him and put him in prison."* The story corresponds to his own experience, since the client is one of those who survives on the street by theft.

The need to be offered another chance. Young homeless people have various problems that they are unable to resolve or which they react to impulsively. The topic of suicide crops up repeatedly and the picture containing the dark silhouette of a person sitting by an open window provokes such thoughts very easily. *"He is deciding whether to jump and getting ready to. Perhaps he would like another chance. How things pan out* **depends purely on him**." *(KB, male)* The client offers his hero a chance, at least to the extent that his fate depends on how he decides. At present the client is in rehab for drug addiction, which also represents a certain hope.

"He wants to jump and commit suicide. He no longer has any expectations. He is thinking about life and **would like to end the suffering he is going through**. *In the end he thinks twice about suicide and visits a psychiatrist." (DČ, male)* In this case too the central character receives another chance when he decides to seek help. The client has hopes of a better life and is not sleeping rough at present.

"He is sitting and looking at the stars. He is waiting for a star to fall. He is thinking about his life and **would like to return something**. *It ends up with a star falling down and him seeing it." (MM, male)* Even though the client is still sleeping rough, he clearly imagines that his life could take a different path.

The central character in the story told by PK (male) does not expect a second chance. *"He is looking, watching, waiting. He is waiting for something to happen, for something to change in some way. Maybe he's thinking about life, love and death.* **He would like to find love but will only find death**." The client is still sleeping rough and has many problems. He is a drug addict who has had his possessions seized, and his pessimism is justified. The story told by PP (male) about a junky does not offer hope. PP himself does not take drugs. *"He is off his head and waiting to escape by jumping out of the window.* **He has no expectations**, *he has decided to jump. He is wondering why he even began taking drugs. He would like to return to a time when he didn't even know that drugs existed. The story ends up with him going to rehab and ending up yet another cured junky who falls back into bad habits from time to time, like*

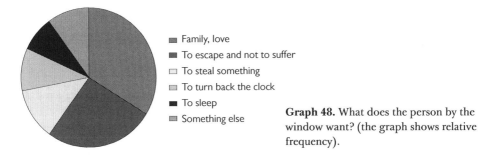

■ Family, love
■ To escape and not to suffer
□ To steal something
▨ To turn back the clock
■ To sleep
▨ Something else

Graph 48. What does the person by the window want? (the graph shows relative frequency).

every other junky." The story appears to express a fear of drugs, the consequences of which the client sees on the street every day, and a distaste for drug addicts. This also features in his interview.

The need for assistance and support. The story told by TD (female) expresses the hope that **someone will come and rescue the central character**. *"He wants to jump. He is waiting for someone to rescue him. He is wondering whether he has the bottle to do it. He would like someone to rescue him. It ends up with someone maybe rescuing him and him living.*" The expectation of assistance from someone else and reliance on such assistance is clear in the story. The story told by ŠP (male) ends badly. Nobody helps the central character. *"He wants to commit suicide but is waiting for someone to rescue him. He is thinking about it. He would like a faithful woman, but in the end **he jumps and dies.**"* The client would like a more permanent relationship but does not have anyone at present. Though his story ends unhappily, he himself has found work and a place to stay.

The need for intimacy and maintenance of a partnership. *"He has just found out that his girlfriend has split up with him and is missing her. He has no idea of what comes next, but he is wondering whether it all makes sense and why she did what she did. He would like everything to be settled and calm, but it isn't. In the end time heals and **he finds himself another girlfriend.**" (JJ, male)* The client places great store on sexual partnerships. Though he has had considerable problems with them, at present he has a job and is living with a new partner who is pregnant with him. The next story is more optimistic, even though it is only in the fantasies of MP. *"This person is observing the stars in the night sky. He is waiting for a lunar eclipse. He is thinking about love, and **would like to be nicer towards his girlfriend**. He rings her and they spend the night observing the sky together.*" The client is an alcoholic who does not have a girlfriend and realises that it is unlikely in his situation that he will find one. Nevertheless, it seems that a relationship is what he would like. He reverts to the theme of partnership often.

The need for a home. The open window might be the entrance to a squat. *"He enters the building. He is hoping nobody is in and he'll find some peace and quiet. He is wondering what's inside and whether he can stay there for a while. **He would like a home** that he didn't have to enter via a window. Perhaps it all works out well in the end, though possibly the police arrive.*" (VS, male)* The client slept rough for a rela-

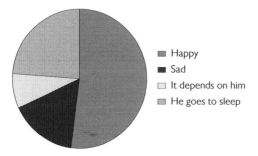

■ Happy
■ Sad
□ It depends on him
▨ He goes to sleep

Graph 49. The story's outcome (the graph shows relative frequency).

Picture 21. A person walking up stairs

tively short time only and was not satisfied with the life of a homeless person. We currently have no information regarding his whereabouts. The pointlessness of running away from home forms the main theme of the story told by TM (male). *"He **wants to run away from home**. He is convinced that nobody will catch him. He is wondering what the best thing to do is. He would like to stay at home and hopes that everything will work out for the best in the end. **Finally he decides to stay**, and he will never regret this decision."* The client grew up in an extremely dysfunctional family and ended up in a children's home. He had no opportunity to choose for himself, because he could not have remained at home under the circumstances.

Graph 50. Where the person is heading and what they are doing (the graph shows relative frequency).

The open window does not only evoke ideas of the future and a better life, but also concerns that things will turn out badly. The stories sometimes have specific contents that correspond to experiences from the clients' real lives, e.g. that the window provides a point of entry to a thief or someone who wants to sleep in the building. The theme of suicide also appears, with the possibility of jumping out of the window or running away from problems if a new opportunity does not appear on the horizon or nobody provides any assistance. The window is both the way out of an undesirable situation as well as a possible route to a better life.

The fifth picture is also part of the TAT test. It shows someone climbing up a spiral staircase, though it is not clear where the stairs lead. The picture might evoke the future and the idea of heading in the direction of a better life, or thoughts of one's own ambitions and the possibility of their realisation, as well as the risk of failure and hopelessness. The height might offer a good view, but it would also be possible to jump off.

The need for an open future. A upward path symbolically represents a **change for the better** that is not always easy. The interpretations offered by young homeless people often focus on their own future and the hope that life will get better. *"This person wants to go up. He expects the stairway to end. He's thinking about life. He would like a normal life and family. The stairs end and he starts to live a normal life." (SŽ, female)* This story is reminiscent of a fairytale in which someone is given a task and if they complete it they are rewarded. SŽ does not want to sleep rough and has found work and accommodation. KB (male) also knows that he has to do something for his future. *"He is walking so as to get somewhere. He is thinking about himself.* **He would like a good life**, *but knows that this depends on him."* The client, who is a drug addict, has not thus far managed to change for the better.

IK (female) also takes the stairs to be a symbol of the future. *"Logically speaking the stairs mean going forward into the future. He expects things to be better when he gets to the top.* **He is thinking about the future.** *He would like what everyone needs, a family and a future. The story ends well."* IK is unquestionably an intelligent woman but has been unable to deal with her situation up till now. The fact that she is a foreigner with no networks in Prague whatsoever does not help. She has a child with another homeless person, though the little boy is in alternative family care with the project Klokánek (Kangaroo). She is not a drug addict, is interested in working and usually has a job.

The theme of other stories is the need to keep from going under, i.e. the need to keep off the street. *"He wants to go up. He is waiting until he finally reaches the top. He is wondering whether he will once again end up on the bottom. He would like some stability in life. The story ends well and he remains on top." (ER, female)* The culmination of the story corresponds to reality, since ER has managed to remain "on top" and has a job and accommodation. The next story is less optimistic. *"This person is walking upstairs because the elevator is broken. His legs are hurting and he would like to be at the top. When the staircase ends, he collapses because he's sixty years* old and lives on the 12th floor. He has a heart attack, is taken away by an ambulance and dies on the way to hospital, because this is his third heart attack." (KM, female) The conclusion can be interpreted as meaning that **it is too late for change**, that nothing can be done, no matter how hard a person tries. KM is a client who suffers depression and anxiety. She lacks self-confidence and does not believe that anything will end well. Her approach to life is exemplified in the story. She is still sleeping rough though she is not a drug addict.

The need for self-realisation. Some of the stories are about **work**: what kind of work, whether it is satisfying, difficult, poorly paid, etc. *"He is going to work. He's building something. He starts to work. He's wondering whether it's nice outside. He would like more money and a beautiful girlfriend. But instead, he'll complete the daily plan and return home." (ZK, male)* It is clear that this person is not entirely satisfied with his work. It is a necessity, but a duty that he complies with. In reality ZK works only occasionally and admits that he is incapable of holding down a job for long. However, the idea of more stable work appears in his material often. Dissatisfaction with work features in another story. *"He's walking to a vantage point, so it's clear what he's doing. It will be a relief when the stairs come to an end. He'll say, at last I'm at the top. He has to walk up these stairs every day. He works on an observation tower. He would like better work where he didn't have to walk up stairs. And so **one fine day he decides to jack it all in**." (RB, male)* The story reveals a tendency not to do anything involving exertion. This reflects the client's real life. He does not have a job and relies on charities.

The existence of the need for self-realisation, even if unachieved in the end, is the basis of another story. *"He is climbing the stairs to a vantage point. When the stairs end there is a wonderful view of the landscape in front of him. He would like to climb even higher. **He would like to become a guide** to the regions of Bohemia and Moravia. But he can't pass the exams, he flunks them and becomes just a tourist." (LS, male)* The central character in this story would like to find a better job, but is incapable of completing the necessary task and remains a traveller who does not do anything useful. This corresponds to the client's own life.

The need for a home base. In the story told by KB (female) keys play an important role as a symbol of opening the way home. *"Maybe the person is on his*

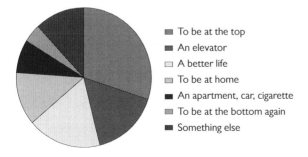

- To be at the top
- An elevator
- A better life
- To be at home
- An apartment, car, cigarette
- To be at the bottom again
- Something else

Graph 51. What the person climbing the stairs wants (the graph shows relative frequency).

way home. He is waiting to open the door to his apartment and wondering if he has the key on him. He would like to have the key. The story ends with him finding his keys and making himself a cup of coffee." The story ends happily, though given the client's circumstances (she is a drug addict with hepatitis C), this is more a case of wish fulfilment than a realistic possibility. The concept of home sometimes appears **in the form of memories** of what the client has lost. "*He is going up to the attic. He's going to look at some photographs and ask himself what he used to do. He would like to turn the clock back. He goes to the top of the stairs and remembers.*" (*JH, female*) The client left home of her own free will, but appears dissatisfied with her decision. One problem she has is that she spent most of her childhood with a foster family and never fully got over the loss of her biological mother. It is unclear which of her two homes she is thinking of.

The need for intimacy and a partner. Some stories relate to partnerships, either finding a partner or mourning their loss and hoping to find another. "*He is walking up the stairs in order to get where he needs to be and to be at peace. He walks along a long corridor into a large hall. He is thinking about his partner. His partner left him and he would like her back. He will sit at the top of the stairs and wait to see if she returns.*" (*MC, male*) The client does not have a girlfriend, though it is clear he would like one. He himself admits that his alcoholism and homelessness make this unlikely. The story can be interpreted as the client mourning his disappearing hopes. The central character in the story told by SK (male) finds a new girlfriend and more, though his interpretation of the picture belongs more to the next category (see the following paragraph).

The need to find meaning in life. "*He wants to walk upstairs. He wants to take in the wonderful view or get some fresh air and clear his head. He expects to feel good about himself, to feel that he's at the peak of his possibilities. He is thinking about the fact that this is a long trek. He would like to have a wife and kids. In the end he meets a single mother with a daughter and they get together. This person **finds the meaning of life.**" (SK, male*) The character receives his reward after making an effort. In real life the client has not been so lucky. He still sleeps rough and we do not know if he has any kind of ongoing relationships. The central character in the story told by TŽ (female) says openly that her **life has no meaning** and she does not want to carry on living. "*Perhaps he is going to commit suicide. When he gets to the top*

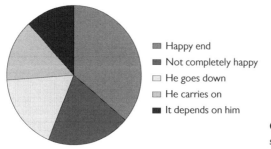

Happy end
Not completely happy
He goes down
He carries on
It depends on him

Graph 52. The story's outcome (the graph shows relative frequency).

of the stairs he will jump off. He is thinking about the fact that he has no pleasure from life. He would like everything to be different. In the end he hurls himself off." The client has experienced many traumatic situations and is dissatisfied with her life. She is a drug addict and most of her current problems stem from this. She has no support from her family. Stairs leading up can evoke feelings of depression and **suicidal tendencies**. *"He wants to climb to the top, and when he gets there he will hurl himself down. He is wondering about how long he will fall. He wants to kill himself. He jumps and dies." (LR, male)* The theme of suicide appears repeatedly in the case of this client. He is a drug addict who has been sleeping rough for four years.

A theme common to many of the stories regarding the last picture involves reflections on a better life and the hope that a change will take place that will bring something positive. Resignation, a lack of faith in the possibility of improvement and an attempt to end life also appear. Many young homeless people would like a job, a home and a relationship that would give life some meaning, but this tends to remain merely a dream. The central character of their stories usually waits passively to see what happens. Only a small number of clients concede that it is up to them and that they must do something in order to attain the desired objective.

4.2 THE TRANSFORMATION THAT TAKES PLACE AS A CONSEQUENCE OF LIFE ON THE STREET

If someone spends a considerable period of time sleeping rough, many changes take place. These changes affect their **habits, attitudes, abilities and personality traits**, as well as of course their self-identity. Certain abilities and skills may gradually be lost (a fact the homeless themselves admit), though others may be acquired that help a person survive under the circumstances in question. Often this will involve competencies that are not useful in other environments and may be even undesirable from the perspective of mainstream society. Such skills would include theft and the ability to survive without maintaining person hygiene. The longer a young person is on the street, the more they lose the chance of maintaining the skills and habits that are needed for a life in society and the more difficult their reintegration will be. Many studies bear this out, e.g. Auerswald and Eyre (2002). When a homeless person returns to society they have to undergo the reverse process and divest themselves of everything that would create a barrier.

The transformation of the personality of young homeless people takes place in four linked stages (Farrintgon and Robinson, 1999; Boydell et al., 2000):
- Phase 1, which lasts approximately a year. This can be called the **period of orientation and familiarisation with the street subculture and lifestyle** to which the individual must adapt. During this phase the main emphasis is laid on an ability to survive, independence, and the ability to cope with the bur-

dens faced by people sleeping rough. Their self-identity does not yet change because they are convinced that this is a temporary situation and that they will not be homeless in the future. *"**I don't regard myself as homeless**. Not at all. Sleeping outside doesn't mean anything." (LR, male)* The problem is that the change to their personality traits takes place regardless of what they themselves think of their life on the street. During phase 1 they have no doubt that they will return to society and most are convinced that the question is not if but when.

- Phase 2 is the second year on the street and is the **period of adaptation**. It is a time of relative stability. A person experiences the change of seasons and the specific features of their new social context, and deals with this in some shape or form. They accept their new lifestyle and acquire the necessary skills. As soon as they have learned to survive and to satisfy their basic requirements under these circumstances, they achieve relative composure. For a certain time they align their habits and attitudes with what is useful on the street, but may impede reintegration into society. However, most homeless people are unaware of this fact. They gradually become used to a life without any great demands, focus mainly on the present and do not think about the future, or put off thinking about a possible return indefinitely. They are more experienced and realise that life on the street is far from idyllic. They know that strong rivalries and a fight for scarce resources are being played out and that relationships between homeless people are not always problem free. They still have a tendency to rationalise occasional conflicts and dissatisfaction, though from time to time their equilibrium is disturbed and they consider making a change (Auerswald and Eyre, 2002).

  During this phase they commonly **deny that they belong to the homeless community** and define themselves using less pejorative terms. For instance, young homeless people may call themselves squatters. A certain ambivalence may arise and they may make an effort to differentiate themselves from the homeless community while at the same time becoming aware of their drift away from mainstream society. At this point they do not know exactly where they belong. *"I don't want to talk to people who can't understand how someone might be on the street. And I avoid those who are living on the street. **I don't want to belong to them**. I don't want people to see me entering this squat." (ES, female)* Another common strategy involves differentiating themselves from "typical" homeless people, who are filthy and smell. *"I wouldn't want to be like that on the street, all smelly. **I make every effort to be clean**, that's what I call being **normal**." (PV, male)* The gradual transformation of opinions into those characteristic of homeless people is a signal of a change in the understanding of their own existence. *"For me it was a slap in the face to suddenly find myself at the Salvation Army, among people I had always viewed as garbage. That's how I felt while I had somewhere to live, but over time I got used to them and realised **they're just normal people** like everyone else." (MP, male).*

This client is not yet willing to accept the identity of a homeless person, but realises that he has adapted to life on the street and is not happy about it. *"You get used to things. The problem is I hate the fact I'm adapting. Because **I'm starting to regard the situation I'm in as normal**. At certain moments it really bothers me that I'm so used to it that it seems normal to me. I see it in myself and I'm not at all happy about it."* (MM, male)

*"When I used to see a homeless person it was like, hey, look at them, what a sight! I'll never be like them, never ... **and now I am**. Now I've been sleeping at Central Station for six months, filthy..."* (TK, male) During this phase many young homeless people concede that a change of lifestyle is possible, but emphasise that they will maintain themselves on a suitable level and that this will not prevent them from reintegrating into society whenever they feel like doing so. Their opinion regarding the ease of returning to society usually changes after they have been sleeping rough for two years (Farrintgon and Robinson, 1999).

- **Phase 3. The consolidation of a homeless lifestyle** and the change of self-identity ensuing therefrom. During this period most people identify with some kind of homeless group and draw attention to its positive qualities. *"We're a kind of close-knit family and we don't let just anyone join us. Here I have loads of friends who help me."* (MB, female) During this period young homeless people now know that nothing much distinguishes them from other people on the street, even though they draw attention to certain differences as part of a defensive mechanism. *"The worst are the other homeless people, because **you see how you're identical to them**. I live on the street and I belong among them, that's the fact of the matter. It wasn't always like that."* They often say: we're not like them. We may be on the street but we're different from the old homeless people even if we worry that we'll end up like them. *"I don't like the dirty old geezers who smell out half of a tram so that you have to get off and wait half an hour for another. I don't understand how people can live like that. I hope I never end up sitting on the tram myself in that state."* (PČ, female)

"I'm also homeless, but I don't walk around so dirty. It's disgusting. When some old bloke sits on a bench pissed off his head on a carton of wine... It's horrible." (IH, female)

Phase 3 is an important milestone because during this period people gradually **lose control over their lives** and it becomes less and less likely they will be able to return to mainstream society. It is generally the case that the longer a person is sleeping rough the more they change and the more easily they take on the identity of a homeless person. *"I'm not ashamed. Ok, so I'm homeless. To be honest I don't give a damn what other people think, I've accepted it."* (MD, male) This client is getting used to a different lifestyle, his competences are changing, the negative consequences of various risky activities (drug addiction and alcoholism) are intensifying, his health is deteriorating (he has hepatitis C), and his social station is plummeting still further (he has spent time in prison). The accumulation of negative characteristics increases the tendency to identify with people who are in a similar situation, and this in turn makes leaving the street that much more difficult. More experienced homeless people have already made a few such attempts. Having failed, they are aware that returning to ordinary life will be more difficult than they thought. *"The worst thing is that **you can never drag yourself up**. Not to the top, but so that you can say to yourself 'I hit rock-bottom but now I'm better off than I used to be'. I'm afraid that I'll die on the street. I don't know if I'll ever drag myself out of this."* (KM, female) Client MT accepts things might change in the future, but right now has no plan to resolve anything. *"The worst thing is that I've become used to everything. I have everything I need, really, I'm used to things. **Maybe things will change in the future**, but right now I'm free to do what I want and I don't care if I get drunk or what I look like."* This client's main problem is his addiction to psychoactive substances.

- **Phase 4. Continuing desocialisation and personality deterioration.** This phase is typical for individuals who have been sleeping rough for some time and use drugs or alcohol. They now identify unambiguously with the homeless community and reject any kind of change. They are aware that there has been a change for the worse, that mainstream society has rejected them, but they are indifferent to this fact. They do not wish to concern themselves with problems that appear irresolvable and distance themselves from anything that would bother them or require that they make an effort. A typical strategy involves systematically escaping by means of alcohol and drugs and resigning themselves to survival and nothing else. Young homeless people only rarely reach this phase.

4.2.1 YOUNG HOMELESS PEOPLE'S OPINION OF THEIR OWN TRANSFORMATION

Our study's outputs show that a period of time spent living on the street influences not only opinions and attitudes but also self-conception. It is clear from what our cohort of young homeless people told us that their experiences change their overall **attitude to the world and life**. *"The biggest change was that **I hadn't realised what life is like, how difficult it is** in absolutely all aspects. I had everything I needed. It's that much more difficult when you had everything and then you lost it all."* (JŠ, male) The client left home without thinking about the consequences of his decision and only then began to realise what was involved. At the time the interview was conducted he had been living on the street for two years. TK (male) is an experienced client. *"I've started to **look at the world in a different, more detached way**. I don't see things in the normal way, it's different."* The experience of life on the street offers an overview that is not always positive. A person sees themselves and their surroundings and compares the present with what used to be in the past. Some people realise the extent of what they have lost and are sometimes able to admit that this was their own doing. *"I think that **you realise what mistakes you've made** and what situation you're in. What you had and no longer have." (PV, male)* In his case the awareness of his own errors did not result in his looking for a remedy.

Day-to-day confrontations with shortages and discomfort result in young homeless people **appreciating more ordinary items** such as food, warmth and a shower, i.e. things that they no longer take for granted. They begin to realise that they have to look after their basic needs and that this is not always such an easy matter. They are also aware that their demands have dropped. They do not always regard such a change as positive, but sometimes take it as proof of their own decline. *"Nobody who hasn't experienced it knows what it's like to search for food, to be starving hungry and to be glad to receive at least a bowl of soup. I'm grateful for it because now **I appreciate the fact that I have somewhere warm to lay my head**. You start to really appreciate the small things in life." (MB, female)*

*"You start to appreciate the traditional things, a shower, some food and warmth… **The normal things that wouldn't occur to most people**." (JB, male)* Values change. **The need to survive now takes precedence**, with other requirements less important.

"I have less money and people look at me differently. Right now the important thing is to have somewhere to sleep, something to eat, and, I don't know, to find some clean clothes from time to time. It's not important to have loads of money but to survive somehow." (VS, male)

This confrontation with reality leads young homeless people to **the awareness that nothing can be taken for granted**, and some of them begin to realise that it is up to them how they live in the future. They often ended up on the street as the consequence of an impulsive, ill-conceived reaction that exposes them to new burdens that they have to learn how to deal with. *"When I was still at home, when I had somewhere to live and had food on the table and everything I needed, I used to think that things grew on trees and that that's how things always would be. And now, when suddenly I'm on the street, I realise that **what I don't do for myself won't get done**, and so I've finally left the world of illusion and arrived in reality." (MP, male)* Acquiring an overview may be useful, though the question remains as to what extent this will influence his future actions. A factor standing in the way of any

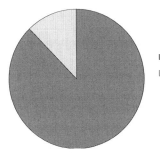

I've changed
I haven't changed

Graph 53. Clients' understanding of how they have changed under the influence of life on the street (the graph shows relative frequency).

change is the client's drug addiction and alcoholism and the lack of any functional base.

To most young homeless people it is clear that **their social status changed** as a consequence of opting for life on the street. They became part of a community that they themselves had previously despised but which they had gradually to become used to. The change in their opinion is manifest in a **more tolerant attitude toward other homeless people**. The company of individuals living on the street ceases to be unacceptable to them and as a means of retaining some self-respect they begin to perceive it as a standard social group. They accept a homeless existence as part of their identity, albeit with certain reservations, and for the moment do not admit that it will remain thus forever. Many of them begin to think about homelessness itself and the status of such people.

*"I didn't used to notice people living on the street. But now I'm also on the street **I can see how others despise them**, how they look at them, and I think that if they found themselves in the same situation they also wouldn't feel fantastic." (ŠZ, female)*

*"Now **I have a completely different attitude toward these people who live on the street**, because I understand their problems." (SŠ, male)*

*"I've begun to look differently at people living on the street. You can be accustomed to it and see it differently. Not all of them are to blame for their situation. Maybe **they would like to change but it isn't that easy**. I didn't judge them even before I found myself on the street, and now I understand them more." (MC, male)*

People living on the street feel that there are no clearly delineated boundaries between the various levels of mainstream society and homeless people and that the disdain of those in a better position is not always justified. This opinion acts as a defence mechanism, since they too belong among the homeless.

Young homeless people tend to judge themselves differently too. They are astonished by their own decline, something they couldn't have imagined previously, and have to deal with this disappointment. They have to admit to themselves that they have ended up like those that they previously condemned. *"**I would never have imagined that I would end up here**. I used to despise all such people. I wanted nothing to do with them, to my mind they were pariahs... even though I'm now one of them." (JP, male)*

*"I began to tell myself that it's a fucked up world and that I hate it. I was angry, but most of all I was angry at myself. I started to think about myself a lot and **to hate myself**. Yeah, things changed, the way I used to need everything. I used to visit restaurants and now I'm glad if I can get my hands on some crappy yoghurt." (TN, male)*

The awareness of one's own social decline is unpleasant and is countered by **various defence reactions**. This often means escaping with the aid of alcohol or drugs, or into fantasy. Mythomania provides a more acceptable version of one's own story. *"I don't think I'm completely stupid, I've got the feeling that I could achieve something, change something." JB (male)* On the whole young homeless people do not deny their social decline and the associated deterioration. Their **self-image suffers** as a consequence, they are angry at themselves, they sometimes express self-hatred, and over time resignation takes over. A person gets used to the idea that they are no longer what they used to be. *"To begin with I hated myself. I thought* **I was a loser***. Now I'm used to the idea. You have no choice, you have to get used to things." (AK, female)*

"I used to think that one day a prince would come and sweep me off my feet. I don't think that anymore. Now **I'm toothless, tattooed and ugly***, no prince would go for me. I know this because it's all behind me. He came and then escaped from me, poor thing."* *(IK, female)* This client is a drug addict and lived on the street for three years. At present we have no news of her whereabouts. LR (male) is also aware of his situation. *"I'm losing my self-confidence. I say to myself, 'come on you idiot, you're a junky'.* **I'm a homeless junky and everyone can see it***."* In this and many other such cases the client's deterioration is largely the result of the use of drugs and alcohol, which was also often the reason they found themselves on the street in the first place.

Many young homeless people **lose their self-confidence**, especially when they compare the current situation with the past or with people from mainstream society. Defence mechanisms prevent them from doing this too often. Instead they rationalise their situation and throw the blame on their circumstances, etc. However, it remains clear to them that they are worse off than previously. *"I began to believe that everyone was better than me. I don't have as much self-confidence,* **I don't believe in myself***. I think in terms of appearance I look normal. But what they have, I lack. I don't know how to behave like them, I don't have their knowledge, their property, etc. I don't do anything I could enjoy and that's the problem. Doing what I want whenever I want no longer does it for me. It's weird... you lose your ideas and you become more and more boring. Because try as you will, either you don't have the money or you've tried everything you can. You've forgotten languages, you've forgotten absolutely everything. Recently I've had a real problem with my intelligence.* **I'm really stupid***. Not even my vocabulary is what it used to be." (JP, male)* This is a client who lived on the street for more than three years. He takes drugs and has problems with relationships. From what he says it is clear that he is aware of his deterioration but is unable to change his lifestyle. In this respect, neither a relationship (which ended) nor fatherhood (the child ended up in temporary foster care organised by the Kangaroo project) has helped.

Young homeless people often believe that life on the street entails a certain deterioration, and that because of this **they have lost certain abilities** (though they have acquired other competences). The more experienced of them know that lazing around as a lifestyle choice has its negative consequences and that a person will pay dearly for their comfort. *"When you don't do anything but just laze around the whole time, you take a walk, sit down somewhere and look around and smoke, basically do fuck all, you go completely bonkers. In the last 14 months I've become completely thick." (JP, male)*

"I see the change in the way **I've become a complete fucking idiot***." (BČ, male)* This client is a drug addict and the deterioration in his abilities is unquestiona-

bly linked to this. He has now been on the street for four years. TK (male) also senses the unfavourable impact of using psychoactive substances. *"The more I took drugs, **the more they fucked up my head**. And yet when I was normal, I knew exactly where I was heading and how I should behave."* These are the words of a junky who has been sleeping rough for four years and died during a fire in a squat.

Other young homeless people tend more to notice **changes to their personality and a deterioration in social skills**. *"I didn't have what I had at home and had to look after myself. I began to realise that **what used to be a nice boy was turning into a bastard**. Loads of people told what was going on, so I let them think what they wanted to think and simply acted as I wanted."* (LC, male)

*"The activity when you're looking for work or, I don't know, when you're making an effort to get out of this rut… you no longer make the effort. **I've become lazier** is how I'd put it."* (MM, male)

*"**I began to become indifferent**. Some things that I used to consider important I stopped taking seriously."* (LS, male)

Illustration 22. Figures corresponding to regular representatives of the majority that are not conspicuous in any way. Those that drew the pictures, a man and a woman, have not identified with the homeless lifestyle. They would like to reintegrate into society and one of them has managed to.

Illustration 23. Idealised figures whose beauty and style do not correspond to reality. Those that drew the pictures have not identified with the homeless lifestyle. Both are trying to find work but have many other problems.

These are the voices of various clients who have been sleeping rough for different periods of time (from one to four years) but whose opinion of themselves is similar: 'I'm not what I used to be, something has happened to me and I'm unhappy about it'. However, it seems that again this does not provide strong enough motivation to encourage them to try to change their lives.

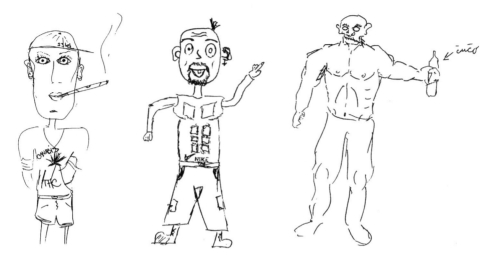

Illustration 24. Figures displaying typical signs of homeless or rebellious culture. Those that drew the pictures have identified emphatically with the homeless lifestyle. They have been living on the street for several years, take drugs, and show no signs of changing.

Illustration 25. A drawing symbolically depicting personal decline and the conviction that the future holds no hope (the broken branch on the right). The person who drew this picture is incapable of holding down a job and was thrown out of his family because of his intolerable behaviour. He is incapable of attempting to find a more effective solution to his life and remains in a passive, parasitical position.

Several homeless people are aware of the fact that under the influence of life on the street their **experience and perception of various events** has changed. They have become more indifferent and apathetic, or, on the contrary, are more irritable than they used to be. It is clear that these effects do not only have to be caused by a homeless lifestyle, but can sometimes be the result of using psychoactive substances, either alcohol or drugs.

*"I've definitely changed. I used to be a sort of clown, nothing could unsettle me. **Nowadays the slightest thing can completely throw me.**" (MM, male)*

*"**I've lost a sense of inner calm**. I have no idea what I'll be doing tomorrow." (MH, male)*

*"**I'm beginning to become pessimistic in outlook**, kind of depressed, as though a light has been switched off in me. But I don't do anything about it. I simply sit and scowl at people." (JP, male)*

Life on the street obliges a person to **pick up new skills** that from the perspective of mainstream society are unacceptable or demeaning, and to begin with homeless people view these skills in the same way. However, over time they begin to take them for granted or even as a source of entertainment and excitement. It is clear that after a certain time they stop distinguishing between what is acceptable and what not. *"**I picked up a few habits, street habits**. Rummaging around in garbage cans, 'mining' as we say. To begin with I felt terrible. People were walking past and looking at me as I rummaged around in garbage cans and I thought that was as low as I could go. I didn't want to do it, but then I became used to it. I told myself I had to survive somehow. And then it started to be fun." (MH, female)* The question is how something of this kind can amuse or excite someone. Is it the manifestation of a need to provoke a society that rejects the homeless, a search for substitute stimulation, or simply a reaction consisting of a change of approach to the activity in question? One thing is clear: thanks to these kinds of activities the gap between the homeless and members of mainstream society gradually widens.

The opinions homeless people have of themselves and their transformation under the influence of sleeping rough is not always negative, but sometimes **contains positive characteristics**. Maintaining a reasonable level of self-respect requires that a person find something in themselves that can be respected and thus ameliorate the frustration caused by the increase in negative characteristics. This is most often the ability to survive and look after oneself. *"I hated myself for how low I'd fallen. On the other hand I said that **I had proved something, I had proved I could survive here**." (TN, male)*

"The fact that I have to look after myself, that things have changed and I have to provide for myself. My self-confidence has grown." (MK, male)

The character of **self-identity is manifest in the drawing**. (Clients were asked to draw a human being in any way they wanted to and were able. Some of the drawings simplified the figure, but many were interesting.) The drawing did not always have to be a self-portrait. It was often a depiction of a certain type that the individual in question accepted as the identification standard. This might be average and inconspicuous, idealised, as well as possessing signs of the homeless community.

4.3 SUMMARY OF HOW YOUNG HOMELESS PEOPLE PERCEIVE THEMSELVES AND RATE THEIR TRANSFORMATION

Young homeless people rate themselves somewhat differently to their contemporaries in mainstream society. However, **their opinion of themselves corresponds to reality** and the results obtained using various different methods match up. They regard themselves as sociable, gregarious, good at striking up contact with others, but also unreliable and incapable of maintaining long-term relationships. These may be their primary characteristics, though may also reflect the fact that life on the street both requires and therefore intensifies such attributes. Nobody has sufficient privacy and if other people bothered them it would be difficult to survive for long. The facts also bear out something else that young homeless people say of themselves, namely that they are not very responsible, that they enjoy having fun without taking into consideration the consequences of their behaviour. The postponement of a more effective resolution is also a manifestation of irresponsibility. Some young homeless people admit that they are emotionally unstable, hot-tempered, get angry easily and lack self-control. This last point is another reason why they are unable to live in mainstream society. On the street they do not have to control themselves to such an extent. They are aware that they are unable to meet duties and abide by ordinary rules. In addition, they do not regard a lack of self-regulation as a negative trait, but more as a manifestation of their individuality and independence, something they rate more highly than conformism.

Personality traits intensify a tendency to a certain lifestyle. Young homeless people are conspicuously more impulsive in their actions, something that is visible in their tendency to react without forethought. This relates to their lack of persistence and self-control, which then feeds into difficulties managing ordinary demands and escape strategies. Impulsiveness is linked with a craving for new, intense experiences that is manifest in the case of young homeless people in an affinity for an unconventional lifestyle, insufficient social inhibitions, and the use of psychoactive substances. We can assume that some young homeless people are temperamental in character and that this increases the risk of non-standard behaviour, though in the case of many their upbringing and family background was also inadequate. Their parents may have evinced similar traits, which may be one possible reason for the breakup of the family and the poor upbringing provided the offspring.

It is clear that there is a decrease in tolerance for many stimuli and an increased **tendency to react aggressively**. Young homeless people are unable to control their behaviour and gauge what effect it will have, and for many this is not even important. They are prepared to punish anyone who offends them in any way. Faced with depression and feelings of unpleasant stress, often related to drug use, they react aggressively. They are used to acting in this way and in their community aggression is accepted as something that is unpleasant for those around but relatively common. Mainstream society on the contrary requires control and management of unacceptable conduct, which means that from the point of view of a possible return to society, these traits as evinced by the homeless represent a significant barrier.

Young homeless people are aware of how they have changed during the course of their time on the street. It is clear to them that this change is not a good thing but **sometimes a change for the worse**. They steal, cheat each other, anaesthetise themselves with drugs and alcohol, and in order not to suffer prefer not to reflect on their life. They know that they are incapable of controlling their conduct so as not to create unnecessary problems. They are unable to bring themselves to meet even the minimum duties and cannot deal with ordinary levels of frustration. If they do not want to do something, they do not do it. They express a lack of interest in and indifference to what happens to them or what the future will bring. They have no ambition and many lack any kind of motivation. Sometimes they regret the way they have ended up. Sometimes they are capable of seeing their own situation objectively and not regarding their failure as being exclusively the fault of other people. Despite this, however, they are usually unable to do more than regard their own decline with resignation. On the other hand they appreciate their ability to survive on the street and look after themselves. The freedom offered by a homeless lifestyle is sometimes highly regarded for a certain period of time, especially if the individual concerned has not suffered an especially traumatic event. (Similar conclusions were reached by Thompson et al., 2006.) It will be interesting to examine how they visualise the future.

5. HOW YOUNG HOMELESS PEOPLE VISUALISE THEIR FUTURE

Young homeless people are focused on the present and do not concern themselves with anything that could harass them in some way. Most do not reflect on where life will take them. They accept what it brings and make no attempt to change anything. If they begin to think of the future at all, they tend to be more optimistic than the older members of this community and have more positive expectations. Though they speak of their anxieties and worries, they believe that their situation will improve over time. *"I simply make the most of life. I don't accept anything negative and I think positively. You have to learn how to live this way and **I hope things turn out well**. I have hope and **I don't allow myself to get down thinking about what happened in the past**, because this doesn't help you." (LL, male)* This client did not have it easy in the past. He comes from a dysfunctional family dominated by an alcoholic father. In his early adolescence he started taking drugs and developed hepatitis C. He was also prosecuted for theft.

Most young homeless people think that opting for a life on the street is a matter for them to decide and that everything else will follow naturally. After a certain period of time they discover that returning to society will not be as easy as they had imagined. They react in various ways to this realisation, usually by putting off such a move. Life on the street involves falling into an undemanding routine and an unwillingness to do anything requiring effort. Comfort, indolence, a lack of willpower and the absence of that persistence that is essential if change is to take place form an impediment. Some young homeless people **speak of their dreams and wishes**, which include stable accommodation, a job, the need for a more permanent relationships, etc. However, they are unable and unwilling to raise a finger to realise them. They present such dreams as a desirable alternative to their future that is still far off, but do not exclude the possibility of attaining it. (Boydell et al., 2000; Miller et al., 2004).

Leaving a life on the street is fraught with difficulty, if it takes place at all, and often lasts a long time. It involves the **necessity to undergo the inverse initiation**. The individual must learn how to operate within the framework of mainstream society, create a new identity, establish new bonds with people (or renew old bonds), and change their mode of behaviour. It is not easy to adapt to such a radical change of lifestyle, because someone who has been homeless lacks the necessary habits and abilities. One of the main **impediments to returning to society** is an inadequate education that makes an individual's position on the job market precarious, and undesirable habits, e.g. the inability to keep to a given timetable. Other significant problems include accumulated debts, a criminal record, drug addiction and alcoholism, and the hepatitis C ensuing therefrom (in other countries this would be AIDS) (Garrett et al., 2008).

An anchorage in the homeless community, which is important in terms of survival on the street, can also put the brakes on attempts to change. Leaving the street is also influenced by the **degree of identification with a homeless lifestyle**, the level of desocialisation, and personality changes that have taken place. If their attempt is to be successful, an individual must have strong internal motivation and must be willing to accept the rules of mainstream society and the ensuing restrictions. Meeting these demands is difficult for young homeless people. When they speak of a possible return to society, they often link this with considerations of all manner of problems and impediments, which then serve as an argument as to why they have thus far been unsuccessful. *"Everyone would like to get off the street, but it's not as easy as it sounds." (JH, male)*

"It's not easy to change. You have to be in it for the long haul." (LR, male) Neither of these clients has yet found the motivation to make the attempt.

Many young homeless people **return to society for a limited period of time**. They are unable to deal with normal life and soon find their way back to the street. The cycle of departure and return may be repeated several times. *"**The street is a vicious circle. Everyone returns here at least once**. It's difficult. I've tried it a few times, but ... I found a job and a place to stay, but after six months I was back among the same people. And then I found a job, for six months I had accommodation, and then back again. It was because of alcohol and also because in a way I missed the freedom of the street." (MP, male)* As is clear from what he says, this is a client who is an alcoholic and has no base of any kind that would oblige him to find a more effective solution to his situation and would support him. The attempts made by other people follow a similar course. For a third of them the demands of mainstream society are so unpleasant and onerous that they give up the idea of a normal lifestyle. They often portray their return to homelessness as liberation from a stereotype and the various restrictions of normal life, including the necessity to subordinate their daily regime to duties, to manage their finances, not to steal, take drugs, etc. Life on the street requires nothing of this kind from them and may appear all the more attractive for that. Sometimes this is simply a rationalisation of their failure and a need to explain it in such a way that they maintain at least some acceptable level of self-respect (Ayerst, 1999; Garrett et al., 2008).

It is clear from the interviews we conducted that young homeless people are aware of what has happened to them and the fact they have changed for the worse. However, it is not clear whether they are able to prevent a further decline and willing to do something to change their life. Most of them say that **they would like to return to society and believe they will succeed**. *"It's a horrible life on the street. You look for any way you can out of it. If they accept me for that job on Tuesday, **I think things will be ok** and I should be off the street by winter." (KB, male)*

The client was successful and after two years on the street now lives in a boarding house and has a job. KV (female) is realistic regarding her chances. *"I would like to have a job and some kind of base, a place to stay, and if I had a child some day, then I hope it won't end up in a children's home but has a proper family. I need to find a job, I don't care what I do as long as it's paid. Even if I were in a refuge, the main thing is a job, because without work it's not possible."* The client spent a considerable part of her life in an institution and knows what she is talking about. Although she lives on the street, she is attempting to resolve her situation and so far succeeding. During the two years following the interview she found accommodation in a refuge and has a job.

However, the dreams and wishes of young homeless people are **not always realistic**. Sometimes they represent an idealised image that not even the individual themselves believes could be realised. They nevertheless provide interesting information regarding their personality. *"Of course I'd like to have a house, a car, a beautiful young girl who's stupid and who I can treat as I want, who's not a gold-digger."* *(RK, male)* This is a client who moved back and fro between a problematic family and a children's home. He is addicted to crystal meth, has served a prison sentence for grievous bodily harm, and during this time was diagnosed as suffering dissocial personality disorder. It is clear from the interview we conducted with him that he has been handicapped by early emotional deprivation. The outlook does not look good. MS (male) also has a completely unrealistic idea of his own life. *"The main thing I would like is a job paying CZK 25,000 (approximately USD 1,260). I'd like to have my own apartment paid up, so I had some security and couldn't lose it, and a good car. Another thing I'd like is one of those mobile homes."* This is a person with a low IQ and dissocial personality disorder who is unable to think realistically or act appropriately.

Not only does the **return to society** involve overcoming many problems, but people used to complete freedom may find such a life boring, stereotypical and restrictive. As a result, several of them reach the conclusion that it is not worth the effort. They have become used to not having any duties and we can assume

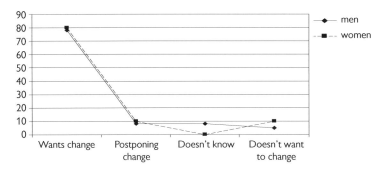

Graph 54. How young homeless people view their future life (the graph shows relative frequency).

that the complete collapse of a daily regime has damaged their self-regulatory abilities (which had never been particularly advanced). Adaptation to a homeless lifestyle sees people make **less of an attempt to change things** and become increasingly indifferent to negative consequences. Homeless people gradually reconcile themselves to their situation and are less and less willing and able to attempt to achieve an objective. They are aware of the way they are and though dissatisfied by this fact they do nothing to improve their situation. *"It's Catch-22, Why look for work, achieve a certain standard of living, walk around with a mobile telephone, well dressed, looking good… then suddenly suffer another setback and you go right back to the beginning. So I'd rather not go anywhere so as not to end up where I started." (RK, female)* The client is still sleeping rough two years after our interview, has no accommodation or job, and has given up the search.

Despite all the doubts they have and their aversion to a fundamental resolution of their problems, most young people **at least think about changing their life**. For the time being they do not wish to concede the possibility that life on the street might last forever. They are aware of the possible negative consequences of a homeless existence, would like to live like other people, but often get no further than expressing this desire in words. However, even thinking about an acceptable future may alleviate the unpleasant feelings of exclusion. When someone talks about something, then at last they draw closer to the desired outcome on a symbolic level. *"I am always trying to leave life on the street. I don't want to start liking it here. I'm always looking for some kind of work. But the paradox is that I didn't give a thought to finding a job for more than six months. I simply couldn't be bothered. I switched my brain off and I wasn't bothered whether I was on the street or wherever. Then something happened, I don't know what, but I do know that **I started wanting to live a normal life**. I suddenly knew that life on the street simply wasn't for me, because you've got nowhere to go. You start to envy those people and their comfortable lives." (JJ, male)* The client finally managed to quit the street. He has accommodation, a job and a girlfriend, with whom he is expecting a child.

MM (male) is dissatisfied with his life. *"I never thought that when I was twenty-five I'd be here. I thought I'd have a job, a relationship, a kid on the way, an apartment with a mortgage… something along those lines. I'm not happy with the way things have worked out. **I want to get myself out of this rut and operate normally**. That's my aim for the future."* Despite his dissatisfaction, the client is still sleeping rough. During the two years since the interview he has spent more time in prison and the future for him does not look bright.

From the perspective of young homeless people, **putting off the moment when they have to resolve their situation** may represent an acceptable compromise. This does not mean that a client wishes to remain on the street, though neither does it mean that they want to resolve matters immediately and are willing to take the necessary measures. They will resolve matters later, when the moment is right, when the conditions are ideal, etc. Deferring matters is a typical strategy of young homeless people that, while resolving nothing, maintains the hope that someday their life will improve. *"I want to change everything and nothing. Ok, I want to change things, but **gradually**. It would help if I had some kind of base, my own accommodation or a boarding house, so I knew that after work I would be returning home, that someone would be waiting for me who provided me with support."* (MS, female) The client is still sleeping rough. Given that she is a drug addict, resolving her situation will not be easy. Her relationships have not been very successful and have certainly not provided her with support. If anything, they have had the opposite effect.

TN (male) feels similarly, *"For once in my life I would like to achieve something and I think **I still have enough time for that**. I would love to make a living through music. I'd like to go to university. It's not certain, but they're crossing their fingers and saying* (at the centre) *that it's clear I have what it takes. It's really my dream, even though I don't always do everything I could to achieve it because I lack the psychological strength. But if you want something enough you'll achieve it."* Thus far the client has made no fundamental change. He was diagnosed as having depressive syndrome and borderline personality disorder and was hospitalised in a psychiatric ward. Nevertheless, thanks to the support he receives from his family he has a certain chance. The interviews, especially those we conducted with men, reveal an **ambivalence as to what the individual actually wants**. *"I regard sleeping rough as a kind of holiday. On the one hand I like it, on the other it depresses me. I'm trying to quit the streets as quickly as I can. Yeah, on the one hand I get off on it and on the other I want out. I say I want out, except I don't seem to be heading uphill but downhill."* (JŠ, male) In this client's case, the endeavour to improve his situation prevailed. Over the past two years the client has found a job and lives in a lodging house.

An important reason why young homeless people consider giving up life on the street, despite the difficulty involved and their repeated failure, is the fear that they might become as decrepit and neglected as those they see on a daily basis around them. *"I'm trying not to sink any lower."* (LS, male) From their perspective this lifestyle is acceptable only for the **young, in whom similar excesses are expected** (prolonged adolescent moratorium) and when it should not have such fateful consequences. *"I'm fully aware that **things can't carry on like this forever**. But it's ok to live this lifestyle for a certain period of time, but not forever of course."* (MD, male) This client managed to return home and slept rough for just under a year. The age limit at which a lifestyle without responsibilities is acceptable has been pushed back to 30 years, which corresponds to the tolerance shown by mainstream society toward similar experiments. LB (male) believes thirty is the right age to think about changing lifestyle. *"I can't imagine still sitting here and taking drugs at the age of 30. **At 30 I'd like to life in a different way**."* Though the client, who was 26 at the time the interview was carried out, would like to live differently, it is far from clear whether he will manage this because of his drug addiction.

Our group included people who **did not want to change their lifestyle**. These are often drug addicts, individuals suffering psychological problems, e.g. depression, or people who have nobody close to them who might help them.

"I don't even want to change my life. I have a job (she sells the street magazine Nový prostor [New Space]), *I have everything I need. I'm not lacking in anything, and in any case nobody and nothing is going to help me." (LB, female)* The client rejects all offers of assistance and is one of the few who says openly that she enjoys life on the street. It is possible that she is putting on a brave face on things, since she has attempted to commit suicide several times, a fact that hardly indicates satisfaction and a balanced mind. However, it is highly likely that she is not planning to reintegrate into mainstream society, something that is also true of IC (male). *"Firstly, I have everything I need here, and secondly, everything other people have I can have too, and thirdly, **it suits me the way things are.**" (IC, male)* This client has slightly different reasons for being against change. He grew up in a children's home and has been living on the street for four years. He is one of a small number of young homeless people to walk around dirty and unkempt. He claims he has no reason to make an effort, since he has no family or partner. At present he is serving a prison sentence for theft.

5.1 THE REQUIREMENTS AND BARRIERS TO RETURNING TO MAINSTREAM SOCIETY – THE OPINION OF YOUNG HOMELESS PEOPLE

An important condition underpinning a return to society is finding a job. However, the question arises as to where a young homeless people would look for work, if at all. It is interesting to see how many people worked, even if only occasionally, during their time on the street. A quarter of them managed to find at least temporary work, and this can be taken as one of the conditions of a possible improvement of their social position. However, it is clear that finding a job as a homeless person will be difficult. As Marek, Strnad and Hotovcová (2012) point out, the lack of personal documents, a criminal record, insufficient

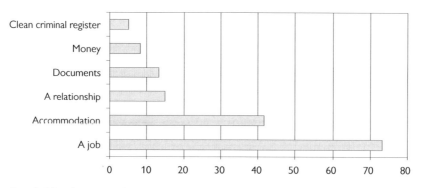

Graph 55. What young homeless people think might help them return to society (the graph shows relative frequency).

qualifications, no contact address, as well as an untidy appearance and the poor reputation they have as workers, are factors that reduce their chances. In addition, some of them have unrealistic ideas regarding their own abilities or the wages they might expect to receive, and this prevents them from accepting what work might be available to them. Many employers have a poor experience with them, because they are unreliable and often absent. Others reject them out of hand because the status of homeless person is automatically linked with various negative attributes. On the other hand, homeless people are often abused by certain employers, especially if they work without a contract, something that is common. Temporary and cash-in-hand jobs do not only mean that the employer does not pay national insurance contributions, but often that an individual does not receive any money for the work they have done, or far less than was agreed on. It is difficult for someone in this situation to fight back.

If young homeless people reflect upon their future realistically, it is clear to them that they must first find a job and stable accommodation. *"When spring starts we'll find a job. During winter there's nothing much available. But come spring we'll both go to work and look for some small cottage where we can at least take a shower. The main thing is to **find a job and a place to stay**, and then things become possible."* (VL, *female*) At present the client is living in a hostel, has a new boyfriend, is working, albeit without a contract, and her situation has stabilised somewhat. More experienced homeless people tend to have more modest ambitions as regards the work available to them, because they are aware that without the requisite qualifications and experience it is not easy to find a job. *"I don't want to live on the street. What would help me? A job, definitely, in my area of expertise, though **I'd take anything on offer**. Work always helps. Nothing else saves you from this shit."* (*JH, female*) Though the client has found temporary work, two years on she still lives on the street because she does not have enough money to pay for accommodation.

MD (*male*) is actively trying to find work. *"**I want to find a job as quickly as possible** and accommodation. But if I can't find a place to stay, it doesn't matter. The important thing is a job. I looked on the internet and I went to that JOB club on the internet. I rang around a few places and had a few interviews. So far I've had no success,*

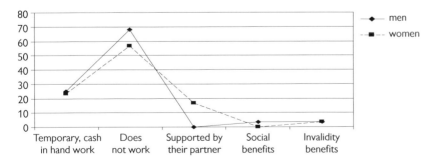

Graph 56. Work on the street (the graph shows relative frequency).

though I meet their conditions. I've had four interviews. As soon I have accommodation and a job I'll feel calmer inside, more composed, and I'll know that if I have a job and manage to hold it down, then in a month's time I'll be paid and I'll live a bit better than I do at present. After that **things will gradually get better**." In the end the client found work and returned home. SP (male) feels similarly. "*I know that it's important to have a job and to hold it down **even though it might be less well paid**. But you have to hold onto that job. When you work your values are slightly different.*" This client too has found a job and no longer lives on the street. Both these clients slept rough for less than a year and had had experience of work before leaving home.

Many young homeless people **worked while there were jobs available** and had no problems. But now **the jobs have dried up** or there is nothing for unqualified people like them. "*I'd like to find a permanent job, somewhere to rent and maybe save for a holiday. I went for a job, just as a cleaner, and they wanted the baccalaureate. I mean that's a pretty tough requirement. I have to have gone to university to clean an office, that's a bit crazy, isn't it?*" (ZK, female) This is the third time the client has found herself sleeping rough. She says she does not want to live in this way, but has been unable up till now to change her life. This may be due to her drug habit. LC (female) also had a problem finding work. "*I went to work as a cleaner with a Ukrainian woman in Smíchov. It seemed to me at that time that it was poor work. Because I never had any problem with work. Even at the agencies there was loads of work. There was never no work. There was always some kind of cash-in-hand job for a day. But now not even the agencies… They want to see your criminal register. I travel to Žižkov, to the job centre, and there's simply bugger all.*" The client has a criminal record, which makes it difficult for her to find work. Nevertheless, from time to time she is successful and has a chance of improving her life situation. She is held back by problematic partners, who by no means offer assistance and support.

Most young homeless people are disadvantaged by the fact that **they have no qualifications** and would therefore earn very little even in a full-time job, always supposing they could find one. Sometimes their wages do not even cover the cost of accommodation. If in addition they are supposed to repay debts, they stop being motivated to work. Furthermore, they have never learned how to manage their finances, and life on the street has intensified this problem. Some of them have high expenses related to drug use. Their close contact with a group that is used to spending any funds acquired immediately is yet another burden. Their inability to manage their finances and the knowledge that those without work will leech off them further reduces their willingness to work.

Our cohort contains many people who have experience of **employers failing to abide by their original agreement**. It is difficult for them to do anything about this and they tend to accept the fact, because otherwise they would lose the hope that things will work out better next time around. "*I worked for an agency in T. They promised me the world. They said that we would celebrate Christmas in a warm hostel. **We worked there for four days and then they told us that our contract had terminated** and we could go home.*" (IK, female) This client found another job, but her income was insufficient for accommodation. JŠ (male) ended up in a similar situation. *"I had a temporary job at the airport. I was one of the cleaners. My job was to drive around on one of those carts cleaning the floor. They problem was that **they didn't offer me any contract and got rid of me**. I should receive some back pay but so far I haven't."* This client returned home and resolved his situation at least temporarily. JB (male) was another not to receive pay for a cash-in-hand job. *"Yeah, **I have a cash-in-hand job** digging trenches. This time round I've probably got work until next Wednesday, though it's not certain. **So far I haven't received any money**. I've worked three days, but you how it is. They know I need the money because I made it clear that they weren't going to intimidate me."* The client travelled to England to be with his relatives and we have had no information regarding his whereabouts since then.

There is no doubt that it is not always easy finding work. However, the conduct and attitudes of young homeless people can also militate against their chances. Though most say they would like to find work, many of them are also aware that **they have no real desire to take on commitments**. They are inclined to be sceptical about the possibility of finding work right from the outset. *"I believe that I'll get out of this rut. I don't want to remain on the street. But for instance tomorrow, when I again fail to get that temporary job, my whole situation will again be complicated. I'm afraid of not getting myself off the street. It's no easy matter finding work these days. And another fuck up is that when you don't have anywhere to live, **when you're sleeping rough, it's difficult to go to work**. It's not really on, living on the street and going to work." (ZK, male)* This client is an alcoholic, which is one of the reasons he is unable to find and hold down a job. In addition, he has a criminal record. He has been living on the street for four years.

Many young homeless people know that they would find it extremely difficult to get up every morning and spend a considerable part of their lives at work. The idea of permanent work and a regular salary is attractive, but inertia and indolence tend to prevail. *"I would like to find a job and somewhere to live. I would do anything to make a bit of cash to start with. You have to want to find work and **also you have to want to go to work**. In any case, half of the people sitting here will be back on the street in a few years." (MH, female)* The client never held down a job for long. As she says, *"I used to go to work. I had a job for a month recently, but I came back to the street. I handed in my notice and told them I was heading back to the street."* It is not clear why she acted in this way and what she has in mind, but it is clear that she will not hold down a job. She has no base and her experience of life is such that she has no useful skills. She spent her childhood alternating between an alcoholic mother who was also a drug addict and a children's home. After temporary episodes she keeps returning to the street.

MK (male) makes no special effort to find work. *"I need to find work and live normally. It's no problem finding a job, though **I haven't yet looked for one**."* He worked for a while, but left his job because it didn't interest him. *"I worked for a cleaning firm. I started in winter when we cleared the snow, cleaned the pavements. Then came spring when we cleared up the mess left by winter, and then started cutting grass.*

I left because the pay was rubbish, and because I didn't get on with the people. I simply stopped liking the work." The client is not interested in working and if he finds a job he is incapable of holding onto it. He is a drug addict who has been sleeping rough for four years and has no work at present.

MS (male) justifies his unwillingness to work by citing low pay. *"I'm always hearing that I should find a job. But my answer is always the same. As soon as someone offers me CZK 15,000 (approximately USD 760) a month or more, then I'll work. But not a single crown less. So if they offer twelve or thirteen thousand, then the job's not for me, I'm not interested. **After the probationary period I need at least twenty thousand net**, because with ten thousand I'd still have to rummage around garbage bins. If someone gives you CZK 10,000, what kind of salary is that? It's shit money. I can't find work where I'd earn decent money. If I had some money I could pay rent. I don't have money so I can't pay rent."* This is a client with a low IQ, no professional qualifications and a criminal record, who receives invalidity benefit because of psychological problems. He has been sleeping rough for four years.

TD (female) openly admits she has no desire to work. *"I wanted to find some kind of work, but somehow or other didn't. **It's kind of nice not having to go to work**, just lounging around somewhere. When you realise that you live fairly well without any work, you don't really feel much like working."* This woman has never worked. She lives with her mother and looks after her daughter, whom she had with another homeless person. PČ (female) feels similarly. *"**I kept on putting off getting a job**. I used to say to myself, 'Ok, this is the last year I'll just have a good time. Come winter I'll get a job'. But I've been saying that for three years now. It's a right old fuck up."* During the past two years the client has served a prison sentence. She is a drug addict and there appears little chance of her turning her life around. She has been sleeping rough for five years.

TK (male) is another who felt little inclination to work. *"When I came out of prison I didn't really want to work. I had money, I wasn't stealing or anything. I lived on this and then I lost my documents. I had new documents drawn up and right now I'm on holiday. I'm recharging my batteries. This isn't laziness, I just don't feel like working. Especially right now. Right now I wouldn't be able to find any work I liked. If I could, I'd like to work in a hospital, but firstly the work is physically and psychologically tiring, and secondly it pays really badly. **Right now I'm on holiday recharging my batteries.**"* The client died during a fire at a squat and had been sleeping rough without a job. The people who do not want to work tend to be drug addicts or alcoholics. Their addiction to psychoactive substances is the main cause of their problems, including the very fact that they are homeless. The argument that there is no work to be found or that they cannot find anything they would like to do is clearly an example of rationalisation.

Some young homeless people frown on laziness and an unwillingness to work in others, especially in the case of those whom they place in a different category, and yet do not work themselves. *"I try to avoid other homeless people, the boozers sitting around parks and so on. Other homeless people get on my nerves. For instance, here where Naděje is based.* **Every day I hear them bullshitting about how they'd like to find a job and yet every day I see them here.** *After two months I ask them if they're working and they tell me they're not but that they're looking for a job. Yeah, well I'm looking too,* **but I'm really trying.** *They say they are and then I see them with a carton of wine in their hands and that doesn't much look like looking for work to me."* (PP, male) People are often critical of precisely that which they themselves are guilty of too. They are not happy with their situation but are unable to deal with it and shift their condemnation onto someone else. They are better than the rest because they are making an effort. After two years PP is in a similar situation to the homeless in Naděje, though the truth is that if he finds a temporary job then he works. He does not have a problem with drugs or alcohol.

Young homeless people claim there are many reasons preventing them from working. One of these is a **lack of documents and the difficulties of obtaining new ones.** Someone with no documents is totally anonymous. They do not exist in the eyes of society and are not taken into account (though nobody can have any expectations of them either). As soon as they have documents, they become a tangible person with rights and duties in the eyes of the authorities. Obtaining replacement documents, especially an ID card, in which endeavour they are given assistance by the employees of Naděje, is not objectively demanding but from a subjective point of view means crossing the boundary of anonymity. This, along with inertia, is another possible reason why certain homeless people attempt to put off the evil moment with the excuse that *"I would have left the street long ago, but without an ID card I can't do anything."*

AM (male) had to sort out problems with documents. *"I definitely want to go to work and begin to live a normal life and find a hostel. But* **I can't find work because I haven't got a single document.** *I'm waiting for them. I've been trying to obtain*

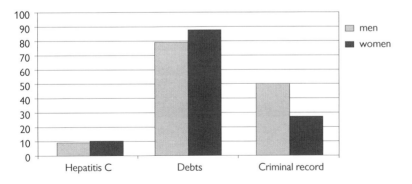

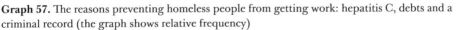

Graph 57. The reasons preventing homeless people from getting work: hepatitis C, debts and a criminal record (the graph shows relative frequency)
NB: The debts that are common within the homeless community include unpaid national insurance, fines, fees for various services, e.g. a stay in a drunk tank or refuge, etc. Other categories involve debts arising from credit fraud and outstanding loans.

documents for a whole year unfortunately. And my birth certificate, which I received in March, I lost the very next day. I'm lazy, I have to change a bit because I'm incredibly lazy." Despite all his protestations the client eventually received his documents and is currently working and lives in a hostel. An ongoing quest for documents is a feature of IK's (male) life. "*The thing is, I get drunk and lose my ID card, so I have to wait a month, and then I get drunk again and have to wait for another. I hope all this comes to an end soon, because right now I'm just waiting for an ID card. I'm going to wait until I find a job or I lose my ID card again. I spend my life waiting. **I'm always waiting for something, and when I get what I was waiting for I lose it again**.*" The client is an alcoholic who has been sleeping rough for three years. As well as losing his documents he has other problems. He is incapable of going to work regularly even when he finds a job. He became homeless because of alcohol. It is unlikely there will be any fundamental change to his lifestyle in the foreseeable future.

Young homeless people know that someone with a criminal record will find it difficult to get work. "*It's really difficult to find work with this suspended sentence hanging over me. Everyone wants an extract from the criminal record.*" *(PP, male)*

"*People who have documents can have an extract from the criminal register and they're clean. People who, for instance, have hepatitis C can't get normal work because nobody will take them on.*" *KM (female)* Only of course if they admit to this fact, something they do not have to do, because not every employer asks about an applicant's state of health.[6] It is more likely that their health problems will render them incapable of working.

Homeless people often have **debts**, which because of their lax approach accrue to such an extent that they are unable to repay them. Many of them are convinced that they could manage to find work, but because **they face repossession proceedings**, they would lose the money that they earned. This is far from being a motivating thought, and so repossession proceedings constitute a significant impediment to returning to normal life. "*Right now I'd like a temporary job or something like that in order to save some cash. For the first time since I started sleeping rough I'm going to claim benefit, so at least I'll be able to save the odd crown. Then either I'd rent a little cottage... But I'll be up front about it: if I get a proper job as I wanted to do, because I've now got documents, then they'll take everything I own because the repo man is after me and I haven't paid my health insurance. **So they'd take everything I have**. So simply temporary work, rent a cottage or find a hostel. I'll deal with the repo man when I get myself back on the rails again.*" *(LP, male)* The client works but only on an informal basis, and lives in a hostel. He had the opportunity to escape the street, but his debts currently represent an unmanageable burden.

---

6 Hepatitis C is a inflammation of the liver caused by a virus. In more than half of cases it proceeds to a chronic state with the threat of cirrhosis and hepatocellular carcinoma. Other people can be infected, and in the case of homeless people this most often takes place through shared use of a needle or through sexual contact. In the case of homeless women the foetus is also sometimes infected (Vokurka, Hugo et al., 2004).

KM (female) is in a similar situation. *"I don't know. Maybe I'll never escape the street, **maybe I'll never repay the debts I have**. I don't owe much, but if you add up the transport fines and health insurance, the whole lot comes to at least CZK 250,000 (USD 12,500). So if I found full-time work, the repo man would automatically take my pay away from me. I've already made enquires. I wanted to start living a normal life. What would help me? Winning a million in the lottery. If you realise that you may be at rock bottom, but you can crawl up again or at least reach a normal level among normal people, it doesn't have to be all that bad."* The client is still sleeping rough and her debts have grown. Winning the lottery is hardly a realistic prospect, as she knows, but thus far she does not accept an alternative. The thought of repossession proceedings has demoralised her to such an extent that she is doing nothing, even though she is not the kind to be unable to resolve the accumulated debts. She is not a drug addict or an alcoholic.

JJ (male) also has problems with high levels of debt. However, he is thinking of how to resolve the situation. *"I'm afraid of repossession proceedings. **I have loads of debts** and the situation is a mess. I definitely want to change my life, but up till now there has been no work. However, we're supposed to start work on Tuesday, so I should have some funds. I'll try to spend as little as possible and whatever I save I'll put to one side. I'll do my best to turn this job into a full-time job. The problem is that when I have full-time work the repo man cleans me out and I'm back where I started from. But I don't have to deal with it until then. I can only do one thing. Get a job, stick with it three months and then go to the courts and **declare myself bankrupt**. I could get out of the situation that way. How much do I owe? Half a million crowns (USD 25,000). It's a vicious circle. I find a proper job, the repo man comes after me, takes all my money, and I'm back on the street. It's incredibly difficult to drag yourself back."* At present the client is working and has accommodation and a partner. We do not know how he dealt with the debts he had.

The most serious impediment to a return to society is an **addiction to drugs and alcohol**. Even if such individuals would like to live differently, they are in-

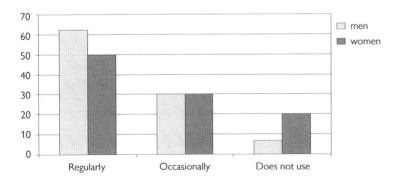

Graph 58. Reasons preventing the homeless from working: drug use and alcohol (the graph shows relative frequency).

capable of doing so and many of them are aware of the fact. *"I have a perspective on things and an aim. I don't possess a single thing, but I have a target in that I'd like to get off the drugs. If I don't make the effort, then I've lost again and then another day will come when I once more say that I want to kick the habit. I've told myself so often that I'll give up. I don't need drugs anymore to boost my self-confidence and I want to live a normal life. I really did want to live a normal life, but **everything started to get fucked up and I'm back here.**" (JB, male)* The client has frequently been in rehab but has been unable to give up and keeps returning to drugs. At present we have no information as to his whereabouts.

IH (female) is a drug addict, as is clear from her appearance and conduct. She adopts the customary stance to her addiction. *"I want to find a job and stop doing drugs. I'm completely fed up of the whole thing. I like being clean for a week or more, but then I start again and I can't decide what I prefer. **So I give in and start doing drugs again.** I don't know what I want and that's the worst thing of all."* Drugs are the reason she is incapable of working or indeed doing anything else. They also prevent her from forming a stable relationship with someone who does not take drugs. The client herself is aware of this fact, but has not yet been able to deal with her addiction. EK (female) also takes drugs regularly. *"I would like to change my life and to start working. **But I can't say I want to stop doing junk.** That would be crazy. I can't say that it would entirely suit me, but of course I'd like to change things. I'd like to find a job and live normally. That's the most important thing. Work would help."* The client would like to work but does not want to give up drugs yet. At present she lives with different friends and sometimes works. However, her prognosis is less than positive.

MP (male) is an alcoholic and realises that this is his main problem. *"Without alcohol I could hold down a job and find myself a normal girlfriend. I want to live normally, but right now, living on the street, **alcohol is the only pleasure I have in life.**"* The client was not set a good example by his parents, who were both alcoholics with all the consequences for the family that entailed. He is well aware that because of alcohol *"I am losing the chance of living a normal life"* and that he will not find a girlfriend this way: *"When I say that I'm homeless and an alcoholic, girls beat a hasty retreat."* However, he does not want or is unable to change, and rationalises his approach by claiming he has no reason to. He has been sleeping rough for four years.

Young homeless people often have very **unrealistic ideas** regarding the work they might do. Some of them are unaware of their limits or refuse to admit that certain things are beyond them. This may be a sign of mythomania serving as symbolic compensation for the failure and humiliation they have experienced. If they were to try to achieve an unrealistic objective, they would in all likelihood be disappointed. Although this would provide useful feedback, they would in most cases be unable to learn from it. They would like to achieve something tangible, but quickly and without any great effort if this were possible. In this respect they are not so different from their contemporaries in mainstream society.

Young homeless people do not have much in the way of satisfactory opportunities and prefer to dream of something better, since fantasy does not have to respect reality. *"I'd like to change my life from the base up, with the proviso that I'd be the same as I am now. However, I must admit that I want to be a decent bloke. **I'm not stupid, I'm a pretty talented writer**, I could maybe work on the dancing and make a go of it. This is Prague, there's loads of opportunities." (JB, male)* The client is unqualified and has no idea how he would achieve such objectives.

Young homeless people are aware that successful reintegration into society **depends above all on the desire, will and persistence they exhibit**. *"If you really want to, you can escape street life. But you have to really want to and you have to do something about it." (JJ, male)* Many of them have learned that a desire to escape is not enough. They have experienced many failures and sometimes their faith that they will finally succeed is their only support. They cling to the illusion that everything will turn out right in the end even though they are not making any effort, and hope that a miracle will take place. *"In my head I can't help but think with some certainty that things will get better." (TN, male)* This is their defensive shield in situations that they are unable to cope with and postpone resolving.

The attempt to drag themselves out of street life is sometimes conditional upon an **impulse that would activate them** and afford their behaviour some meaning. They expect someone or something to turn up, in which case they will begin to act differently because they will finally have reason to. Their attitude reveals a need to shift responsibility to some external force that would induce them to react differently. This is another manifestation of their immaturity and inability to cope with their own adulthood. They imagine that an incentive will arrive from somewhere that will provide sufficient motivation for them to change. Many of them do not believe that they are capable of managing change on their own and need someone to give them a kick up the behind. This would involve some kind of authority who would encourage them – unreliable, irresponsible and easily prone to the temptations of immediate gratification – to start acting in a more mature way.

*"I know for a fact that a child would help. I can say one hundred percent that I wouldn't hesitate for a minute. And a boyfriend. If I met a bloke who was worth it. I'd like to change my life one day definitely. I'm not able to say when right now. I can't say that in a year I'm going to be living a decent life, because I don't know. **I'm waiting for the right impulse**, but I hope that I won't have to wait too long, so long that it's too late. Whenever I start to feel happy something happens to spoil everything." (PČ, female)* This client's main problem is her personality. She already has a child but does not look after it. She has had many partners, but most were men who caused her problems, and she continues to wait for someone better. The question remains as to what kind of partner she could meet on the street and whether such a person would provide a sufficient impulse for her to make a fundamental change to her life. Nevertheless, a relationship is one of the ways of increasing self-confidence and creating the resolve to change one's lifestyle (albeit often temporarily). *"If*

*I manage it on my own, then I'll be surprised, because **I've always needed someone supporting me by my side**, someone who offers me psychological assistance. I need to be given a kick up the arse."* TŽ *(female)* Thus far nobody has provided her with this service and the client is still sleeping rough, taking drugs, supporting herself through prostitution and not looking after her daughter. However, it is not only women who have a tendency to transfer responsibility for their life onto someone else. *"Someone would have to give me a kick up the arse. I need to be supervised. I need a pistol to be pointed at my head and someone to tell me to look for work, to go to an agency."* *(VS, male)* The client was on the street for a relatively short period of time and then disappeared from records. At present we have no information as to his whereabouts and activities.

Young homeless people often justify their apathy when it comes to making a change by appealing to the **meaningless of such conduct** or the non-existence of someone close to them for whom they would be willing to become more engaged (as they see it). *"I don't even particularly want to change things. I don't have anyone to change for. If I found myself a girlfriend that I wanted a serious relationship with and she likewise, then that would definitely force me to start acting normally. But right now I'm single and **nobody is forcing me to do anything**."* *(MP, male)* However, the main cause of the client's reluctance to change anything is alcohol. This is yet another example of the rationalisation of passivity, which resolves nothing but simply explains why the individual in question has so far done nothing fundamental.

Reintegration into society also depends on the **social network a person has at their disposal**. Many young homeless people are aware that remaining within the homeless community is blocking their endeavours and that they should make some effort to tear themselves away. *"It would help if I could put some distance between myself and this community. If you live with these people on the street, it's a never-ending process."* *(LS, male)*

"I'd prefer to meet the kind of people who are a level up, who live a normal life. I'd like to get somewhere and live like a normal person." IK *(female)* On the other hand, the homeless community is the only group that accepts these individuals without judging them or wanting anything from them. Many young homeless people are no longer in touch with other people and therefore have no source of potential support.

The interviews reveal that young homeless people tend to be sufficiently self-critical. They are able to admit that the reason they are still sleeping rough is down to their own **incompetence, laziness and lack of effort**. (Almost a third of them are of this opinion.) However, they can be acquiescent and passive too, looking for ways of explaining their apathy: *"This is the way I am and I can't do anything about it."* MH (male) explains his failure thus. *"If you want to return to the old life, then someone can help you, but you have to want it yourself. I understand this, but **I don't know if I can be bothered to want it**. It's true that I'm incredibly lazy and can't be bothered to be otherwise. That's always how it's been. I do something and then suddenly I'm like, I've had enough."* This is a client who was unwilling to recognise any duties even when living at home. He stole and got into debt. He is not happy with life on the street, but at present is unable to live in any other way.

Young homeless people are often **unwilling to accept any restrictions** and do what is necessary or avoid what is undesirable. Freedom and independence is much more attractive. They admit that they do not want to concern themselves with problems and question whether something is appropriate or not. They do not want to have to resolve issues and so prefer to remain on the street where they do not have to concern themselves with such matters. (The suppression of problems is a common defence mechanism that is not typical only of homeless people.) Any other option is beyond their capabilities, especially if they are addicted to drugs or alcohol. Passive resignation is the only acceptable alternative for many of them.

Our findings match those of S. Garrett et al. (2008), who discovered that many young homeless people are tired of life on the street. An important part in their considerations of a possible return to society was played by their experience of older homeless people, i.e. of the kind they themselves might become. Important events, e.g. pregnancy, could act as the impulse to change. The young people in Garrett's group emphasised the motivation that would drag them out of their daily routine. A lack of persistence and loitering around with others was one of the main themes of the young homeless people examined by P. Miller (2004). Some of them were aware that they would not quit the street on their own and would need assistance from someone. Half of those questioned cited the use of drugs and alcohol as a serious barrier to returning to mainstream society, as indeed did our clients. They recognised that their link with the homeless community would put the brakes on their efforts. A third of the group knew someone who had failed in their efforts to return to society and were convinced that repeated adaptation to a majority lifestyle was difficult. It was clear to them that dragging themselves off the street would require more than simply a job and accommodation and represented a fundamental change in lifestyle.

C. Raleigh-DuRoff (2004) looked at what young homeless people believe would help them quit street life. She found that this was faith in a positive outcome, the hope that there was a chance to change something, the expectation of a better future, and sufficient self-confidence. Wishes and plans indicate hope for the future. Assistance from other people was also important: relatives, friends and professionals. A certain support is provided by small successes, e.g. finding a job, something that fortifies the conviction that the objective set will one day be attained. However, the young homeless people in her group were not unanimous in respect of their opinion regarding a return. She also found individuals who were not attracted by the restrictions on personal freedom this would necessitate. For some the difference in the extent of stereotype and adventure of both lifestyles was important. Another limiting factor was also the fact that some of these individuals had nowhere to return to, while on the street there was a community that accepted them.

5.2 CHANGE TO THE SOCIAL STANDING OF YOUNG HOMELESS PEOPLE AFTER TWO YEARS

Two years after the first interview was conducted there had been many changes in the group of young, Prague-based homeless people. Several of them had returned home or found work and accommodation, while others remained on the street. Many had managed to leave the street (usually by acquiring a regular job and accommodation in a hostel), albeit only temporarily in some cases. Some had returned to the street, often because they had been unable to hold down a job and as soon as they had made some money they stopped going to work and were laid off. A third of those we spoke to remain on the street and had not made any attempt to change matters. (Similar figures were reported by Thompson et al. (2006). C. Raliegh-DuRoff (2004) says that 40% will remain on the street.) One person died during a fire at a squat. We have no information regarding a fifth of our cohort. We do not know where or how they are living, and it is possible that some of them are no longer homeless. Others served a prison sentence and nobody knows what happened to them when they came out of prison.

We can assume that the longer a person lives on the street, the less likely it is that they will manage to return to society and lead a normal life. The greater probability of the short-term homeless returning was confirmed by Milburn et al. (2007). People who sleep rough for a prolonged period of time deteriorate more and lose the requisite habits and skills (always supposing they possessed them in the first place). However, the results of our study do not lend themselves to clear-cut conclusions.

From the table it is clear that in the case of men it is not decisive **how long they spent sleeping rough**. The situation is different in the case of women. The longer they remain on the street, the more likely it is they will remain homeless. (The difference between homeless women and women with a job and accommodation was statistically highly significant: t=3.38, p≤0.01). It is possible that women who live longer on the street have more problems than men, which makes

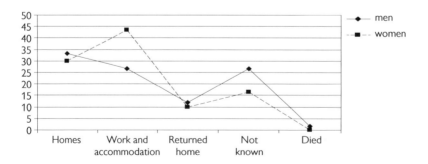

Graph 59. The social situation of young homeless people two years after the first interview (the graph shows relative frequency).

Table 6. Average duration of homelessness in the case of people with different social statuses (the table shows the number of years these individuals spend sleeping rough)

	men		women	
	average	SD	average	SD
homeless	2.32	1.49	4.44	1.57
has a job and accommodation	2.45	1.83	2.19	1.51
not known	2.81	2.82	2.6	1.36

it more difficult for them to change their status. The results might be distorted by missing information regarding certain men who lived on the street for several years and regarding whom we no longer know where they are and what they are doing. The relatively high standard deviation in the group of these men indicates a considerable diversity regarding the duration of their time on the street. It includes those who became homeless at the start of their adolescence, i.e. slept rough for seven to eight years.

The age at which an individual became homeless is not a decisive factor. It cannot be unambiguously said that people who have been homeless since adolescence automatically have a lower chance of improving their social status than those who only became homeless after the age of 20. However, a qualitative analysis of the information acquired shows that people who worked for at least a certain period of time have much in the way of useful experience and skills, and if not addicted to drugs or alcohol will manage the return to normal life more easily. Whether a person **quits life on the street** or remains homeless is influenced by a **large number of factors**, the combination of which will decide in the end how the individual will deal with them and whether they will return to the street after a certain period of time. As Miller et al. (2004) remind us, the homeless population is very diverse, and this is reflected in the likelihood of a person being able to return to mainstream society. Other researchers have reached the

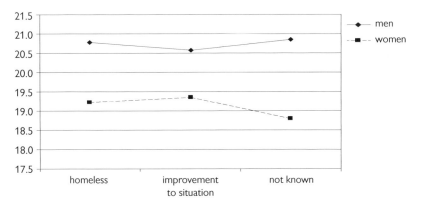

Graph 60. Mean age at which people with different social statuses became homeless.

same conclusions, e.g. Hyde (2005), the group working with Bearsley-Smith (2008), van den Bree et al. (2009), and others.

5.3 A SUMMARY OF WHAT YOUNG PEOPLE THINK OF THEIR FUTURE AND A POSSIBLE RETURN TO SOCIETY

Some young homeless people are satisfied with their life. However, **most would like to change things**, even though they tend to postpone this to the more distant future. They are usually aware of what they should do, but only rarely do they manage to act upon this knowledge. Many are aware that their failure is the consequence of laziness, insufficient effort or an addiction to drugs or alcohol. Others blame objective causes for their failure (lack of work, lack of money, the absence of anyone who could help them). Most young homeless people say that they would like to quit the street, but follow this up by saying that **it is too difficult**, that it does not have to be immediately, and that perhaps there is actually no reason to attempt something of this kind. They claim that they want to live a normal life, but realise that they are too comfortable, unwilling to abide by rules, and refuse to do anything that would require any real effort. It is simpler not to do anything but simply survive on the street, and so this is where they remain or where they return. Many of them are convinced that if someone helped them or if they had a reason to change, they would manage it. Waiting for an external impulse and postponement of a definitive solution represents a subjectively satisfactory coping strategy. A person does not have to admit that they have failed and does not have to give up their objective, because as they see it they are simply putting off a fundamental turnaround in their lives.

It has been shown that a return to society is always complicated by a factor that depends on the individual in question, whether this be the consequences of their behaviour in the past or their current lax attitudes and inability or unwillingness to resolve their problems. However, it is important to take into consideration the absence of a reason for making an effort. If the homeless are not sufficiently motivated to change and cope with the resulting strain, they will not manage to return to society even if different institutions offer the best assistance they are capable of. **Effective help should be based on the possibilities the homeless have** and focus on objectives that are attainable. The important thing is whether the difficulties relate to initiating the necessary changes (finding work and accommodation) or an inability to live otherwise, with an awareness of duties and responsibilities. It is clear that in the first case assistance will be easier and in the second more difficult and time consuming.

CONCLUSION

The life stories told by young homeless people are many and varied. There is no one typical story that explains why a person ends up sleeping rough (or suffering some other social decline). As always, the **family** is crucial. What is important is what opportunity the child has to create stable emotional bonds, as well as the security of the family environment and the influence of a model of a certain lifestyle. It is not insignificant that 20% of the homeless were raised in institutional care or by a foster family.

Also of great importance is the **personality of the individual** and how they react to various stimuli and how capable they are of managing stress in an acceptable way. Emerging adulthood is a milestone when problems can arise and decisive reversals can take place. Failure at school complicates matters since it means professional qualifications cannot be obtained. This in turn puts a person at serious disadvantage on the jobs market, whether this involves difficulties finding a job, dislike of the daily grind, or very low wages.

Drugs, alcohol and criminality during adolescence are important factors that impact unfavourably on a person's life trajectory and create an obstacle to returning to society. Some people have up until this point not suffered any real problems. However, the influence of their peer group and their own immaturity and irresponsibility lead to problems they are unable to cope with. As a result they find themselves sleeping rough. The chance of returning to society is greater at the start of adulthood than at any time later.

The findings of our interviews with young homeless people are not surprising and correspond to those of other researchers. Their value resides in the fact that they indicate when it is necessary to work with risky individuals so that their failure is not needlessly intensified.

APPENDIX

Map 1. Where homeless gather and sleep in Prague, 2012

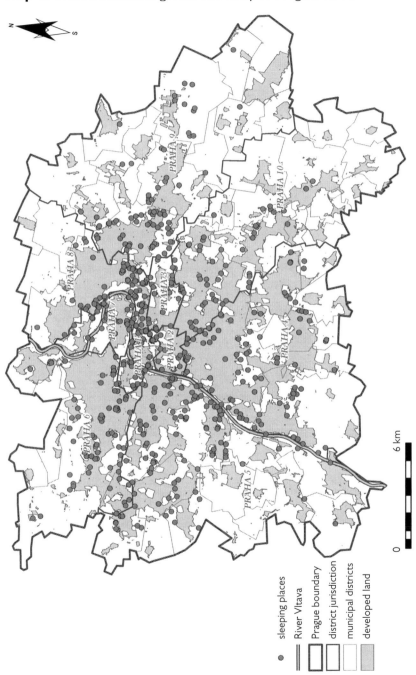

Map 2. The availability of the social services in Prague, 2012

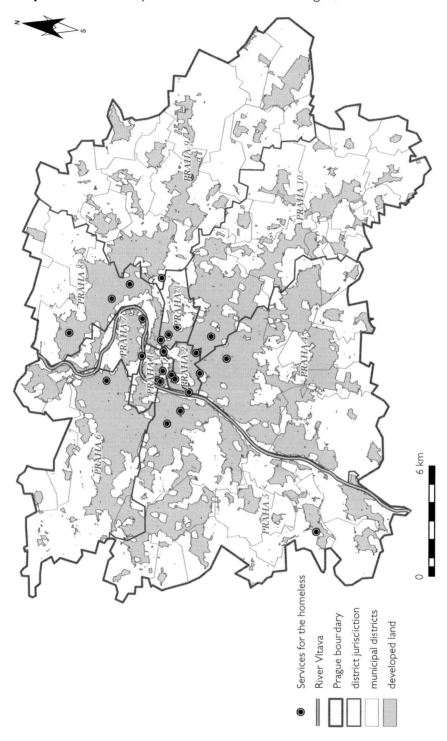

Services for the homeless

River Vltava

Prague boundary

district jurisdiction

municipal districts

developed land

BIBLIOGRAPHY

Auerswald, C. L., Eyre, S. L. (2002): Youth homelessness in San Francisco: A life cycle approach. Social Science and Medicine, 54, 1497–1512.

Ayerst, S. L. (1999): Depression and stress in street youth. Adolescence, 34, 567–575.

Bao, W. N., Whitbeck, L. B., Hoyt, D. R. (2000): Abuse, support, and depression among homeless and runaway adolescents. Journal of Health and Social Behavior, 41, 408–420.

Baron, S. W., Hartnagel, T. F. (1998): Street youth and criminal violence. Journal of Research in Crime and Delinquency, 35, 166–192.

Bearsley, C., Cummins, R. A. (1999): No place called home: Life quality and purpose of homeless youths. Journal of Social Distress and the Homeless, 8, 207–226.

Bearsley-Smith, C. A., Bond, L. M., Littlefield, L., Thomas, L. R. (2008): The psychosocial profile of adolescent risk of homelessness. European Child and Adolescent Psychiatry, 17, 226–234.

Bender, K., Thompson, S. J., McManus, H., Lantry, J., Flynn, P. M. (2007): Capacity for survival: Exploring strengths of homeless street youth. Child Youth Care Forum, 36, 25–42.

Bender, K., Ferguson, K., Thompson, S. et al. (2010): Factors associated with trauma and posttraumatic stress disorders among homeless youth in three U. S. cities: The importance of transience. Journal of Traumatic Stress, 23, 161–168.

Blazer, D. G., Kessler, R. C., McGonagle, K. A., Schwartz, M. S. (1994): The prevalence and distribution of major depression in national community sample: the National Comorbidity Survey. American Journal of Psychiatry, 151, 979–986.

Booth, S. (2005): Eating rough: food sources and acquisition practices of homeless young people in Adelaide, South Australia. Public Health Nutrition, 9, 212–218.

Boydell, K. M., Goering, P., Morrell-Bellai, T. L. (2000): Narratives of identity: Re-presentation of self in people who are homeless. Qualitative Health Research, 10, 26–38.

Buhrich, N., Hodder, T., Teesson, M. (2000): Lifetime prevalence of trauma among homeless people in Sydney. Australian a New Zeeland Journal of Psychiatry, 34, 963–966.

Caton, C. L., Shrout, P. E., Dominguez, B. et al. (1995): Risk factors for homelessness among women with schizophrenia. American Journal of Public Health, 85. 1153–4456.

Cauce, A. M., Paradise, M., Ginzler, J. A.. et al. (2000): The characteristics and mental health of homeless adolescents: Age and gender differences. Journal of Emotional and Behavioral Disorders, 8, 230–239.

Chamberlain, C., MacKenzie, D. (1994): Temporal dimensions of youth homelessness. Australian Journal of Social Issues, 29, 1–25.

Chen, X., Tyler, K., Whitbeck, L. B., Hoyt, D. R. (2004): Early sexual abuse, strees adversity, and drug use among female homeless and runaway adolescents in the Midwest. Journal of Drog Issues, 34, 1–21.

Chen, X., Thrane, L., Whitbeck, L. B., Johnson, K. (2006): Mental disorders, comorbidity and postrunaway arrest among homeless and runaway adolescents. Journal of Research on Adolescence, 16, 379–402.

Cougnard, A., Grolleau, S., Lamarque, F. et al. (2006): Psychotic disorders among homeless subjects attending a psychiatric emergency service. Social Psychiatry and Psychiatric Epidemiology, 41, 904–910.

Coward-Bucher, C. E. (2008): Toward a need-based typology of homeless youth. Journal of Adolescent Health, 42, 549–554.

Crawford, D. M. (2009): Traumatic history and adult transitions. In: Whitbeck, L. B. (2009): Mental health and emerging adulthood amon homeless young people. Psychology Press, Taylor and Grancis group, New York, Hove.

Csémy, L., Vágnerová, M., Marek J. (2011): Duševní poruchy mezi mladými bezdomovci? přehledová práce. Psychiatrie, 15, 26–32.

Čírtková, L. (2009): Forenzní psychologie. Nakl. A. Čeňka, Praha.

Dachner, N., Tarasuk, V. (2002): Homeless „squeegee kids": Food insecurity and daily survival. Social Science and Medicine, 54, 1039–1049.

Darbyshire, P., Muir-Cochrane, E., Fereday, J., Jureidini, J., Drummond, A. (2006): Engagement with health and social care services: perception of homeless young people with mental health problems. Health and Social Care in the Community, 14, 553–562.

Derogatis, L. R. (1977): The SCL-R-90 Manual I: Scoring, administration and procedures for the SCL-90. Baltimore, MD: Clinical Psychometric Research.

Derogatis, L. R., Melisaratos, N. (1983): The Brief Symptom Inventory: An introduction report. Psychol. Med. 13, 595–605.

Dragomirecká, E., Kubisová, D., Anděl, M. (2004): Duševní zdraví pražských bezdomovců. Psychiatrie, 8, 274–279.

Embry, L. E., Vander Stoep, A., Evens, C., Ryan, K. D., Polock, A. (2000): Risk factors for homelessness in adolescents released from psychiatric residential treatment. Journal Am. Acad Child and Adolescent Psychiatry, 39, 1293–1299.

Endermann, M. (2005): The Brief Symptom Inventory (BSI) as a screening tool for psychological disorders in patients with epilepsy and mild intellectual disabilities in residential care. Epilepsy and Behavior, 7, 85–94.

Ensign, J. (2004): Quality of health care: The views of homeless youth. Health Service Research, 39, Part I., 695–707.

Farrington, A., Robinson, W. P. (1999): Homelessness and strategies of identity maintenance: A participant observation study. Journal of Community and Applied Social Psychology, 9, 175–194.

Fazel, S., Khosla, V., Doll, H., Geddes, J. (2008): The prevalence of mental disorders among the homeless in Western Countries. PLOS Medicine, 5: e225.doi: 10.1371/journal.pmed. 0050225.

Ferguson, K. M. (2009): Exploring family environment characteristics and multiple abuse experiences among homeless youth. Journal of Interpersonal Violence. 24, 1875–1891.

Fischer, S. N., Shinn, M., Shrout, P., Tsemberis, S. (2008): Homelessness, mental illness, and criminal activity: Examining patterns over time. American Journal of Community Psychology, 42, 251–265.

Folson, D.P., Jeste, D. V. (2002): Schizophrenia in homeless persons: a systematic review of the literature. Acta Psychiatrica Scandinavica, 105, 404–413.

Garrett, S. B., Higa, D. H., Phares, M. M., Peterson, P. L., Wells, E. A., Baer, J. S. (2008): Homeless youths' perceptions of services and transitions to stable housing. Evaluation and Program Planning, 31, 436–444.

Goering, P., Tomiczenko, G., Sheldon, T. et al. (2002): Characteristics of persons who are homeless for the first time. Psychiatric Services, 53, 1472–1474.

Greene, M. J., Ennett, S. T., Ringwalt, L. C. (1999): Prevalence and correlates of survival sex among runaway and homeless youth. American Journal of Public Health, 89, 1406–1409.

Gwadz, M. V., Nish, D., Leonard, N. R., Strauss, S. M. (2007): Gender differences in traumatic events and rates of post-traumatic stress disorder among homeless youth. Journal of Adolescence, 30, 117–129.

Hollander, D. (2008): For some newly homeless youth, living situation and substance use are linked to risky sexual behaviour. Perspectives on Sexual and Reproductive Health, 4, 122.

Hradecký, I. (2007): Definice a typologie bezdomovectví. Naděje, Praha.

Hyde, J. (2005): From home to street: Understanding young people´s transitions into homelessness. Journal of Adolescence, 28, 171–183.

Johnson, K. D., Whitbeck, L. B., Hoyt, D. R. (2005): Predictors of social network composition among homeless and runaway adolescents. Journal of Adolescence, 28, 231–248.

Jones Johnson, R., Rew, L., Kouzekanani, K. (2006): Gender differences in victimized homeless adolescents. Adolescence, 41, 39–53.

Kamieniecki, G. W. (2001): Prevalence of psychological distress and psychiatric disorders among homeless youth in Australia: A comparative review. Australian and New Zealand Journal of Psychiatry, 35, 352–358.

Kidd, S. A., Kral, M. J. (2002): Suicide and prostitution among street youth: A qualitative analysis. Adolescence, 37, 411–430.

Kidd, S. A. (2003): The need for improved operational definition of suicide attempts: Ilustrations from the case of street youth. Death Studies, 27, 449–455.

Kidd, S. A., Carroll, M. R. (2007): Coping and suicidality among homeless youth. Journal of Adolescence, 30, 283–296.

Kidd, S., A., Davidson, L. (2007): „You have to adapt because you have no other choice": The stories of strength and resilience of 208 homeless youth in New York City and Toronto. journal of Community Psychology, 35, 219–238.

Kidd, S. A., Shahar, G. (2008): Resilience in homeless youth: The key role of self-esteem. American Journal of Orthopsychiatry, 78, 163–172.

Kushel, M. B., Yen, I. H., Gee, L., Courtney, M. E. (2007): Homeless and health care access after emancipation. Archives Paediatric Adolescence Medicine, 161, 986–993.

Levinson, D. (2004): Encyclopaedia of Homelessness. Sage Publication Inc., London.

Mallett, S., Rosenthal, D., Myers, P., Milburn, N., Rotheram-Borus, M. J. (2004): Practising homelessness: a typology approach to young people's daily routines. Journal of Adolescence, 27, 337–349.

Mallett, S., Rosenthal, D., Keys, D. (2005): Young people, drug use and family conflict: Pathways into homelessness. Journal of Adolescence, 28, 185–199.

Mallett, S., Rosenthal, D. (2009): Physically violent mothers are reason for young people´s leaving home. Journal of Interpersonal Violence, 24, 1165–1174.

Mallett, S., Rosenthal, D., Keys, D., Averill, R. (2010): Moving out moving on. Routledge, London, New York.

Marek, J. (2010): Psychosociální bariéry v reintegraci bezdomovců. HTF UK.

Marek, J., Strnad, A., Hotovcová, L. (2012): Bezdomovectví v kontextu ambulantních sociálních služeb. Portál, Praha.

Martijn, C., Sharpe, L. (2006): Pathways to youth homelessness. Social Science and Medicine, 62, 1–12.

Martinez, R. J. (2006): Understanding runaway teens. Journal of Child and Adolescent Psychiatric Nursing, 19, 77–88.

Mersham, C., van Leeuwen, J. M., McGuire, M. (2009): Mental health and substance abuse indicators among homeless youth in Denver, Colorado. Child Welfare, 88, 93–110.

McAdams, D. P. (1996): Personality, modernity, and storied self: A contemporary framework for studying persons. Psychological Inquiry, 7, 295–321.

McAdams, D. P. (2001): The psychology of life stories. Review of General Psychology, 5, 100–122.

McAdams, D. P. (2006): The Person: A new introduction to personality psychology. Hoboken, J. Wiley.

Milburn, N. G., Rotheram-Borus, M. J., Batterham, P. et al. (2005): Predictors of close family relationships over one year among homeless young people. Journal of Adolescence, 28, 263–275.

Milburn, N. G., Rotheram-Borus, M. J., Rice, E. et al. (2006): Cross-national variation in behavioral profiles among homeless youth. American Journal of Community Psychology, 37, 63–76.

Milburn, N. G., Rosenthal, D., Rotheram-Borus, M. J. et al.(2007): Newly homeless youth typically return home. Journal of Adolescent Health, 40, 574–576.

Miller, P., Donahue, P. Este, D., Hofer, M. (2004): Experiences of being homeless or at risk of being homeless among canadian youths. Adolescence, 39, 735–755.

Morgan, C. J., Cauce, A. M. (1999): Predicting DSM-III-E disorders from the youth self-report: Analysis of data from a filed study. Journal of American Acad. Child and Adolescent Psychiatry, 38, 1237–1245.

Mounier, C., Andujo, E. (2003): Defensive functioning of homeless youth in relation to experiences of child maltreatment and cumulative victimization. Child Abuse and neglect, 27, 1187–1204.

Neale, J. (2000): Suicide intent in non-fatal illicit drug overdose. Addistion, 95, 85–93.

Nesmith, A. (2006): Predictors of running away from family foster care. Child Welfare, 85, 585–609.

Noom, M. J., de Winter, M., Korf, D. (2008): The care-system for homeless youth in the Netherlands: Perception of youngsters through a peer research approach. Adolescence, 43, 303–316.

Nyamathi, A., Wenzel, S. L., Lessser, J., Flaskerud, J., Leake, B. (2001): Comparison of psychological and behavioral profiles of victimized and nonvictimized homeless women and their intimate partners. Research in Nursing and Health, 24, 324–335.

Olivan, G. (2002): Maltreatment histories and mental health problems are common among runaway adolescents in Spain. Acta Pediatrica, 91, 1274–1275.

O'Sullivan, J., Lussier-Duynstee, P. (2006): Adolescent homelessness, nursing, and public health policy. Policy, politics and Nursing Practice, 7, 73–77.

O'Sullivan Oliviera, J., Burke, P. J. (2009): Lost in the Shuffle: Culture of homeless adolescents. Pediatric Nursing, 35, 154–161.

Pears, J., Noller, P. (1995): Youth homelessness: Abuse, gender, and the process of adjustment to life on the streets. Australian Journal of Social Issues, 30, 405–424.

Průdková, T., Novotný, P. (2008): Bezdomovectví. Triton, Praha, Kroměříž.

Rachlis, B. S., Wood, E., Zhang, R. et al. (2009): High rates of homelessness among a cohort of street-involved youth. Health and Place, 15, 10–17.

Raleigh-DuRoff, C. (2004): Factors that influence homeless adolescents to leave or stay living on the streer. Child and Adolescent Social Work Journal, 21, 561–572.

Reid, S., Berman, H., Forchuk, C. (2005): Living on the streets in Canada: A feminist narrative study of girls and young women. Issues in Comprehensive Paediatric Nursing, 28, 237–256.

Rew, L. (2000): Friends and pets as companions: Strategies for coping with loneliness among homeless youth. Journal of Child and Adolescent Psychiatric Nursing, 13, 125–132.

Rew, L., Taylor-Seehafer, M., Fitzgerald, M. L. (2001): Sexual abuse, alcohol and other drug use, and suicidal behaviour in homeless adolescents. Issues in Comprehensive Paediatric Hursing, 24, 225–240.

Rew, L., Taylor-Seehafer, M., Thomas, N. Y., Yockey, R. D. (2001): Correlates of resilience in homeless adolescents. Journal of Nursing Scholarship, 33, 33–40.

Rew, L. (2002): Relationships of sexual abuse, connectedness, and loneliness to perceived well-being in homeless youth. Journal for Specialists in Pediatric Nursing, 7, 51–63.

Rew, L. (2003): A theory of taking care of oneself grounded in experiences of homeless youth. Nursing Research, 52, 234–241.

Rew, L., Horner, S. D. (2003): Personal strengths of homeless adolescents living in a high-risk environment. Advances in Nursing Science, 26, 90–101.

Robert, M., Fournier, L., Pauzé, R. (2004): La victimisation et les problemes de comportement. Deux composantes de profils types de fuguers adolescents. Child Abuse and Neglect, 28, 193–208.

Robert, M., Pauzé, R., Fournier, L. (2005): Factors associated with homelessness of adolescents under supervision of the youth protection system. Journal of Adolescence, 28, 215–230.

Rohde, P., Noell, J., Ochs, L. (1999): IQ scores among homeless older adolescents: characteristics of intellectual performance and associations with psychosocial functioning. Journal of Adolescence, 22, 319–328.

Rohde, P., Noell, J., Ochs, L., Seeley, J.R. (2001): Depression, suicidal ideation and STD-related risk in homeless older adolescents. Journal of Adolescence, 24, 447–460.

Rokach, A. (2005): The causes of loneliness in homeless youth. The Journal of Psychology, 139, 469–480.

Rosenthal, D., Rotheram-Borus, M J. (2005): Young people, drug use and family conflict: Homeless and runaway youth. Journal of Adolescence, 28, 185–199.

Rosenthal, D., Mallett, S., Myers, P. (2006): Why do homeless young people leave home? Australian and New Zealand Journal of Public Health, 30, 281–285.

Rosenthal, D., Mallett, S., Gourrin, L. et al. (2007): Changes over time among homeless young people in drug dependency, mental illness and their comorbidity. Psychology, Health and Medicine, 12, 70–80.

Ryan, K. D., Kilmer, R. P. Cauce, A. M. et al. (2000): Psychological consequences of child maltreatment in homeless adolescents: untangling the unique effects of maltreatment and family environment. Child Abuse and Neglect, 24, 333–352.

Salomonsen-Sautel, S., Van Leeuwen, J. M., Gilroy, C. et al. (2008): Correlates of substance use among homeless youths in eight cities. The American Journal of Addictions, 17, 224–234.

Sekine, Y., Iyo, M., Ouchi, T. et al. (2001): Methamphetamine-related psychiatric symptoms and reduced brain dopamine transporters studied with PET. American Journal of Psychiatry, 158, 1206–1214.

Shelton, K. H., Taylor, P. J., Bonner, A., van den Bree, M. (2009): Risk factors fo homelessness: Evidence from a population-based study. Psychiatric Services, 60, 465–472.

Sleegers, J., Spijker, J., van Limbeck, J., van Engeland, H. (1998): Mental health problems among homeless adolescents. Acta Psychiatrica Scandinavica, 97, 253–259.

Slesnick, N., Prestopnik, J. (2005): Dual and multiple diagnosis among substance using runaway youth. The American Journal of Drugs and Alcohol Abuse, 1, 179–201.

Smart, A. J., Walsh, G. W. (1993): Predictors of depression in street youth. Adolescence, 28, 41–53.

Stein, J. A., Dixon, E. L., Naymathi, A. M. (2008): Effects of psychosocial and situational variables on substance abuse among homeless adults. Psychol Addict Behav, 22, 410–416.

Stewart, A. J., Steiman, M., Cauce A. M. et al. (2004): Victimization and posttraumatic stress disorder amon homeless adolescents. Journal Amer. Acad. Child and Adolescent Psychiatry, 325–331.

Svoboda, M. (1999): Psychologická diagnostika dospělých. Portál, Praha.

Šupková, D. a kolektiv (2007): Zdravotní péče o bezdomovce. Grada, Praha.

Taylor-Seehafer, M., Johnson, R., Rew, L. et al. (2007): Attachment and sexual health behaviors in homeless youth. Journal for Specialists in Paediatric Nursing, 12, 37–48.

Taylor-Seehafer, M., Jacobvitz, D., Holleran Steiker, L. (2008): Patterns of attachment organization, social connectedness, and substance use in a sample of older homeless adolescents. Fam. Community Health, 31, 581–588.

Thompson, A. J. (2005): Factors associated with trauma symptoms among runaway/ homeless adolescents. Stress, Trauma, and Crisis, 8, 143–156.

Thompson, A. J., McManus, H., Lantry, J. et al. (2006): Insights from the street: Perceptions of service and providers by homeless young adults. Evaluation a Program Planning, 29, 34–43.

Thompson, A. J., Maccio, E. M., Desselle, S. K., Zittel-Palamara, K. (2007): Predictors of posttraumatic stress symptoms among runaway youth utilizing two service sectors. Journal of Traumatic Stress, 20, 553–563.

Tyler, K. A., Hoyt, D. R., Whitbeck, L. B., Cauce, A. M. (2001): The effects of a high-risk environment on the sexual victimization of homeless and runaway youth. Violence and victims, 16, 441–455.

Tyler, K. A., Cauce, A. M. (2002): Perpetrators of early physical and sexual abuse among homeless and runaway adolescents. Child Abuse and Neglect, 26, 1261–1274.

Tyler, K. A., Whitbeck, L. B., Hoyt, D. R., Johnson, K.D. (2003): Self-mutilation and homeless youth: The role of family abuse, street experiences, and mental disorders. Journal of Research on Adolescence, 13, 457–474.

Tyler, K. A., Whitbeck, L. B., Hoyt, D. R., Cauce, A. M. (2004): Risk factors for sexual victimization among male and female homeless and runaway youth. Journal of Interpersonal Violence, 19, 503–520.

Tyler, K. A. (2006): A qualitative study of early family histories and transitions of homeless youth. Journal of Interpersonal Violence, 21, 1385–1393.

Unger, J. B. Kipke, M. D., Simon, T. R. et al. (1998): Stress, coping, and social support among homeless youth. Journal of Adolescent Research, 13, 134–157.

Vágnerová, M. (2010): Psychologie osobnosti. Karolinum, Praha.

Vágnerová, M., Csémy, L., Marek, J. (2012): Osobnost mladých bezdomovců. Psychiatrie, 16, 9–14.

Van den Bree, M., Shelton, K., Bonner, A. et al. (2009): A longitudinal population-based study of factors in adolescence predicting homelessness in young adulthood. Journal of Adolescent Health, 45, 571–578.

Votta, E., Manion, I. (2003): Factors in the psychological adjustment of homeless adolescent males: The role of coping style. Journal Amer. Acad. Child and Adolescent Psychiatry, 42, 778–785.

Whitbeck, L. B., Hoyt, D. R., Ackley, K. A. (1997): Abusive family backgrounds and later victimization among runaway and homeless adolescents. Journal of Research on Adolescence, 7, 375–392.

Whitbeck, L. B., Hoyt, D. R., Bao, W. (2000): Depressive symptoms and co-occuring depressive symptoms, substance abuse, and conduct problems among runaway and homeless adolescents. Child Development, 71, 721–732.

Whitbeck, L. B., Johnson, K. D., Hoyt, D. R., Cauce, A. M. (2004): mental disorder and comorbidity among runaway and homeless adolescents. Journal of Adolescent Health, 35. 132–140.

Whitbeck, L. B., Hoyt, D. R., Johnson, K. D., Chen, X. (2007): Victimization and post-traumatic stress disorder among runaway and homeless adolescents. Violence and Victims, 22, 721–734.

Whitbeck, L. B. (2009): Mental health and emerging adulthood among homeless young people. Psychology Press, Taylor and Grancis group, New York, Hove.

Yoder, K. A., Longley, L., Whitbeck, L. B., Hoyt, S. R. (2008): A dimensional model of psychopathology among homeless adolescents: Suicidality, internalizing, and externalizing disorders. Journal of Abnormal Child Psychology, 36, 95–104.

Zerger, S., Strehlow, A. J., Gundlapalli, A. V. (2008): Homeless young adults and behavioural health: An overview. American Behavioural Scientist, 51, 824–841.

Zweben, J. E., Cohen, J. B., Christian, D. et al. (2004): Psychiatric symptoms in methamphetamine users. American Journal of Addictology, 13, 181–190.

SUBJECT INDEX

accommodation 9, 88, 189, 195, 206
acquired helplessness 130
adaptation to life on the street 144
aggression 23, 154–158, 188
aggressive behaviour 154
alcohol use 64, 138–142
alcoholic parent(s) 21
anxiety disorder 130
AUDIT (Alcohol Use Disorder Identification Test) 139

begging 74, 77
behavioural problems 50, 51, 59, 63, 134
BSI (Brief Symptom Inventory) 132, 133, 135, 136, 142, 143

criminal activity 68, 98
criminal record 194, 199
crystal meth (methamphetamine) 140–143

depression 129, 136, 142, 144, 149
depressive disorder 129
desocialisation 180
devalued self 148
domestic violence 22, 23, 24, 154–158
drug use 64, 138–142

extraversion 143, 148, 151
Eysenck Personality Questionnaire (EPQ/S) 143, 150, 152–154

failure at school 46, 48–50
finance 65, 66
foster family 42, 209

foster parents 41
friendship 119, 120, 121, 145, 151

hepatitis C 199
homeless community 110, 124, 147

identification with a homeless lifestyle 166, 190
identity 12, 73, 147, 148
indebtedness 66, 67
institutional care 20, 41, 42, 134

leaving the street 180, 190
life on the street 60, 70, 71, 96, 105, 177, 189

marihuana 140
mental health 129, 132
mental illness 25, 63, 138
moral code of the street 108

need for
    an open future 174
    assistance 163, 167, 172
    self-realisation 175
    a sense of belonging and acceptance 161, 162
neuroticism 143, 149, 151, 153

parenthood 17, 126, 127, 145
partnership 111, 119, 121, 145, 172, 176
post-traumatic stress disorder 101, 131
prostitution 74, 75, 83, 86, 87, 100, 105, 131
psychoticism 133, 135, 136, 141, 142, 143, 149, 151, 154

NAME INDEX

Marie Vágnerová / Ladislav Csémy / Jakub Marek

HOMELESSNESS
AMONG YOUNG PEOPLE
IN PRAGUE

A NARRATIVE ANALYSIS
OF DEVELOPMENTAL TRAJECTORIES

Published by Charles University in Prague, Karolinum Press

Ovocný trh 3–5, 116 36 Prague 1, Czech Republic

http://cupress.cuni.cz

Prague 2014

Editor vice-rector Prof. PhDr. Ing. Jan Royt, Ph. D.

English translation by Phil Jones

Editor Martin Janeček

Cover by Anna Issa Šotolová, layout by Jan Šerých

Documentary photo by Dana Kyndrová, Anna Pospíšilová and Ladislav Kážmér

Typesetting and print by Karolinum Press

First English edition

ISBN 978-80-246-2517-1

e-ISBN 978-80-246-2587-4 (pdf)